Deaf Women's Lives

Deaf Women's Lives

Three Self-Portraits

Bainy Cyrus,
Eileen Katz and
Celeste Cheyney, and
Frances M. Parsons

Frances M Parsons

My deep appreciation and
gratitude for opportunity to

GALLAUDET UNIVERSITY PRESS
Washington, D.C.

know you more—
Love, Peggie

Gallaudet University Press
Washington, D.C. 20002
http://gupress.gallaudet.edu

Cover painting, *Smelling Rose*, 2002, by Chuck Baird, oil on canvas and wood cut out, courtesy of Gallaudet University Archives.

Library of Congress Cataloging-in-Publication Data

Deaf women's lives : three self-portraits / Eileen Katz . . . [et al.].
 p. cm.—(Deaf lives)
 ISBN 1-56368-321-0 (alk. paper)
 1. Cyrus, Bainy. 2. Katz, Eileen. 3. Parsons, Frances M., 1923– 4. Deaf
women–Biography. I. Katz, Eileen. II. Series.

HV2373.D43 2005
305.9'082'0922–dc22 2004061968

Contents

Introduction
Let Them Write

Brenda Jo Brueggemann

It is by writing, from and toward women, and by taking up the challenge of speech . . . that women will confirm women in a place other than that which is reserved in and by the symbolic, that is, in a place other than silence.

<div align="right">Hélène Cixous, The Laugh of the Medusa</div>

I am fairly certain that none of the authors whose words fill the pages that follow have read the work of French feminist theorist, Hélène Cixous. They have probably not read her work, in general, nor more specifically, have they likely encountered Cixous's critical and creative encouragement for women to write that fill the lines of her text, *The Laugh of the Medusa*.[1] Yet they seem to have been "listening" anyway:

> Write! Writing is for you, you are for you. . . . I know why you haven't written . . . Because writing is at once too high, too great for you, it's reserved for the great—that is, for "great men"; and it's "silly" . . . Write, let no one hold you back, let nothing stop you. . . . (1525)

Bainy Cyrus, Frances Parsons, and Eileen Katz (with Celeste Cheyney) claim writing as their own in this triple-text memoir of deaf women's

lives. The three (or four, depending upon how you want to count them) authors featured in this autobiographical triptych all grew up and became young adults—also as deaf/hard of hearing persons and also as women—in different times, circumstances, and locations. Each of their memoirs is quite different. Yet each is also similar in its confirmation of the other's experiences.

Bainy Cyrus writes in "All Eyes" of her predominantly oral education, beginning at the Clarke School, one of premier and longest-standing oral-deaf institutions in the United States. She writes poignantly of her (delayed) language development as a deaf child in the 1960s and 1970s, working hard to comprehend the nuances of structure in both spoken and written English. Yet despite her struggles to achieve literacy equal to that of her hearing peers at the time, Bainy's story always remains positive and forceful in her recognition of not just what she is missing but also with what she has and excels at. Deaf people, she tells us, are "all eyes." And with their eyes, they "read" much.

So it was that Bainy herself stood before an audience in the Gallaudet University Conference Center auditorium in November 2004 and read to us some of her writing from this book.[2] In her "reading" at the "Narrating Deaf Lives" conference, she had indeed taken up the challenge of speech (and following from it, the challenge of writing) as she threaded together several passages from her memoir, "All Eyes," to delight us with her humor and to make us not only marvel at, but be thankful for, the fact that Bainy had herself now become *a writer*. Her stories about mis-reading English/American idioms such as "paint the town red" and "elbow grease" are all the more poignant when we realize that Bainy has herself now managed to "paint the town red" through the successful completion of this memoir, and she has surely also applied some "elbow grease" in that creation and completion. Writing may be "too high" and "reserved for the great men" and even at times "silly" for women—as Cixous suggested—but it is also obviously possible, potent, and promising in Bainy Cyrus' hands.

Much like Bainy, but living in a very different time and situation, Eileen Katz's story of her earlier life as a young Jewish girl in London during World War II, is also a story of being "all eyes" and working hard, very hard, to make sense of it all at a time when everyone—deaf, hearing, young, old, man, woman—was surely working hard to understand

things. In "Making Sense of It All," Celeste Cheyney has helped Eileen Katz shape and write some of her earliest memories about trying to understand what was happening during World War II as a young deaf Jewish girl at the residential school for Jewish deaf children, a leading oral school in England (where sign language was also used). Eileen herself is just learning to master and understand language—both written (English) and British sign language—as she works hard to patch together various images and texts she encounters about the war and its impact on London. The children have to learn how to even just ask questions—and to translate them between sign language and English—about such previously unknown objects as barbed fire fences, airplanes dropping bombs, trenches, radar towers, and an angry looking man who appears often in the newspapers with his arm extended out stiff in some kind of salute. The Battle of Britain begins and Eileen works even harder to make sense of it all.

Much like Bainy Cyrus then, Eileen Katz learned to patch together the sense of a "foreign language" and to construct meaning from her eyes as aided considerably by their engaged and curious intellects. They also shared a history as letter writers. Both young girls wrote much while they were students in these oral schools, distant from the rest of their family, and even though Eileen and Bainy's stories are separated by several decades and an ocean, their letter writing somehow also unites them.

Additionally, it joins them to Frances (Peggie) Parsons, the third author in this set. Like Bainy and Eileen, Peggie was the product of oral school education (although she boasts of failing four such schools in her younger days). And like Bainy and Eileen, she found some familiarity through writing. While Bainy and Eileen often wrote letters home as young students, Peggie's writing consisted largely of journal writing—a kind of letter to herself—during the years she traveled throughout the world to teach other deaf schools about "total communication" (TC). As an ambassador for the combined method (oral instruction plus sign language) of education for young children in a day that such instruction was just dawning, and as a self-professed advocate for many of the deaf children she met who were oppressed and even abused in places like Argentina, Peggie Parson's memoir excerpt, "I Dared," resonates with the same pride, poise, and communicative yearning that threads through the memoir excerpts that share the binding with her in this triptych.

These are remarkable women. These are remarkable writers. These are remarkable deaf people.

Living in quite different times and situations, these three (deaf) (women) authors still all placed themselves (or were placed) between oral and signed methods of instruction. Likewise, they all three find it hard to clearly distinguish between densely interwoven aspects of their identity; at the "Narrating Deaf Lives" conference, for example, none of them could—or would—separate out what part of their narratives or lives were about being "women" as opposed to, or in conjunction with, being "deaf" (or the many other things they are). They all relate narratives that are consumed by—and created with—writing, with words, and with a rich and yet sometimes troubled journey into and through literacy in print and spoken languages.

As we move between "All Eyes," "Making Sense of It All," and "I Dared," I hope we will all come to understand how it is that, through writing and with writing, as Hélène Cixous suggests, "women will confirm women in a place other than that which is reserved in and by the symbolic, that is, in a place other than silence." Daring, with their eyes, to make sense of it all, these three (deaf) (women) authors take up the challenge of such confirmation in the world by writing some of their own life stories. As the audience for such texts, we listen, we read, we dare, we make sense of it all—and we too are then confirmed in a place other than silence.

Notes

1. Hélène Cixous. "The Laugh of the Medusa." Trans. Keith Cohen and Paula Cohen. In *The Rhetorical Traditions: Readings from Classical Times to the Present*, ed. Patricia Bizzell and Bruce Herzberg. New York: Bedford St. Martin's, 2001.

2. All four authors gave presentations and readings from their memoirs at a Gallaudet University Press Institute event, November 3–5, 2004: "Narrating Deaf Lives: Biography, Autobiography, and Documentary." This three-day event was intended to highlight the issues and intricacies involved in "narrating deaf lives" by showcasing recent, current, and forthcoming projects in these areas. See http://gupress.gallaudet.edu/gupiconference/index.html

All Eyes

Bainy Cyrus

It was indeed a wondrous day for my mother, having finally gotten her wish after bearing a string of three wild little boys. Mom collapsed on the delivery table with a sigh of relief when she saw the absence of a tiny weenie as soon as I slipped out of her womb. As an adult, I can imagine that excitement with a chuckle, but I also wonder what it was like for my mother to be deceived with my normal appearance. Although no one knew at that time, I had been born with a hidden disability.

By the time I was eighteen months old, my parents sensed something wasn't right with me. My grandmother Donnie had long suspected that I didn't seem to act like any other baby so she urged Mom to take me to the family pediatrician. I did not demand as much attention as my brothers did. Nor was I aware of comings and goings in the house. I did not wail at the sound of the front door shutting, even with my playpen only ten feet away, and I never turned at my mother's homecoming. Most of all, I had not spoken a single word, not even "Ma" or "Dada," as I should have long ago. My brothers had not shown these "symptoms" when they were my age.

When Mom took me to the pediatrician, she was assured that I was still too young to talk and that I might have "the last child syndrome."

That is, the baby in a particularly large family was usually spoiled as a result of constantly being waited on by older siblings who interpreted the baby's words. Nevertheless, Mom became increasingly concerned with my lack of speech. She brought me to the doctor for a couple more visits, only to be assured that I would eventually produce my first word out of the blue.

But Donnie wasn't convinced. "I don't believe it. There *is* something wrong with Bainy," she insisted to Mom and Dad. Hearing these words, Dad, who was a doctor specializing in internal medicine, began to think that his mother-in-law was right. Since he was out working all day, he hadn't seen enough of me to notice my lack of baby words. Yet, I always beamed at my dad's tickle game every evening as he rolled his finger around before zapping me in the tummy, eliciting giggling squeals from me.

Mom fearfully suspected mental retardation, but Dad didn't think so because he had seen me put toys together, most of the time, flawlessly. In fact, I was more coordinated with toys than my brothers. Donnie assumed that I was deaf because I had never turned in reaction to the door slamming. So she and Mom once again took me to the pediatrician and asked for hearing tests. Without hesitation he brought out a bell and rang it behind my back. *Ding, ding, ding.* Nothing. I hardly moved a muscle as I sat there and stared at my mother. Frowning, the pediatrician realized for the first time that there was definitely a problem. He decided to try making a louder sound. Standing behind me, he held an inflated balloon and burst it with a needle. *POP!* Still no response. My face remained blank, staring straight ahead. The pediatrician stepped back in concern. This time he knew better than to tell my mom to wait for my first word.

Finally, the pediatrician placed a tape recorder behind me and turned it on. It emitted the deep, rounded tones of a male voice. He increased its volume and inched it closer to me. I did look up with a puzzled frown, my eyes still transfixed on the wall ahead of me. After staring at me, the pediatrician hesitantly asked my mother, "Does she hug you?" Mom and Donnie were taken back by his question and wondered what a hug had to do with these hearing tests. Mom replied, "Of course, she hugs me. Just like any other child. Why did you ask?"

"She seemed to hear the tape recorder but didn't know where the sound came from. She could've turned her head to the recorder," the

pediatrician said, obviously reluctant to add more details. What he had in mind was autism and he didn't want to upset Mom with his assumption. So he suggested that she take me to an otologist for more accurate hearing tests.

My parents saved copies of medical reports written by the pediatrician and other doctors about my diagnosis. In those flimsy yellowed letters, the pediatrician described my actions to doctors at Johns Hopkins University Hospital. His typewritten words, fading over thirty-five years, show that he really did care. Mom told me that this pediatrician expressed remorse for not noticing my abnormality sooner. I understand that back then in the early 1960s, pediatricians knew little about the symptoms of any disability.

More hearing tests were performed, eliciting very little response from me. The otologist believed I had a very definite loss, but he was uncertain about deafness because other conditions such as autism or aphasia could be possible. He explained that, like deafness, these other disabilities could show symptoms in toddlers such as not recognizing sounds and not developing speech. And it was too early to find out exactly what the problem was, he told my parents.

The otologist immediately referred me to the Speech and Hearing Center at Old Dominion University. There, an audiologist placed me in a small alcove, putting a headphone on my head, and began performing tests with an audiometer. He found that I responded to bell and flute sounds over 70 decibels between 500 and 2000 cycles per second. My response indicated that, at a high volume, I could hear low-frequency sounds better than high-frequency ones. That technical language may sound confusing to you, so I'll explain a little of it to you now and more later when I explain the oral education method. What is important to understand here is that a decibel is a measurement of loudness. The range runs from 0 decibels to 140 decibels. The level of 0 decibels represents the softest sound a typical ear can hear, like the sound of a pin dropping. And *that* is a normally hearing person's threshold. At the level of 55 decibels is loud conversational speech. The level of 75 decibels includes the sound of city traffic. The level of 140 decibels includes the sound of a jet engine at take-off. Well, the audiologist found that I could start hearing at 70 decibels in the low-frequency range.

However, the audiologist advised that no definite conclusions about hearing or not hearing could be made with certainty at the moment because of my young age. Instead, he suggested further observation of my responses before confirming the diagnosis. He then counseled Mom and Dad about speech stimulation, instructing them to talk to me as much as they could, only face to face. Knowing that this method of stimulating speech would be a burden at home, the audiologist suggested that I work with a speech therapist at Old Dominion. Mom and Dad agreed, eager for me to say *something.*

Several months passed, and all attempts at motivating me to vocalize and imitate vowels had been fruitless. Mary Jane, a speech therapist, had worked with me two or three days a week. I do vaguely remember her as an affectionate person who seemed to work awfully hard at motivating me. Mary Jane and I met again thirty years later at a coffee café and had a captivating conversation because she told me how everyone had believed that I had a complex communicative disorder. Deafness was the last thing on their list because I did have some hearing, particularly of loud sounds. Aphasia was what everyone assumed. This disorder, which is a complete absence of the communication and comprehension skills, provides an explanation for the child's failure to speak. An aphasic child cannot follow the meaning of the words he or she hears. According to Mary Jane, I showed these symptoms. She would set small things on the table and ask me to pick up a pen. After many unsuccessful attempts, I would finally pick up the right item. But the next day, I'd completely forget. Not knowing what the "pen" looked like. Back to the drawing board. Mary Jane would have to start all over again. But she persevered.

As our therapy sessions progressed, Mary Jane realized that I watched her lips intently. I had finally speechread some words such as "yes" and "no." But still I couldn't vocalize. Instead, I began talking to myself silently in front of the mirror. The medical reports explain that I jabbered without any sound coming out of my mouth, making livid facial expressions and gestures. Boy, I must have looked nutty! But I had a perfect reason for my puppetlike actions. Because I didn't know that voices and moving lips were often associated together, I began to think it was natural for everyone to mouth words. No wonder I began to imitate facial expressions, especially Mom's. I'd just frown hard and shake

my index finger up and down, babbling in silence. That's how Mom scolded me whenever I knocked over a glass of fruit drink or threw a plastic toy block. When scolded, I'd place my hands over my eyes. You guessed it, I didn't want to see my mother's lips!

Now I was two and a half years old and still not speaking. It was time to take me to Johns Hopkins Hospital which had pioneers in the field of deafness. That trip involved a four-hour drive to Baltimore, which would be the first of many in several months. To rule out autism, the local doctors made an appointment for us to meet with the specialist, also in Baltimore, who was famous for his research on autism. Mom and Dad feared a visit to the specialist because autism still might be a possibility. They knew autistic children lacked the ability to communicate and responded to sounds inappropriately. I had those symptoms; that's why Mom and Dad were scared out of their wits when they pulled up in front of a small colonial ranch house which was the specialist's office.

When we entered the foyer, the specialist descended the stairs with a broad grin and took one look at me in my dad's arms. He told Mom and Dad flat out, "Bainy is not autistic." My parents were caught off guard and looked at each other. The specialist explained that he was watching by the window upstairs when we parked in front. When Dad removed me from the back seat, he knew instantly that I was not autistic. It was because I wrapped my arms around Dad's neck. If I were autistic, my arms would have gone limp or pushed Dad away. Much to my parents' relief, the specialist ruled out autism and, instead, suspected deafness after reading the reports from my local doctors. He didn't think I had aphasia because I watched lips.

That consultation led to the beginning of my numerous hearing tests spanning eight months at Johns Hopkins. The doctors found that, if I was visually engrossed, I didn't react to sound. However, if visual stimuli were removed and my attention was centered on listening, they could observe a variety of reactions to sound. Loud sounds of 70 decibels were enough to break into my visual preoccupation. I also reacted better to low-frequency sounds and required more decibels to hear high-frequency sounds.

Any of those doctors could have immediately suggested the use of amplification once the hearing impairment was diagnosed, but back in

the 1960s, technology wasn't well advanced. Today, a deaf baby can even be diagnosed *on the day he or she is born,* thanks to high technology and a better understanding of deafness. Back then, the doctors didn't know the exact degree of my hearing loss, so they decided to use structured auditory listening games as a way to see whether I could discriminate sounds. They instructed Mom and Dad on how to stimulate my language and speech development at home by using a face-to-face only approach. We were sent home, knowing we would come back in the following weeks for more hearing tests.

Mom and Dad decided to rely on oralism because I had spent a considerable amount of time watching lips. That choice was fairly common for a hearing family who wanted their deaf child to be like them, able to speak. If I had come from a deaf family, it might have been different; sign language would have then been the likely choice.

During our visit at the coffee café, Mary Jane went on to tell me that I still forgot to pick up a pen during one session after another. She explained that it was easy for me to forget new words when there was no auditory sense. Hearing babies, even those in wombs, remember the sounds of the words they hear, so they learn spontaneously. Deaf babies? No way. That's why a deaf child needs to be taught the same word over and over again, usually *thirty-five times.* In contrast, it takes only three repetitions for a hearing child to learn a word because it's much easier to remember the *sound* of each word. Hearing people learn by *hearing;* deaf people learn by *seeing.*

That's why I had to watch Mary Jane's and my mother's lips to understand speech. Actually, no one told me to speechread; I just happened to pick up the habit myself. Lips seemed to be the only thing moving on everyone's face, so why not watch the action? I just thought, and still think, lips are so full of character that they have a mind of their own. If lips are moving in a restricted way with frequent tightening, then whoa, I better step back and not aggravate that person. If lips are chapped, shredding like a river birch bark, then I assume that person must have spent a lifetime worshiping the sun.

Mom and Dad ordered the John Tracy correspondence course, which was designed for parents of oral-bound deaf children. This course was

developed in the 1940s by the wife of Spencer Tracy, the movie actor who had a deaf son. The course encouraged my parents to teach me to associate things with lip movements. One of the step-by-step activities it recommended taught them to play matching games with me. Mom and Dad would scramble pairs of items on the floor, then pick up, for example, one shoe and mouth this word to me, and ask me to pick up another shoe in the midst of other items. I'd watch the lips carefully and pick up the right item.

However, I didn't always get things right. I would forget by the next day, and the same teaching would have to be started all over again. I bet my parents and Mary Jane wanted to wring my neck, but they knew that teaching a deaf child required top-level patience. The process was complex because so many words looked the same on the lips. To me, the spoken word "doll" may have looked like "dog" or "all." In the future, I would have to learn to watch the tongue formation in the mouth, the placement of teeth, and the vibrations of the cheeks.

Even the most skilled speechreaders get only between 30 percent and 40 percent of what is said, especially on fast-talking lips. That's why deaf people need to be spoken to slowly and clearly. Even though many words look alike on the lips, the speechreaders manage to understand by figuring out the right words to fit in, as I have learned over the years. For instance, you say, "Oh great!" On the lips, it could've been "grade" or "grain." Of course, I cannot hear the difference between those three words, but I can quickly grasp what the right word is given the context.

※

After taking more hearing tests at Johns Hopkins, I was given a final diagnosis: bilateral sensorineural hearing impairment. That diagnosis was what the doctors considered a very severe, close to profound, nerve deafness. The doctors suggested that I try mild amplification so I could learn to hear at a comfortable level and then eventually settle with a permanent hearing aid. The final diagnosis, of course, saddened my parents but what hit my mom twofold was the realization that I would never have a normal education and that her pregnancy was the cause of my deafness. She told me the first insight affected her most because she couldn't bear to send me away to a residential school. She and Dad were informed that I required long-term special education. Norfolk, Virginia,

had no oral school that was appropriate. Mom was disheartened to learn that the closest reputable oral school, Clarke School, was 700 miles away in Massachusetts.

Mom was not too concerned about why I was born deaf because she had no plan to have any more children. Four was enough. She was too busy making sure my brothers and I stayed off the railroad tracks or didn't run through thorny bushes. Our health and safety occupied her mind. Still, the doctors were curious about my birth defect, and they had questions for my parents. Mom and Dad sat down, prepared to answer yes or no.

"Any history of genetic deafness in the family?" "No."

"Now about your child . . . Any type of illness?" "No, just flu and colds, that's all."

"Has she had meningitis?" "No." "Scarlet fever?" "No."

"Middle ear infection?" "No." "Any ear injury?" "No."

"Did she develop skin rash?" "No." "Mumps?" "No."

"Okay . . . now about your pregnancy. Any trouble with it?" "No, it was uneventful."

"Mrs. Bilisoly, did you develop skin rash during your pregnancy?" "No."

"Did you have high fever during that time?" "Uh, yes. I was really ill for three or four days. The fever was very high. I remember it happened during the third month."

There it was. The real reason for my deafness. The doctors nodded at each other, one saying, "High fever during the third month could be the result of a case of rubella." Mom didn't know what to feel as she sat there confused and heartbroken. Dad, as a doctor, had heard of rubella but had not seen the symptoms among his patients before. He quickly assured Mom that it wasn't her fault, that rubella was something unavoidable like a flu bug, and that rubella was a form of viral infection known as German measles. This virus could have temporarily deprived my auditory nerves of oxygen, and the damage was done. It was the absolute cause of my hearing impairment, the doctors said. Mom knew she couldn't have done anything about this virus. I would never want her to feel guilty anyway.

Mom said my three brothers, the last one five years older than me, reacted well to my diagnosis because they were immediately informed

that deafness was manageable. Nash, Lindsay, and Harvey, all before their adolescent phases, vowed that they would protect me but still treat me the same. They sure did. They made sure that I didn't get ridiculed or didn't date a jerk. But they still beat me up or turned my doll inside out, trying to turn me into a whiny little sister. Actually, I liked that because they were treating me just like a normal person.

Lindsay told me that he noticed I was different before the diagnosis because I hardly ever cried. Possibly entranced by *The Twilight Zone* episodes, he even suspected I had supernatural powers, so he challenged his pal Hamil to hit me in the arm, bragging that I'd never cry. Hamil, though known as a prankster of the neighborhood, refused. Lindsay said to watch and socked me in the arm. He thought *Uh-oh* when my face slowly shriveled up, mouth arching downward, and I finally wailed WAAAAAAAH! He felt bad enough about it that he grew up to be the most tenderhearted brother of all.

Things began to make more sense now that I was wearing a hearing aid. With this aid, I could turn up the volume to any level and feel comfortable with it. It was a shiny, silver Zenith Royal, the size of a dental floss pack, tucked in a white cloth pocket with straps all around my torso. I remember so vividly receiving this first hearing aid at age four and a half that I can play it back in my mind like a videotape. Lindsay came rushing into the house with excitement and dragged me outside in front of Dad who was surrounded by the entire family and some neighbors. After removing a new hearing aid from the bag, Dad placed the straps over me and then jiggled the earmolds into my tiny ears with my mother's help. He then glanced at me as if to say, "Are you ready?" and that caused everyone to circle around me like they were peering into a fish tank.

Dad turned on the hearing aid and said, "Hello, hello, hello." Bam! I heard his voice and grinned, driving everyone to excited laughter. Actually, that wasn't the first time I had heard a voice, since I had heard Mary Jane and others talking through mild amplification at Old Dominion. But this time was different—right here on the sidewalk—so many voices at the same time! Something else struck me, too. As I looked around with the hearing aid and straps and all, I realized that no

My preschool photograph.

one else had one on. I was the only one. At that moment, I learned of my deafness. Really, I had long thought everyone was just like me, not hearing anything. I even thought every single soul on earth took hearing tests as if they were a daily routine.

In the future, there would be questions and comments about the strange-looking thing on my chest. "What's that on you?" "What music are you listening to? Oh? It's not a radio?" "My gosh, it looks like a one-cup bra." Many more would follow. Years later, my sister-in-law Vickie found a picture of me wearing these straps and hesitantly asked why I had a harness. Her innocent question made me feel like a flesh-eating jungle beast caught in a net. I had never thought of that in the past!

Mom and Dad had made a decision to send me to Clarke School in Northampton, Massachusetts. Although they knew it was going to be painful not to have me home, they felt confident about this school that had earned an article in *National Geographic* for its reputable oral

program. I had gone to Clarke for orientation and had been pleasant the whole time. But the second time, they *sent* me there, and I was a mess, screaming the whole way up. Mom was so frustrated because she couldn't tell me anything, even with my hearing aid, that would reassure me that I wasn't being left there for good. That's what made the situation so hard. Mom knew that I would be greatly upset being away from home, or worse yet, that I would be angry with her for "deserting" me. Being left at an unfamiliar place could be traumatic for any five-year-old. So the lack of communication wasn't the only factor.

Whenever Mom tells the story about sending me to Clarke School, she dwells on the light blue smocked dress I had on. She had stitched it and was proud enough to parade me around in that dress nearly every-day. Mom still has a portrait of me wearing the dress, sitting and smiling, taken before the screaming incident. I am sure she is reminded of my piteous screams every time she sees that portrait. She has said that seeing the dress became so disturbing after the incident that she never put it on me again.

When it was time for my parents to leave, I started to scream again. Miss Miller, my new teacher, restrained me from running after them. I don't remember any of that. But, whenever I think of the story Mom has told me many times, I can feel the powerful trauma of being separated from the two most important people in my life, particularly at such a young age of five.

All Eyes

Clarke School was, and still is, a beautiful place with century-old brick buildings and gigantic pines. Hubbard Hall beckons with its green and white colonial sign that reads *Clarke School for the Deaf, established in 1867.* It was where I had my first class, all of us sitting on tiny wooden chairs arranged in a semicircular pattern facing Miss Miller so we could see her lips and one another's. Some of us fidgeted and others just stared ahead. One might think, oh, that looks like a normal preschool class. No, ours didn't look like one at all. Weighed down by ugly head-phones, we all resembled miniature airline pilots. We each had our own volume boxes on the half-hexagonal stand behind us, and the main cord ran a good twenty feet from there to Miss Miller's mike around

her neck. But still, the ample length would not prevent the many cord incidents ahead! Cords ran everywhere like a spider web, ready to trip or snare anybody.

That auditory training program was an extremely important step in the teaching of oralism. We would be learning not only to listen to the teacher's voice but also to hear our own voices. This method provided better amplification than a hearing aid because it cut off feedback. With this system, we would be better able to hear the vowels and consonants that we could not hear otherwise. Later on, we would learn how to make these sounds.

Crucial for our development was learning how to hear and recognize sounds with hearing aids. As preschoolers, we still had more to learn to use our residual hearing—what hearing we still had—to full advantage through our hearing aids. We would have to learn where the sounds came from, how they were made, what they meant. All of us had nerve deafness and, therefore, were unable to discriminate sounds, especially speech sounds, even with our hearing aids (which only made sound louder). In fact, we needed to *learn* to hear.

The hearing aid has its limitations. It cannot help the person hear everything. In most cases, the aid only reduces the hearing loss by 30–35 decibels. It's not at all like a pair of glasses that can correct vision. The aid also cannot help one discriminate sounds as well as hearing people can. It cannot cure distortion from a sensorineural loss that causes the voice to sound distorted and muffled. Even if a voice is very loud, its sound becomes worse and more distorted. These garbled sounds occur because many consonants are high-pitched and use frequencies for which I have the least hearing, as do most other deaf people.

I'll explain how I hear this sentence: *I like to play tennis but not with Betty who always beats me.* Well, all I can hear is *I lie oo ay enny buh nauh weh Beh-ee oo ahway bea me.* That's how most deaf people hear—and how they also *talk*, missing the high-pitched consonants. Imagine suddenly becoming deaf and then having to learn a foreign language. That's the same thing as being born deaf.

My classmates and I were about to begin a long, grueling process of oral education. Our hair would be slightly, if not permanently, squashed on the sides from wearing headphones every day. Auditory training was not a problem for me because I understood its necessity. I had grown to

respect Clarke as a special school where I could always feel secure with kids like me, all of us wearing bulky hearing aids on our chests.

I remember wearing a headphone and sitting next to Miss Miller in front of a two-way mirror about three times a week. To begin teaching, Miss Miller gently took my hand and placed it on her cheek. Holding the mike under her chin, she began, "Ooooo . . . ooooo." With my hand on her cheek, I felt the vibration of speech through my hand. I could also hear Miss Miller's voice through my headphone. As a rule of oral education, I always had my eyes directed to the mirror. Miss Miller wouldn't let me gaze away to an inviting pile of toys in the corner or a housefly buzzing over us. Direct eye attention was what we needed so we could "hear" by speechreading.

Next came the spoken word "ball" along with a red item in Miss Miller's hand. With my hand on her cheek, I watched her lips form, "Buh, buh, *buh*," and then I tried to imitate her sound, uttering, "Bbb-buh" with the mike under my chin so I would learn to hear my own voice. Miss Miller, as many times as she had to, reminded me to look in the mirror to watch my own lips. She would hold up the ball and say, "Can you say 'ball'?" Once again, she would press my hand against her cheek and repeat this word. After many attempts, I would finally say, "Baaaaw," watching my lips in the mirror. Though the word was not spoken perfectly, Miss Miller praised me to boost my motivation. From her thirty-plus years of teaching oralism, she knew it was impossible for me to say "ball" with fullness the first time. It would take time and effort to learn a consonant such as *L*, which was almost invisible on the lips; I would eventually learn that a flap of the tongue over the upper teeth or slightly behind indicated this consonant. That's what speechreading is for—learning to "read" consonants.

Leonard House was a former family home on the edge of campus, a few minutes' walk to Hubbard Hall. This coed dormitory was only a hundred feet from the school infirmary that I always considered a haven. Whenever I sniffed or coughed, Miss Miller would sweep me off to the infirmary in concern, taking only a few long strides. I didn't mind going into this place drenched with the smell of ammoniac and full of red-eyed kids waiting either to be poked, rubbed, squeezed, hammered, and given baby aspirin or to be motioned down the hall to stay in a recovery room. Years later, I even considered faking illness so I could be

placed in a comfortable hospital bed and read *Curious George,* away from the classroom, acting sicker than having just a slight bad cold, honking and snorting loudly only when nurses walked in.

The girls' bedroom, across the hall from boys', was big enough for eight of us, looking somewhat like an army barracks with tiny cots. This room suited me fine, although I longed for my own double bed at home. But still, I enjoyed the company of my girlfriends. At night, Miss Miller, also residing at this dorm with another teacher and a few housemothers, would tuck us in, saying "good night." If one of us had trouble sleeping, she would place our hand over her throat and sing a bedtime tune, knowing we would feel the vibration of her voice. We never went to bed with our hearing aids on since it would be uncomfortable to have our earmolds pushed further in on the pillow.

My new friends and I hadn't yet learned to say names, only associating one another's faces, and other people's, with memorable characteristics—the one with a zillion freckles, the one with buck teeth, the one with Shirley Temple hair, the one with lopsided glasses. Then we began to recognize names in writing, long before we learned to say them. With fifteen of us in Leonard House, we had to have every single one of our belongings labeled—even our underwear—on which was either a sewn cloth name label or inked letters of the last name. Leonard House was so laden with written names that a visitor might suspect it was an FBI investigation lab.

Outside was the playground with the swing set, which would make us all rambunctious, crossing paths and fighting for the last available swing. Of course, we were kept on close watch for fear that we would wander off into the woods or, worse yet, the street. The staff at Clarke School worried about us getting on the street because they knew that we wouldn't be able to hear a car coming. So they had us clustered together like a troop of insects whenever we walked to class. If one of us strayed off the sidewalk, we would receive a serious scolding. Discipline was what we needed to understand the importance of safety.

On weekends, only three of us remained at the school. As the only out-of-state girl in the entire dormitory, I had only the company of our caretakers and two boys: Peter from North Carolina and Mark from Pennsylvania. Only a small percentage of out-of-state students attended Clarke because of the money involved. Families of many students had

moved to Massachusetts to take advantage of the free tuition, but many other students had been born in this state. My parents could have moved our whole family to Massachusetts, but Virginia was home with tons of relatives.

Miss Miller was clever to have the housemother take me, Peter, and Mark out of the classroom for a walk downtown so we wouldn't see parents pick up their in-state children for the weekend. It always worked because our heads were spinning with the excitement of having eaten ice cream or possessing a new wind-up toy when we returned to the dorm on Fridays in the late afternoon. The quietness of this dormitory didn't bother me too much, even though I sometimes felt lonely. Our small group could watch *Flipper* together and munch on popcorn.

My weekend stays at Leonard House didn't last too long, however. The parents of my classmate Cheryl Robbins began inviting me to their home in Greenfield, about twenty-five minutes north. Then the parents of my other good friend, Diane Karas, had me stay with them in Chicopee Falls, about twenty minutes south. These invitations were, at first, sporadic and then more frequent as those two families took turns hosting me every other weekend. Their hospitality would continue for seven years, which made my life at Clarke, a great distance from my family, so much easier.

I have cherished my wonderful friendships with Cheryl and Diane for nearly half a century. Our lives have all had a roller-coaster quality because of deafness. During our now rare visits, we have shared hearing-world dramas, laughed about old times at Clarke, and showered one another with great affection.

❦

I flew home every six weeks, collecting about a hundred of airline pins in my lifetime. I do remember the thrill of coming home. Gazing from my seat out the window after the landing, my nerves would tingle all over at the sight of my entire family waiting at the outdoor gate. At that time, planes were not attached to telescoping corridors, so one could stand several yards from the plane. It was always a beautiful scene on a sunny day, all of my family and our black poodle Winnie clustered together. I loved that sight.

Despite seeing my family every six weeks or so, I was still tickled with their mail, especially a weekly Polaroid™ picture of themselves waving to the camera, with "Hi Bainy" scrawled along the bottom white edge. One week I'd receive one of Mom and then another of Nash, each waving a hand, the same inscription on the edge. Sometimes the entire family was waving to the camera. It may sound a little goofy, but every Polaroid I received was a treasure for a lost little girl five states apart from her family.

Dad's mail was definitely my favorite. Every week I received his animal-photographed card with a drawn picture on the inside. His artistic talent and sense of humor were just magnificent. One in my memorabilia file says, "Your dumb old brothers are studying for the exams," with a drawing of a sleepy boy poring over his textbook while a log above him is being sawed. Another card reads, "We will find another way to get you home this Friday," accompanied by a drawing of a man riding on top of a big bird. All these hilarious pictures were neatly drawn with colored felt-tip pens and remain pristine thirty-five years later. Most of all, I have been grateful for a father who knows how to express his love and affection with humor.

By now, after attending Clarke for a few months, I could now speak short, simple words with low-pitched sounds. One of my favorite words, I know, was "home" because I always associated it with a Polaroid of my family. Fortunately, this word was fairly easy for me to pronounce, although it took me a while to learn to say it. Miss Miller placed my hand in front of her mouth so I would feel her breath being expelled with the first consonant of "home" and then pressed my fingers against the side of her nose so I would feel the nasal quality of the *M* sound. To learn high-pitched consonants such as *K* and *CH*, Miss Miller held my hand in front of her mouth so I could feel the air or she had me watch a fluffy feather flutter as she made the sound. Too often, I was fascinated with the fluffy feather, not Miss Miller's mouth. I'm embarrassed to say she admitted to my unsurprised parents that my attention span was often short and that I was like "trying to pin down a butterfly."

Deaf children have to struggle to achieve not only the method of communication, oral or sign, but also language development. I would say even that it's much harder for them to learn to read and write than

to learn to communicate. Hearing children, on the other hand, learn English or any foreign language spontaneously. It's easy for them to expand their language by listening to others speak, improving sentence structure, and using the right words. That advantage helps increase their ability to read and write, beginning with the kindergartner's attempt to associate written words with letter sounds.

With English or other spoken languages, deaf children have none of that. *They always have to be taught by someone.* That's why their English language development can take longer. In fact, it can take years for a deaf child to learn to write a flawless paragraph for an English paper. He or she is likely to use wrong words, run a sentence in disorder, or miss a necessary word. That's because the deaf child cannot hear others speak in sentences or is likely to misunderstand what is said. The important fact is that the ability to hear is the ability to read and write. Straight language and vocabulary are a never ending problem for all deaf children. The problem is not the learning disability deaf children have; it's just that they *miss out.*

Although our brains were perfectly normal, my classmates and I lacked straight language and, thus, were unable to learn a full sentence, while our hearing peers had already jumped to several levels ahead of us. Our teachers believed that, for us, the best approach for learning language would be, first, to identify an item and then to use verbs. Toward this end, we were to tackle two sets of index cards, one set consisting of nouns and the other of adjectives. We would have to learn to match cards from these two sets and place them under the right picture such as RED BOW or SAD CLOWN. We were learning language with our eyes.

The interesting fact is that deaf people are exceptionally keen with their eyes, able to detect the slightest movement several yards away. Because they have little or none of the auditory sense, deaf people treat their eyes as the number one sense for communication, education, security, and even entertainment. Deaf people are extremely visual. They "hear" with their eyes. They read speech. They read sign language. They read facial and body languages. They read TTYs. They read closed captions. They become alert to blinking lights of special devices. Deaf people are all eyes. That's how I feel about myself. I don't know what would happen if I lost my eyes. How on earth did Helen Keller get by?

That's why Miss Miller began our language education by teaching us to identify things—because of our visual awareness. We would easily learn that the long red strip tied into a knot was RED BOW and that the Bozo-like figure with his mouth arching downward was SAD CLOWN—if we got the adjective-noun order right. Then we would move on to the more difficult language pattern: verbs. We sure had a long, *long* way to go.

During my first two years at Leonard House, Diane Karas and Cheryl Robbins became my best friends. Their mothers had encouraged us to spend time together by inviting me to stay over for the weekends. Because I was with one or the other of their families every weekend, the three of us girls rarely spent weekends all together. Mrs. Karas told me she was saddened by the sight of me screaming in agony and running after my parents on my first day at Clarke. Diane had made numerous trips to Clarke before, so she wasn't at all upset when her mother left her. At that point, Mrs. Karas vowed to look after me. She sure did—for seven years. So did Cheryl's mother. I cannot thank them enough for making my life easier away from home.

Diane and her twin brother David are the youngest of five in the Karas family. David is not deaf because he wasn't affected by premature birth as his sister was. We still made a good trio, watching *The Brady Bunch* and playing board games; David treated us just the same. And I was enlightened with Mr. Karas's dry sense of humor as he constantly poked me in the tummy and teased about any sports team from my home state. A large man with a gentle heart, he certainly knew how to amuse small kids. Mrs. Karas spent a good deal of time boiling her famous Polish sausages. She even wrapped up one for me to take home to feed my family. In addition to being generous, she has always been a tough-talking, feisty lady who doesn't take rubbish from anybody. That's what made me admire her so much.

Cheryl has quite an interesting family because it has genetic tendencies toward deafness in it. She had a brother and two cousins attending Clarke at the same time. It was Cheryl's father who brought this gene to the family; he was mildly hard of hearing in one ear, but we considered him hearing for his normal speech. In fact, the deafness gene can

Me (on the left) with friends Diane and Cheryl.

be present but not active, and thus produce hearing babies. That's why Cheryl today has a deaf daughter and hearing twins. Those genes are unpredictable, continually creating surprises.

Mrs. Robbins was, and still is, the easiest person to speechread on earth. She sure knows how to display the words she is saying on her lips. She could win a medal for that. I was secretly amused with her way of disciplining Cheryl. When exasperated with her daughter's misbehavior, Mrs. Robbins would say in a loud, clear voice, "Cheeerrruuuuylllll!" Her lips would pucker up in a perfect *CH;* then her mouth would move into a neat wide arc for vowel sounds; and finally, her tongue would slap angrily against her front teeth for a perfect *L.*

My classmates and I had finally learned to say some complete sentences and could pronounce easy words without being misunderstood by strangers. Miss Miller had worked hard to drill language into our minds by making us read every sentence and by correcting our errors.

From day one she and other teachers constantly said full sentences to us, knowing that we wouldn't be able to understand every word of them. They did it because they wanted us to catch a flicker of the language rhythm so we would learn that language did not consist of isolated words.

Small words such as *in, an,* or *the* pose a problem for most deaf people who speechread because these words are likely to be missed on the lips. They just whip by so fast that deaf people don't realize these words were ever said. I remember all the Clarke teachers trying to correct our sentences, reminding us not to forget those small, annoying words. Miss Miller had to keep reminding us to say "I have *a* black dog," not "I have black dog."

Despite having learned to use verbs, my classmates and I still lacked proper tenses. We would need more time to learn the difference between "am" and "will be." If you asked one of us, just an itsy-bitsy deaf kid, what we had for supper the night before and what we did afterwards, you would hear all the present verb tenses as if you were now watching the feast.

Every time I received mail from my family, Miss Miller read it out loud to me and explained the meaning of any word I didn't understand. When one of my brothers wrote about a baseball game, I didn't know what "by one point" or "home run" meant. I had no idea that language not only contained simple words with single definitions but also had word combinations and patterns that expressed various meanings. Like my classmates, I didn't know how complex language was.

It wouldn't be too long before my classmates and I advanced to the Lower School and finally learned to use proper verbs. Our English language development was just inching forward like the slow-turning pages of an unabridged Webster's dictionary. And, I was excited about moving to a new dormitory and about interacting with more kids my age. But I would hate to leave Miss Miller who was like a grandmother to me; she would remain the most favorite teacher of all my years at Clarke.

Charlie Chaplins

Clarke School organized its 200 students into four unique education levels according to chronological age, beginning with Preschool and ending with Upper School for students ages thirteen and up. Lower School was

for those of ages six to eight; Middle School for those from nine to twelve. Most Upper School students graduated at the age of sixteen before joining ninth grade in regular school. Because of time-consuming oral education and slow language development, deaf children were likely to be a few years behind their hearing peers. I was now in Lower School, interacting with more kids my age and just taking time to learn.

Our new classroom was up on the second floor of Hubbard Hall, overlooking the hill down to Magna House where I was rooming with Cheryl and Diane. As we sat wearing headphones at our own desks, all arranged in a semicircular pattern, we took pity on the teacher's constant struggle with the microphone cord that tangled around her legs. Not a single day went by without someone tripping over the cord. Those cords were such a hassle that some teachers hung their mikes from the ceiling—a convenient solution, unless a very tall person walked by. BONK! With the overhead mike, one had to avoid making a painful mistake: Never let it go briskly or its elastic cord would spring, causing a smack on the head. Some deaf kids were mean enough to step on the cord behind the teacher and watch her snap back, arms flailing, and then say, "Oh, I'm sorry, I didn't see it."

I cannot remember if another favorite practical joke happened in my classroom, but I've heard stories about it many times. When the students entered the classroom, they had to remove their hearing aids, put on the headphones, and adjust their volume boxes. It was easy to do. After a while, they already knew what level they would be comfortable with, even before hearing the teacher's voice over the mike. Well, this time, when the teacher finally spoke, the students yelped, peeling off their headphones and commenting on how loud she was. Perplexed, the teacher examined all the volume boxes and tried one of the headphones. Then she pursed her lips in suspicion and demanded to know who did it. It turned out that someone had sneaked in before class, taken out all the knobs, turned the volumes way up, and put the knobs back in to make them look like they were off.

Now that I could speak complete sentences, I could take advantage of a new way to communicate long distance with my family: a tape recorder, the old-fashioned type with reels. The teacher directed me to hold a tiny mike and ramble on carefully about what I had done over the previous weekend with either Cheryl or Diane. If needed to, the

teacher interrupted with her corrections of my language, "Say 'I *went* to the circus last Saturday,' not 'go.'" Then, before the three-inch reel was removed from the recorder and sealed in an envelope to be sent off, I said good-bye to my family.

Using their own tape recorder, my family responded with a different reel that contained their voices. Listening to their tapes was a thrill because they sounded like they were right behind me. But I could hear only voices, not words. That's why the teacher wrote down what the tape said and replayed it and ran her fingers along the lines while my family spoke. With my headphone, I tried to distinguish voices, which wasn't easy. Only Mom's voice was recognizable because she was the only female. My brothers took turns speaking into the mike, telling how much they missed me.

Mom and Dad flew up quite often and watched my class before taking me, Cheryl, and Diane out for lunch. They had become immensely fond of my friends and sometimes met Cheryl's or Diane's parents on campus and gave gifts to express their appreciation to them for looking after me on weekends.

Once, my three brothers came to visit me, and it was a nightmare for my mother. She ignored my dad's advice not to take all of those adolescent boys by herself, since he could not escape work to accompany her on a road trip to Clarke. Mom insisted on taking the boys for a cheery family adventure in spite of an absent father. Dad just sat back in a wait-and-see position at home and could not help smirking when Mom returned neurotic and wild-haired with a food-splattered station wagon and declared that she would never, *ever,* take all her kids on any trip without her husband again.

On that trip, Mom was mystified that my brothers were causing an uproar on campus, being chased by all the little Magna House girls. And sharing a hotel room with the three male adolescents rattled Mom. Nash refused to keep his radio down. Lindsay and Harvey constantly wrestled like a cat and dog. So Mom probably went through the whole trip without a single wink of sleep. She and the boys actually came up to bring me home for spring break, planning to take me out of there a day before all the other students departed. But the staff was concerned for the students' feelings and suggested that they wait until the last day to avoid hurt and jealousy. Well, after two days of dealing

with the hype my brothers had caused on campus, the school president phoned Mom at the hotel and announced, trying to sound light and cheerful, "Bainy can go home a day early."

Clarke School was a strict school, demanding good manners, and when I came home, my parents were delighted to hear my polite words such as "Please" and "Thank you very much." But my formal manners made me seem stiff, set apart. And it wasn't only the manners that made me seem that way; it was also my using verbs in a formal way, along with my robotic voice. Because I couldn't hear backup conversation, I didn't know how to use informal verbs, some of which combined with pronouns, for example, *I'm* and *won't*. Instead, I'd cautiously say "I am," "will not," and whatever was full and direct. In fact, that was how any eight-year-old Clarke student spoke. I'm sure all the teachers there would be mortified if we said "ain't" or "Nah" or "y'all."

Like most other deaf children, I had a flat voice that lacked accent and intonation. I sometimes talked through my nose, sounding as if I had a horrible cold. Even though I can pronounce some words just perfectly, my voice still sounds unnatural, like a strange foreign accent. It took me years to learn to speak with varying tones, and my voice is not as flat now as it used to be. Really, no severely or profoundly deaf person speaks in a natural voice, no matter how well he or she can pronounce words, even though the vocal cords are perfectly normal.

The reason we all have "deafy voices" is because we just don't know how to *monitor* our voices. We are unable to imitate sounds we cannot hear. We cannot hear our own voices as well as hearing people do. We just don't know how to make our voices rich with accent and intonation. That's why we are likely to talk flatly or very loudly. Every time my hearing husband Steve and I eat at a restaurant, I usually talk too loud because the surrounding sounds of waitresses clinking glasses or people yapping makes it hard for me to hear my own voice. Steve has to flap his hand down, lowering his gaze, and of course, I lower my voice. But then, I'm not sure if he can hear me okay. So Steve tells me where to stop the volume by quickly saying, "I can hear ya. Hold it right there." That's why I like a very, very quiet restaurant where I can tell whether my voice could wake the dead.

So you can see why it's difficult for most of us deaf people to have natural laughs. Yes, it's true that some of us laugh as if we are croaking

or gagging. We just can't help that. Back in high school, one of my friends remarked that I never made any sound when laughing. So I asked Mom if she could teach me how to laugh. She looked at me aghast and said, "Huh? You laugh just fine. If you smile, then people know you're amused." So I just left it at that and continued laughing silently until after college, when I finally quit worrying about what people thought of my voice. My laugh isn't quite natural, but at least it feels good to let it all out. Over the years, I've noticed that some of my deaf friends laugh silently. I'm always touched to see people, hearing or deaf, smiling in spite of this harsh world. The point is that deaf people are only hearing impaired, not humor impaired.

During my third year at Clarke, I received the news that my former teacher Miss Miller was "very sick"; at that time, I didn't know what cancer was. She was diagnosed as having pancreatic cancer, which wouldn't give her long to live. To my dismay, I noticed that no one ever said she was going to get well. The teachers sure didn't want to tell me it was a fatal disease, not to mention "cancer," because it would upset or confuse an eight-year-old. And I wasn't old enough to understand that life could be so unpredictable.

One early morning, Miss Magner, an assistant to the school president, picked me up, announcing that I would visit my old teacher at the infirmary. At first I was excited, expecting to see Miss Miller running after her fidgety students at Leonard House. But Miss Magner knelt down in front of me with a grave look and said, "She is still sick." Disappointed, I nodded and continued walking up the hill and across the campus, holding Miss Magner's hand.

As we walked into a room at the infirmary, the bedridden Miss Miller quickly held out her hand toward me—a powerful memory I've had for the past thirty-five years. Her pale arm stretched out, her open hand waited to be clasped as if I was the life she wanted to cling to. She was no longer a robust woman; she had lost a great deal of weight. I moved to hold her thin hand and chatted for a few moments, trying to boost her spirits with the new words I could pronounce. Then Miss Miller said to me, "You work hard for me. I want you to do well." I promised, accepting her hug. That was the last I saw of her. She died a

few weeks later and I took it hard, but later, I became grateful for her happy, long life teaching deaf children to speak and read speech.

My friends and I had a variety of housemothers during our years at Clarke, one each year. About half of them were old and feeble, close to retiring; the other half were in their twenties and thirties and much more involved with us. One I remember the most: Miss Adams at Magna House. One evening, she taught me something about hearing people. For some reason, I wanted to get out of the playroom and asked her if I could go to the bathroom. She didn't believe me since we all just went after dinner. I crossed my legs in fake desperation, explaining that I had drunk an enormous glass of milk, and pleaded for her permission. After staring at me with a suspicious smirk, Miss Adams finally granted her permission, knowing very well what would happen. So she followed me to the bathroom and made me leave my stall door open, folding her arms. After pretending to do my business, I piped up, "Okay, I am finished." With a smug grin, Miss Adams said, "No, you're not. I would've *heard* it if you had gone to the bathroom. So you just stay and finish." Defeated, I sank further into the toilet, my butt nearly touching the clean water. That was the hard lesson I learned: *You can never fool hearing people when it comes to sound.*

Once, I received a brand-new raincoat from Mom through the mail, and I ached for rain on the spot. Cheryl and Diane, too, hoped it would rain and envisioned all three of us stomping through puddles, arms around each other. If we could, we would sing "Singin' in the Rain," but no. We would just skip around and giggle at each other. After hearing my pleading for rain all day, Miss Adams inhaled and said, "Okay, now I've heard enough about your raincoat. You should try what I tell you: Pray to God." I stared at her and then at Cheryl and Diane who shrugged as if to say that it might work. We found a corner to huddle, stood shoulder to shoulder, and clamped our closed hands together like a chorus of Christmas carolers. Then we prayed in our flat voices, "God, please make it rain tomorrow. Amen."

Lo and behold, it rained the next day. Cheryl, Diane, and I gaped at each other, standing before our bedroom window splattered with raindrops. Since that day, I have strongly believed in God and sometimes look at the ceiling in a fearful and apologetic way if I have done a bad sin. Although I was born Episcopalian, I went to Catholic mass every

Sunday with either Cheryl's or Diane's families. Going to the services of a different religion never mattered to me because I was thinking only about God and Jesus. Besides, it was good to be with a family that I felt I belonged to. The Karases and the Robbinses never cared about my being a Protestant; they took me along, treating me like a family member.

Years later, I rediscovered something up in the attic and couldn't help chuckling. I had written a letter to God—not too long after the rain-coat miracle, I remember. Mom was so touched that she saved it all these years. I now have the letter in my scrapbook. My handwriting in pencil looks pretty neat and bold with a lot of curves, not bad for an eight-year-old. But my language at that time wasn't perfect; the letter contains improper verb tenses, unnecessary words, missing words, and of course, a few misspellings. It reads:

Dear God,

I am eight years old. I can not hear. I have a hearing aid. I love you because you are good and nice. I have three brothers! I do not have any sister. This morning my brothers are gone to school. I came to our bedroom. I said, "Oh, that's messy!" I cleaned our room. I told the truth! A long time ago I was bad girl! I was little girl. I bite Daddy's arm. My mother was very cross with me. NAUGTY! (There is a drawing of a mean-looking girl labeled "Bainy" biting an arm labeled "Daddy's arm.")

My daddy is going to the hospital because my daddy is doctor. My birthday is July 16. I was born in 1961. I like the beautiful earth! (An awkward draw-ing of the earth and the sun is placed here.) *I live in Norfolk, Va. It is beautiful outside. I am going to ride bicycle. It have two wheels. Can you re-ally do everything? I wish I could to. My brothers' name are Lindsay, Harvey, and Nash. Nash is sixteen years old. Lindsay is fifteen years old. Harvey is thirteen years old. My dog's name is Romeo. Romeo, Pop, and Miss Miller died. Pop and Miss Miller are sick! Romeo did not watch the car. The car hit him. They went in Heaven. You live in the sky.* (A drawing of clouds sits here.) *I love you!*

Love,

Bainy Bilisoly

Although Clarke was dead set against sign language, we communi-cated by waving our hands. They were just informal hand gestures that the staff knew were not official sign language. Out of laziness, we

sometimes talked silently, only mouthing words, which just about drove the teachers up the wall. "Use your voice," one of them would wearily say to us. Who can blame them? We came up to Clarke to learn to use our voices; this wasn't a mime school. But still, my friends and I prided on our expertise at speechreading silent words.

Because most of us were profoundly deaf, we rarely called to each other, so we used many other ways of catching attention. Next to hand waving, the popular method was shoulder tapping. If you were in our playroom, you would've felt like you were in a room full of Charlie Chaplins. We didn't mind walking across the room just to tap a shoulder. We were tapped so many times that we could have developed permanent craters on our shoulders, like those the astronauts saw from one of the *Apollo* capsules.

The next way to get attention was foot stomping. This method created vibrations through the linoleum floor. The housemothers must have had their fill of our little hard-heeled oxford shoes hammering on the floor. Although she won't admit it today, Cheryl was the loudest of all. Even if she was sitting, she would stomp on the floor hard and fast like a jackhammer. Then there was another way to create vibration: table pounding. That drove the staff bananas, especially if we sat at the dining table. We would constantly hear "No pounding!," but would still clobber the table with our clenched fists, a sound even worse than a gavel.

One method involved no sound or vibration: paperball throwing. All we had to do was crunch a piece of paper and throw it at whomever we wanted to summon. Why worry about walking across the room when the paperball could hit someone's face with a painless thwonk?

And one attention-getting method we all hated to the core—having our chins grasped and turned toward the speaker, either gently or roughly. Every one of us found it so irritating that we would balk loudly and rub our chins in fake pain. We detested having our heads jerked around as though we were flimsy stuffed dolls that needed to be posed.

❧

It's true that many small deaf children don't understand humor very well since they don't hear light teasing, jokes, or idioms in daily conversation. Although I learned early to laugh off fake comments concerning

my appearance or even my mind, it was still difficult for me to pick up humor in conversation, even in college. Many of the jokes were hard to understand because they contained backup details that I had missed. So I just acted like a wallflower, grinning politely and silently. Wouldn't I look like an idiot if I were to let out a fake laugh, especially at the wrong time?

My dad's picture-drawn cards were the first to teach me about humor. When he wrote that he would get a big bird to fly me home, I laughed, knowing he was pulling my leg. Then it was my brother Harvey who taught me to laugh off fake negative comments. He has always been the nutty one in the family, drawing satirical faces and writing hilarious poems. My other two brothers, Nash and Lindsay, have never been without humor either. I must say that I come from a crazy family who, including Mom and Dad, know how to deal with sarcasm. We know how to prevent hurt feelings; we just don't pay attention to insulting comments.

Because we were not a perfect family, I did get hurt at times; however, I could see that my family hadn't meant to hurt me. They weren't always patient with me, and I did sometimes feel isolated from my family. It only happened when they were all yapping away during dinner, not acknowledging me. And it still does happen these days, so I haven't lost a sense of isolation.

It can be painfully difficult for hearing children to have a deaf sibling, especially if he or she is close in age. I have heard that many hearing children are jealous of how much attention their deaf siblings get from their parents. Well, of course, the deaf children need more attention in an *educational* way. It would be inexcusable if a deaf child received more love and affection than his or her hearing siblings. The hearing children also have to deal with the pain and embarrassment of having a deaf sibling, as they are likely to hear insults from other kids such as a neighborhood bully.

Because they were much older than me, my brothers didn't seem to have gone through many difficulties in having a deaf sister. The only time my brothers did fear embarrassment was when they had a girlfriend over. In truth, I was insulted by my brothers' fearful glances at me in the presence of their girlfriends, still, I understood that any teenager or college student would desperately try to impress

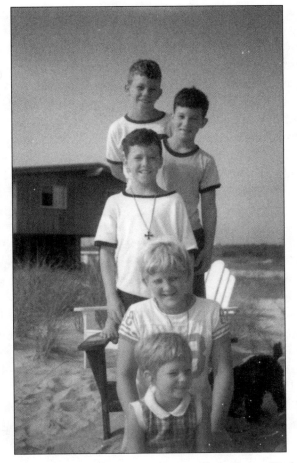

On a family vacation at the beach. From top to bottom: Nash, Harvey, Lindsay, my favorite cousin Kate, and me.

a sweetheart with his "picture-perfect" family. But for the most part, my brothers have long treated me just the same, and we are still close these days.

As a sixteen-year-old, Nash was usually shy and spent a lot of time listening to the Beatles in his attic bedroom. In contrast to Harvey, he wasn't much of a talker or the wrestling type of brother. If his friends today are reading this book, I can imagine them dropping their jaws in disbelief because Nash is now known to be a garrulous attorney, full of snappy quips.

Ever since he socked me in the arm to prove, erroneously, that I wouldn't cry, Lindsay has always been compassionate with me. When I was seven, he rode bikes with me to the neighborhood pool just to keep an eye on me. I remember once darting across the street and turning around to see Lindsay unmoved on his bike. When he slowly came up, I noticed tears running down his cheeks. To my chagrin, Lindsay explained that I would get hit by a car if I wasn't careful and reminded me that I couldn't hear. With a heartfelt embrace, I promised my fourteen-year-old brother I would stop and look both ways. Even today when riding the bike, I think about Lindsay's tears every time I prepare to cross the street. Always look both ways, period.

❦

Mom and the seven other mothers of deaf children from the area went to the legislator in Richmond and urged that the state should pay for the tuition to schools for the deaf, no matter where the school was. After much deliberation, the legislator finally agreed to pay half of the tuition for out-of-state schools while planning new local programs such as mainstreaming. That marked the beginning of Public Law 94-142, the law that encouraged education of disabled students in the least restrictive environment. Today, this act is called the Individuals with Disabilities Education Act, or IDEA.

Because I had been at Clarke for four years and was doing well, my parents decided it was fair enough to pay half of the tuition instead of risking setbacks by transferring me to a school across the Chesapeake Bay that taught both oralism and sign language. I'm glad they decided to have me stay at Clarke because I had real friends there, especially Cheryl and Diane, and felt safe, even though I was way off in another state.

I continued to spend weekends with the Karases and the Robbinses. With the former family, I embarked on interesting adventures that I never had at home. Mr. Karas took us snowmobiling out at a cow farm that belonged to a friend. We rode through the open field at night, watching our headlights sail over the glittering snow. It was awesome. We milked the cows and struggled to aim the squirting white fluid into the bucket. And over at the Robbinses' I enjoyed other outdoor adventures, mostly ice-skating and camping. We slept in a tent and made s'mores over the fire by the river. Mr. Robbins, an avid outdoorsman,

taught me, along with Cheryl and her brother Chuck, how to catch trout in the river.

Years later, Mom expressed her thought that these families had more influence on my life than my own family did. She was probably right. For a long time, I wondered how the Karases and the Robbinses managed to have another family's daughter over every other weekend, putting extra food on the table and buying an extra movie ticket. It was obvious that these families, in which both sets of parents had to work, were trying to make ends meet. One set had to handle two deaf children while the other set tried to support five children. But still those families treated me as if I were their own.

Vocabulary is indeed one of the biggest problems for deaf people. Hearing people learn new words every day by overhearing conversations or listening to them face to face; deaf people cannot. It's pretty much the same with writing. That's why it took me years to develop my English language to age level. When I learned a new word, I still had to learn how to use it. For instance, was that word a noun or an adjective? That's something I was not able to figure out spontaneously. Back then, I used to despise writing and was even afraid to write a personal letter for fear that I would construct a strange sentence or use words improperly. I was totally self-conscious with my insufficient language. But the shame went away when I started teaching myself to read and write in recent years, inventing my own methods. I believe any deaf person can do it, if motivated enough, and can learn to love writing as I do now.

After college, I stopped skimming through a novel or a newspaper and began to labor hard on the word-by-word method. Reluctantly, I became a slow reader, frequently going back to a sentence I didn't understand and trying to figure what it meant. Despite those time-consuming reading setbacks, I was delighted with my language expansion, which I pretty much attributed to my own efforts. I had been taught all my life, so it was time to motivate myself by reading.

If you asked me what I would consider to be the most important thing for deaf children, I would say literacy. I know the choice of communication and education methods comes first for a newly diagnosed deaf child because that choice will affect his or her whole life ahead.

But then, regardless of the communication choice, a deaf child should learn to read and write English on his or her own. I strongly believe that literacy tremendously helps a deaf child become aware of the world, even if he or she is in the deaf community, which has its own language and culture.

At Clarke, we spent so much time on oral education and language development by blackboard that we weren't given a lot of reading material. I don't remember reading fables or any short classic novel. My classmates and I would've had a hard time understanding the novels of Laura Ingalls Wilder or Mark Twain. I'm not blaming Clarke for offering so little reading material; I understand that its main goal was to teach us to speak so we could be prepared to join the hearing world. What we were learning there was definitely time-consuming.

꽃

Diane and I had the same people in our class throughout the Middle School, although Cheryl had left to attend regular school. But her absence at Clarke never affected our friendship a bit because my weekend visits to Cheryl and her family continued. Every time she and her mother came to pick me up, I was full of questions about Cheryl's experiences with the hearing world. It also helped that her brother Chuck not only remained at Clarke but also lived in the same dorm; every time I passed him in the hall, I felt a strong presence of Cheryl and her famous foot stomping!

At Clarke, each class was limited to eight students because the smaller groups worked better for deaf children. Deaf schools typically don't allow large classes. How can a teacher get so many students to look directly at her lips or signing? My small class of children, all sharing the same disability, was a formative place for me and Diane to develop great friendships with those of the opposite sex. Just like any other preadolescent, I had a puppy love, stealing kisses behind the bush.

I even remember my first kiss. Lord, that happened in Miss Miller's class when I was just a tiny front-toothless pip-squeak. Chucky asked me if he could kiss me while Miss Miller was somewhere down the hall. I giggled with a nod. He leaned over and embraced me, kissing me on the lips. My body tingled with the sensation of his lips pressing on mine, although it lasted only for a second. I think even Miss Miller

would have been touched at the sight of six-year-olds giving each other just one little smack on the lips and no more.

During my seventh year at Clarke, my parents met with the staff who suggested that they send me to regular school because my speech, though not always understandable, was good enough after years of oral education. But it was really because the staff feared that I was learning some of the official sign language, which was true. As we got older, my friends and I embedded some real signs in our usual informal hand-gesturing method. My parents were told that it could hurt my chance of functioning in the hearing world; therefore, it was time for me to go.

Mom and Dad decided to send me to a small private school five miles from our home. Knowing that it wasn't going to be easy for me, they discussed with the Clarke staff how to prepare me for a drastic change. They knew that, at first, it would be difficult for me academically *and* socially; therefore, I would need constant help with the homework and advice on how to make hearing friends.

I had mixed feelings about coming home for good. The good feeling was, of course, knowing that I would be with my family every day. The sad feeling was realizing that I would be leaving my deaf friends, especially Cheryl and Diane. Most of all, I was scared to death. How would I be able to interact with the hearing kids on a daily basis? I feared that my intelligence would be tested because I knew my language development was severely delayed. I was once at my hearing friend's house, peeking into her schoolbooks, and was amazed by the words I'd never heard of before. How would I be able to catch up with a hearing person, even if he or she were two years younger than me?

The plan was to make the transfer during spring break to give me more adjustment to regular school before starting afresh the following fall. I was to begin third grade despite my age—a few months before my twelfth birthday. Yes, that would put me three years behind. In fact, I had a vocabulary as scant as a kindergartner's. At that time, I had never heard of the word *transfer* or even *regular*. My deaf friends and I simply used the term *public school* and that was it.

The staff at Clarke began reminding me to use my voice and pay attention in class. I knew talking without a voice, like most of us did out of laziness, would be unthinkable with hearing kids. They wouldn't know how to speechread. And finally, the staff said I would have to work much

harder than my hearing classmates to catch up, and I understood that completely. So I braced myself for the hard road to the hearing world.

Elbow Grease

Many of my friends have said that I have a keen memory of just about everything, and it may be true. March 1973 was when I began energizing my memory to a permanent hustle because it was the beginning of my dramatic years in the hearing world. Because of my deafness, I have relied on sight to keep memories, developing an enormous, sagging photo album inside my forehead. I can even feel its weight. Whenever I see something dramatic, *Click! Hold it right there,* and then this scene is remembered forever.

Emotion is the other way to keep my memories fresh. In the past, deafness had created an emotional roller coaster for me; I think I have experienced just about every single emotion you can imagine—fear, giddiness, anger, pleasure, sadness, joy, despair, and so on. In fact, this disability is extremely sensitive to emotion and to sight, and deaf people remember well by feeling and by picturing scenes.

When Mom dropped me off at Garrison-Williams School, the kids—more than a hundred of them, of all grades—started gawking and following me. I couldn't help feeling as if I were an alien. Overwhelmed by the attention, I quickened my pace toward my classroom. I wanted to be treated like a regular kid, but here, it was all a circus.

As I stood facing my new fellow third graders, a feeling of uneasiness swept over me. I was physically bigger than most of these eight- or nine-year-olds. I was on the brink of puberty, about to develop two bumps on my chest. I was the only hibiscus with crimped petals ready to blossom while my classmates were clamped-shut buds in the midst of large leaves. Towering over those classmates, I didn't, however, feel *mentally* bigger. I knew their language skills were more advanced than mine since I had read their welcome letters and even had to ask Mom for clarification.

I realized that my classmates had been waiting for me to say something, possibly wondering if I could really talk. I awkwardly looked around and said, "Well, where do I sit?" Then came all the little index

fingers pointing to the desk in the front row. I was relieved when Miss Mountcastle, whom I had met the previous week, walked in with a smile toward me, and I sat in my new desk that had no volume box or headphone.

I was struck by how different this class was from those at Clarke. There were so many desks behind me, instead of in a semicircular pattern. I ached to turn around and see whether there was something sneaky going on. I figured I'd be placed in the front row for the rest of my life. As I expected, it didn't do any good to sit in the front row. It wouldn't help me to understand fully what a regular-class teacher had to say. I could understand only a few words here and there in the fast talking, although I could hear the teacher's voice well with my hearing aid. This was a regular class, and it'd be a waste of time if Miss Mountcastle spoke slowly for only the one deaf child. I certainly didn't want that; I wanted regular treatment.

From that day on I developed a habit of daydreaming, which would continue all the way to college. That's why I was never bored. Why worry about trying to piece together missing parts of the spoken lecture when I can pick up only a few scattered words? I highly recommend daydreaming if you've got nothing else to do; it's good for the brain cells to wander around in relaxation like visitors at a museum. Unless you don't know how to look attentive, no one will know that you've got Dali-like scenes in your mind.

People have asked me if I was in a mainstream program and the answer is no. Mainstream means inclusion of deaf children in regular schools that provide interpreters in classes and special classes on the side. I could have been mainstreamed, but my parents felt that a small private school, along with their involvement with my schoolwork, would be worth a try.

Every deaf child is different, regardless of the degree of hearing loss or level of intelligence. Some do well with mainstreaming; others don't. That method has an advantage of introducing the deaf student to hearing peers and encouraging his or her English language development. But it may also cause loneliness and isolation. Opponents perceive mainstreaming as a disaster for deaf children, who are often unable to learn the normal means of communication despite interpreters. Hence, mainstreaming is controversial.

I managed well without mainstreaming because of my family's tremendous support. They always looked over my shoulder to be sure I wasn't going to flunk a test or miss a deadline for a paper. So I was able to muddle through difficult years of normal education before receiving my college diploma. It was a long, grueling battle from the day I entered Garrison-Williams as the tallest and oldest third grader. But it was worth it.

❧

I was delighted to have Lindsay at home during my difficult ordeal; he was the only brother there at that time. Harvey was at a boarding high school in Northern Virginia, and Nash was in California for his freshman year at Menlo Park. I knew I was naive, so I depended on Lindsay for his advice on developing a social life with my hearing peers, many of whom had never associated with a deaf person before.

I realized I had to try everything to be accepted. Trying was fiendishly hard work. I tried not to say or do outrageous things because I still had trouble understanding right from wrong. Admittedly I wasn't always very tactful. I did occasionally blurt out something that caused people's hair to stand on end. One time, late at night, when Mom's company had not yet left, I walked in and cheerfully said, "Oh, you're still here?" Fortunately, my parents were never angry with my tactlessness; instead, they would outright tell me why it was wrong to say this or that.

I tried not to embarrass friends if I was tagging along with them nor my brothers when they had their girlfriends over at the house. More important, I tried not to embarrass myself. I constantly worried about whether my verbal remarks or actions would repel people. I had to rely on facial language to tell what people were really thinking. If I could have heard comments such as "You wouldn't believe what he said to her . . .," I would have been able to learn morality in a snap.

I also tried not to interrupt conversation. Even at a young age I knew deaf children had a tendency to do so. But it was difficult *not* to cut in because some people talked so low or moved their lips so slightly that I may have thought no one was talking. That often happened in a group. If I wanted to say something, I had to look around for unmoving lips before jumping in.

When I was in a conversation with a group of friends, I tried to look included even though I could not decipher the swarm of words flying around. I tried not to look frustrated because I didn't want people to feel sorry for me. I just pretended to listen, my eyes secretly darting around for body language. The hardest part of a group conversation was when everyone suddenly erupted into laughter; I didn't want to be the only one not laughing. Therefore, I felt compelled to let out a fake laugh, which made me feel like an idiot. But I figured that laughing along with the group made me look included.

Despite the feeling of isolation, I was determined not to let group conversation bother me too much. It was something I knew I would have to face for the rest of my life, and I had long gotten used to missing conversation. I never wanted people to feel sorry for me. But now, in the hearing world, I began hearing pitying remarks about my deafness as if it were a death in the family. Inwardly annoyed, I responded by shrugging it off to indicate that deafness was not a tragic thing.

Now that I was dealing with hearing peers on a daily basis, I would have to try with all my resourcefulness to be accepted. I envisioned a long winding road with fallen rocks here and there ahead. With this rough disability, I'd likely either skip around or smash into obstacles, possibly more of the latter. That road was not going to be smooth at all.

I didn't do too well in third grade because of my limited language. All the technical words in the textbooks threw me off, and I had to turn to my parents for help. With her history degree, Mom took delight in teaching me about immigration during the early 1900s. And Dad prided himself in explaining photosynthesis to me, holding up a camellia leaf he had plucked from the yard. Of course, he left out the chemicals such as CO_2 (carbon dioxide) and O (oxygen) and only said, "The sun goes inside and that's what makes the leaf breathe."

My parents and the school staff decided to move me up to fifth grade the following fall so I'd be with those closer to my age. I remember taking a literacy test at the end of school year, and I don't think I even passed it. But that didn't prevent my parents from deciding to let me skip fourth grade; they assumed I'd eventually pull through under their close surveillance.

Fifth grade was even harder because I went through a bad phase. I had befriended a girl who taught me to behave like a bully, picking on

weaker girls. That's why I became difficult at school—just temporarily. I do feel bad thinking about it, but I have apologized to those I hurt. Without realizing it, I had become good friends with the wrong person. I just thought M.J.'s tough attitude was cool, and I was willing to do anything to please her.

Now that memory is hard for me to share. But I want to remind you that it's difficult for a deaf child to understand right from wrong. Some hearing kids know this and take advantage of it. I've heard stories about deaf children being guided into doing something outrageous by their hearing peers who tell them there is nothing wrong with it. Then the hearing kids get a thrill of watching deaf children discredit themselves. That's what M.J. did to me. She told me to strip in front of the neighborhood boys, promising that they would become enamored with me. And I did. That's the truth. I took off all of my clothes, from head to toe. I kept on doing it because M.J. egged me on, praising me and calling me her best friend. Deep down in my heart I didn't feel comfortable stripping, but all I wanted was to be accepted.

She also taught me to bully my own classmates, saying it was cool to push them down on the ground or knock their books off the desks. And I believed her. The school staff was obviously reluctant to tell my parents how difficult I had become, so Mom and Dad never knew I was going around shoving people down, using bad words, or being rude to my teacher.

There was another reason for my toughness: I wanted to hide my vulnerability as a deaf girl in the hearing world. I remember pushing a small girl down on the ground and then feeling my heart wrench with shame. I didn't feel good about what I did. This girl hadn't done anything to me. But in a selfish way, I was more concerned about looking tough to mask an extremely sensitive disability.

When we rode our bikes to a grocery store, M.J. goaded me into stealing a pack of cigarettes, emphasizing the word *sneak* and even demonstrating how to tiptoe. Did she secretly want me to get caught—just to see the excitement of handcuffs slapping over my wrists? For the first time, I questioned our friendship, staring at M.J.'s wicked grin. But I was still too intimidated by her dominance. So I reluctantly went into the store, slipped Marlboros into my coat pocket, and casually walked out. No, I didn't feel good about stealing; I knew it was wrong.

After that, I wanted to get away from M.J. but didn't have the courage or didn't know how. I was all alone and confused with the trap I was in. As I grew to realize, M.J. was not a real friend. But I didn't know what to do and was afraid to turn to somebody for help. I feared that M.J. would retaliate if I told her that our friendship was kaput.

Luckily, the other two girls in the neighborhood pulled me out of the entanglement. I remember that corner of the street where those girls summoned me. They stood so close together with anxious looks that I knew they had rehearsed for this encounter, something unusual for eleven-year-olds. Finally, they declared to me in an alternate fashion, "What happened to you? You've turned mean. You used to be a nice girl but M.J. has changed you. And you're getting a bad reputation. You need to get away from M.J."

I walked home, upset and unsure how I would get out. Then a solution entered my mind, and I hesitated, pushing it off and then pulling it back in. It was going to be a huge risk, but I'd do it to get away from M.J. So I approached my mother after dinner when she was preparing to take a bath. I asked if we could talk, uncomfortably looking at her long green velvet bathrobe. Mom sensed something was wrong and had me sit down on the edge of her bathtub. Then she listened to me confess about smoking and pushing down people. I told her it was M.J. that guided me into it. Because I was too ashamed, I didn't tell her about stripping. So I stopped the confession right there and fearfully awaited for her reaction. This solution was now started but not yet completely done, as I expected. Shell-shocked, Mom stood up and walked around. She then disappeared without a word. I just waited on the edge of the bathtub, my nerves all shot.

Dad barged in, ranting and raving, and it surprised me because he was normally a laid-back person. While Mom stood by in a daze, he slumped down and stared at me in disbelief, which caused my eyes to water. I told him I was sorry and would never do that again. It took my parents several moments to calm down and declare that I was strictly forbidden to see M.J. That's exactly what I was aiming for. I needed my parents to help bring me out of the mess. Fortunately, they didn't ground me because I agreed to stop hanging around with M.J.

M.J. was baffled when I told her I could no longer see her. I lied that my parents had found a cigarette in my coat pocket right after I left her

house. Just a little white lie to get myself out of her retaliation. And it worked. I'm glad I confessed to my parents because it made me a nice girl again. Although it pains me to remember this bad phase, especially stripping and all, I don't feel anger toward M.J. because she was just so undisciplined. As long as my life has turned out well in spite of painful past experiences, there is no reason to hate someone who had treated me badly. Those who are cruel definitely have a problem and need help.

❧

It had been two years since I entered the hearing world, and my grades had improved tenfold with the advantage of a small class of ten or fifteen. My classmates were kind enough to tell me what page to look up or what book to pull out from under my desk. As always, I sat in the front row but still daydreamed while trying to look attentive. What did I daydream about? No telling.

My language development, though still several years behind, had grown steadily in the hearing culture. When I first heard, "a substitute teacher" at school, I waited until I got home to ask Mom if she would spell out the first word for me. Normally for deaf people, it's hard to learn a new word just by speechreading because not all consonants can be heard. That's why I started to concentrate hard on reading. But the problem was, whenever I came across a new word and learned its meaning, I wondered how to pronounce it. So it turned out that I had to learn vocabulary both ways, by reading and oral methods.

I felt accepted by hearing friends who eventually grew to understand my deafness. They treated me like a regular kid, trying to compete with me in running relay races or shooting ball. I had made the school basketball team, and Max the coach invented hand signals for me to read across the court because it wouldn't be a good idea to try to read speech while I was running. I'd end up plowing into other players or smashing into the padded wall like a housefly.

I was invited to slumber parties, where I learned that hearing kids in a gathering don't ever fall asleep once the lights are turned out. They just keep yapping away no matter how sleepy they are. Well, I guess it's more of a comfort for hearing people to talk in the dark. For deaf people? Forget it; they would rather snooze than struggle to speechread or sign in the blackened atmosphere. Whenever I was slumbering with

those friends, I could tell if gossip or jokes were tossed back and forth, although I had removed my hearing aid and heard absolutely nothing. I could see the small hand gestures or feel the one next to me shaking the floor with her laughter.

Now that I was a teenager and becoming more concerned with vanity, it was time to get the behind-the-ear hearing aids. The old hearing aid I had had for years was about to conk out. I was sad about giving it up because it had brought all those first pleasant sounds to my ears. But I wouldn't miss those straps or protruding earpieces that stuck out like corks or those twisted cords that sometimes got caught in a tree branch, yanking off one of my earpieces. When I entered the hearing world, I cut the torso straps, leaving only the one around my neck. I wore my hearing aid like a necklace inside my shirt and that provided comfort. But the trouble was that, whenever I ran down the basketball court, it looked as though I had an abnormally large heart beating violently through my chest. I'm sure it scared the dickens out of the opponents because they didn't know what in the world was thrashing around inside me. I began to tuck the front strap behind my teeny-weeny bra and it helped, though not perfectly.

Mom and I flew to Clarke to receive my new hearing aids, which I could have gotten locally, but this school understood my hearing loss better and would select the right brand for me. I was overwhelmed to be back on this unchanged campus after two years. Diane was delighted to see me, nearly knocking me down with her embrace. To my astonishment, she had shot up several inches above me. So had Cheryl and all the old friends. It was weird how fast adolescents could grow in a short period of time.

Meeting with the school audiologist, I was tickled to once again take hearing tests, which I had done every year at Clarke. The fun thing about hearing tests is that they challenge you, like a game of musical chairs, to catch the lowest sound by raising your hand exactly at the right time. Although I could see the audiologist's face through the tinted glass window between us, I could not see his hands as he manipulated the audiometer, sporadically sending various tones to my headphones. As I attempted to figure out whether I was hearing an actual sound through my headphone or just an echoing in my head, I must have raised my hand a hundred times when there was no actual

sound at all! The hearing test identified that my hearing loss had remained the same as several years before, about a 75 percent loss in both ears. The audiologist then decided on the right kind of hearing aid for me.

I don't remember whether I had earmolds made there or somewhere else ahead of time. In fact, it takes an earmold a few days to harden. The earmold-making process is the most icky part of the whole thing. Imagine sitting there while a big fat syringe injects soft pink material into your ear and you suddenly feel it swish inside like mousse. It tickles, for sure, especially if that foam is cold. When the audiologist yanks it out, it looks like strawberry meringue.

They fit so well, that I knew it would take time to remember that I had these behind-the-ear aids on; I was so unaware of them that I would accidentally crash into bed with them on—and worse yet, dive into the pool, which I did once that year. Hearing aids can be unpredictable, no matter what type they are. I've heard about some hearing aids being ruined simply because of a small splash of water. Yet my audiologist told me a strange story of an old man who forgot about his aid in his pants pocket and threw these pants in a washing machine. Even after being flounced around in soapy water, the man's aid turned out fine. Don't ask me how it survived.

I was thankful for the trip all the way up to Massachusetts, and it was a memorable one because I had a chance to reunite with the Karases and the Robbinses at the former's house where we feasted on Mrs. Karas's Polish sausage. This trip also gave me an unique bond with Mom because she perfectly understood how much a visit to the "old world" meant to me.

But traveling wasn't always so comfortable. Whenever I reminisce about one incident that nearly put me in danger, I shudder and quietly scoff at my own dumb mistake. I made a mistake and never did it again. Mom and I were in New York City with my grandmother Donnie for the Bicentennial celebration. After spending a spectacular Fourth of July on the harbor, we retreated to our hotel dining room where we had dinner and chatted with our waiter. In truth, I thought he was a nice-looking guy with gracious manners. The next day, I happened to run into him in front of the hotel while Mom and Donnie were still packing in their room. He asked if I wanted to get in a taxi with him for a

ride and said something I didn't understand but I just let it go and told him I had twenty minutes.

So yes, I did get in the taxi with the waiter, someone I hardly knew anything about. But he seemed gentle and friendly. As long as we were in a public place with the cabbie, I thought it would be safe to ride along. If this waiter had his own car, I would have said no. When I was seven, my family warned me not to get in a car with a stranger. My brothers kept asking me the same question over and over, "What do you say when a man offers you candy and asks you to get in his car?" After hearing this so many times, I learned to say a firm "No."

Now I was sitting in the back seat with the waiter, zooming down Park Avenue. Just then I began to feel uncertain and asked the waiter where we were going. To my dismay, he responded that we were going to a movie. Since it was broad daylight, I immediately knew something was fishy. My body tensed when the waiter put his hand on my knee. I inwardly panicked when we parked in front of a seedy movie theater with weird names. The waiter held out his hand to help me out of the car but I sat there paralyzed. Finally I told the cabbie to take me back to the hotel pronto. Luckily the waiter didn't protest and rode on without a word.

To my great relief, we ended up at the hotel again, and I quickly climbed out of the taxi, leaving the waiter. After it drove on out of my sight, I stopped in my tracks and tightly shut my eyes in shame. Why did I do this?, I asked myself in a silent shout, clenching my fists. When I hesitantly entered the lobby and saw my mom at the checkout counter, my heart sank as I realized how close I had come to putting my family in agony. Mom turned to me with a pleasant grin, and her unknowing look made me want to hug her. I couldn't hold it in and told her what happened. Mom stared at me incredulously and exclaimed her words that pushed me into further shame: "You're *fifteen*! How could you do this?!"

Visibly shaken, Mom and Donnie barraged me with questions and asked why I got into the car with someone I barely knew, especially in *New York City*. I explained that they, too, thought the waiter was super friendly from the night before. Mom protested that he was still a stranger and that we knew nothing about him other than he waited tables. The whole incident was a hard lesson for me and made me more cautious with strangers, even the friendly ones.

Years later, I babysat my brother Nash's dog at my house, playing ball with her in the front yard. A little girl rode by on her bike and stopped to ask if she could pat the dog. After hearing my resounding "Yes," the girl played with the dog and chatted with me for about a half hour. Well, a few weeks later, the same girl pedaled by and I approached, asking if she would like to see my fish pond. The girl thrust her hand at arm's length and said in her outright tone, "No, I don't know you." It was like a slap in my face, but I was intrigued by how a five-year-old girl could protect herself. She then looked at me in half-recognition and asked if I had a white dog named Molly. After I answered yes, the girl demanded to see my fish pond. As we walked to the back yard, I praised her for giving me that kind of response. The girl continued to come by to feed the fish and chat with me before moving away to another city.

Ever since the encounter with this five-year-old girl, I have been amazed by how quickly small hearing kids can learn to avoid danger by listening to warnings. I understand it takes time and effort to warn any small child to shun a "friendly man" who offers candy or asks for help finding his lost puppy. I cannot help feeling anxious about deaf children who are not able to learn safety the same way hearing kids do, at least, possibly not as fast as they need to. The point is, deaf children are able bodied and can run loose like hearing kids; however, they may be deprived of these important warnings. Just as deaf children have to practice new words over and over, they need to be warned many times about the same thing.

❧

I went to Old Dominion University once a week for my language sessions and learned that people used clichés in their language. When I first heard "paint the town red," I imagined people marching down the street with buckets of red paint and splashing it over everything in sight—trees, buildings, traffic lights, you name it. But then I learned it meant to celebrate. With his laid-back humor, Dad explained what "bite the bullet" and "foot in the mouth" meant.

In college, I still felt that I had missed a lot of this humorous type of language and purchased *The Dictionary of Clichés*. Even today, I still have to grapple with some of the meanings. While my mother-in-law was housesitting for us, she cleaned the bottom of our shower, removing

the gray coating which I had tried to do many times without luck. Well, when we came home and saw the immaculate bottom in our shower, I called my mother-in-law to ask how on earth she did it. She chuckled and replied, "Elbow grease." I paused, picturing a clear plastic bottle with yellow fluid in it. Then came my naive question, "Where did you get it?"

My parents would not allow me to withdraw throughout the entire dinner without saying a word. They were trying to encourage me, as a teenager, to be a better conversationalist. The truth is, I was not as explicit as I should have been. I always gave too short an answer such as "Yes" or "It was fine." Actually I could've rattled on with interesting details if I had heard how people answered questions. No wonder Mom and Dad constantly urged me to "tell more about it." They also tried to boost the way I answered questions or reacted verbally; they taught me how to speak in spirited tones. I remember Mom urging me to say "Ssshhuuuruh!" instead of a flat "Sure." In fact, my deafness had deprived me of expressive language.

Over the years, people had often waited for my reaction, perhaps wondering, "Don't you appreciate what I've just said?" I could see that my lack of response peeved some people, making them think that I was unfeeling. Their perceptions did worry me, but I was more scared of blurting out wrong words. I desperately fumbled for the right words to express my feelings before it was too late. It took me several years to be more verbally expressive. Eventually, I learned the proper words to show my feelings and ways to fluctuate the tones of my voice.

I realized that people spoke differently even though they spoke the same English language. I came home from Clarke, proud of my oral accomplishments but, then, was baffled at the way people here in Virginia talked differently from those up north. Many people here pronounced "house" as "hose" instead of opening their mouths into an "ow" shape as I had seen on northerners. Whenever these people said, "Come by to my house," I wondered if they were asking for help to water their plants. It took me a while to accept the southern accent. And I'd keep the northern accent Clarke had taught me—no sense in turning my expensive oral skills into effortless, tongue-loosening drawls. So these days, I seem to be the only one in the family who pronounces "to-MAY-toe" while everyone drawls "tuh-MAWH-toh."

Regardless of accent, everyone has different lip movements. Some talk from one corner of the mouth, and others move their lips as if they are chewing hard caramel apples. I don't mean to sound critical, but it galls me when someone talks way too forcefully, spraying saliva. As my stomach turns, I try desperately hard not to distort my face. It's nerve-racking when that person begins each word with a *T* or a *P*, propelling a tiny droplet in slow motion toward my face. I scream in my mind, *Yaaaaah!*, before it hits me in the corner of my eye or on the tip of my nose. Of course, I fight the powerful urge to wipe my face because I don't want to hurt feelings. But once I'm alone, I rub my entire face like mad or even throw water on it.

Fragile Leaf

As I had hoped, nobody followed me on the first day I entered Norfolk Collegiate School as a ninth grader. Everyone wove their way through the halls, apparently indifferent about having a deaf girl among them. Fortunately I had already gotten to know many of the people who attended this small private high school, particularly, those who, like me, had gone to basketball camp there during the summer. After having played basketball for Garrison-Williams, I made the junior varsity team in no time. Sports was where I felt readily accepted in the hearing world and where I could prove that deafness did not limit athleticism. That's why I intentionally played sports throughout high school, ending up with tennis as my favorite sport. My efforts in sports would help me achieve the true double-A rating: able-bodied and ambitious.

Still, I did make one sports blunder. It happened when we switched ends of the basketball court after halftime. In the third quarter, I kept forgetting that we were supposed to score at the other end. You guessed it, when I had the ball, I scored for the other team. Proud of my scoring, I spun around only to have my ego deflate at the sight of everyone at the other end. If I had been able to hear my teammates yell for me to come back, I would have turned around. I have seen hearing players head the wrong way, too, but they were saved by the verbal alarm behind them.

I was still the oldest in my class, two years behind, but I considered these kids my age anyhow—except for one huge point: I could drive

and they couldn't. They had just entered puberty, and I had just gotten my first driver's license. So I drove my friends to the mall and wherever ninth graders liked to hang around; that made me feel important, not used. Besides, I wanted to get out of the house on weekend nights.

I've been told that deaf people make the best drivers because they tend to be more attentive to the road for fear of colliding with an ambulance. I do get jittery about missing a warning sound, but my strong hearing aids enable me to hear a low-pitched car horn or even swear words. I don't blame those whose hearing cannot be helped by amplification for being scared of ambulances. But I have not heard of many accidents involving deaf people and emergency vehicles. Apparently, deaf people are able to detect a tiny red blinking light in a heartbeat.

Anyway, I'm not a bad driver, but when I have a passenger with me, well, that can be risky, particularly because I have to swing my eyes back and forth as I watch my friend's lips and the road. Fortunately, this distraction has not caused me to have a wreck. Diane once picked me up at the Hartford Airport in her Lincoln as huge as a Russian tank. I suggested that we, as hard of hearing people, shouldn't chat during the half-hour ride to her house, especially in a car that big. Diane dismissed it with a wave of her hand. Anyhow, we did talk nonstop the whole way while she managed to move her neck every two or three seconds, not once weaving on Interstate 91.

I can imagine how hard it is to sign while driving, but again, I believe deaf people have an ability to avoid accidents. I was once in a car with the three signing girls and it turned out fine, although the car did weave a little. I watched the driver briefly steer the wheel with her knee if she had to sign with both hands. She was driving well below the speed limit, which may have helped to keep everyone safe and happy.

When I started driving, Mom had to keep reminding me to turn off the blinker because I couldn't hear its clicking noise. Poor Mom, with her perfect hearing, had to listen to it for a very long time when I was a nervous, inexperienced driver who thought it was necessary to turn on the blinker at least 2,000 feet before making the turn.

I've had a minor car accident attributed to my deafness, and luckily, no one was hurt. It was rainy and foggy, so all the windows were hard to see through. Trying to get on the road from a convenience store, I asked my two friends sitting in front to look to the right and see if it

was clear to go. They both yelled "No!," but I plunged ahead—and rammed an old Mustang broadside, causing $500 worth of damages. Why did I accelerate instead of wait? I thought my friends said, "Go!" Ever since then, I've tried hard to distinguish between "No!" and "Go!" but I tell people they'll have to either shake a head or wave me forward with a hand.

I had become good friends with Elizabeth Forsberg, and when I first met her in fifth grade, I was touched by her curiosity about my deafness. Always full of pep, Elizabeth asked all kinds of questions such as how much I could hear with my aid. The more she learned, the more she helped. That's why we have remained close all these years, although she now lives a thousand miles away. I will never forget one big lesson Elizabeth learned about deafness when we were looking for homecoming dresses at the mall.

While we browsed in an apparel store, an eager salesgirl asked me to try on a dress she found. So she and Elizabeth waited while I was trying it on in a curtain-drawn room. What I didn't know was that the salesgirl kept asking me questions and waited for me to answer. "How does it fit?" No response. "Ma'am? The dress? Is it okay?" Silence. "Hello? Um . . . how about the dress?" Nothing. All this happened while my idiot friend stood there without a single word, her cheeks puffing out to keep from laughing. She even shrugged when the baffled salesgirl asked her why on earth I had not said anything.

After we left the store with my new dress, Elizabeth told me what happened. Aghast, I asked her why she didn't tell the salesgirl about my deafness. Her answer came out in a pitiful way: "I didn't want to embarrass you." Just then I gave Elizabeth a lecture about how it would be even more embarrassing if people didn't know about my deafness and that she should inform them right away. As she listened, Elizabeth tucked her head with a tiny smirk. Oh, how I wish I had seen that salesgirl talking to a curtain; that would have been great entertainment!

Like a typical high school kid who dated, I went to formal dances and informal parties, and it was in those settings that I realized with dismay that a loud atmosphere would always make it impossible for me

not only to hear but also to be heard. To hear in those settings was, and is, much easier because I could still speechread and understand what people were saying. To be heard in those settings was impossible. I couldn't make myself loud enough, even if I was screaming from the top of my lungs. Because I couldn't hear my own voice in the earsplitting environment, I just didn't know how to monitor it. In addition, projecting my voice at the highest volume distorted my words. People had to lean over to understand what I was saying, but it didn't help, so they just gave up and turned to somebody else. It still happens these days; however, I manage to avoid loud parties. I do like to socialize, seeing old and new friends all together, but only if it's a cocktail party, cookout, or wedding. In recent years, I've come up with a solution to converse with somebody in a loud atmosphere: I suggest that we move to another room or a quiet corner. A friend has no objection to it.

Diane was about to graduate from Clarke after spending twelve years there, and I flew up there to attend the ceremony as well as spend time with my old surrogate families. I met Cheryl's hearing friends at her school picnic and noticed that she interacted with the hearing peers the same way I did, friendly but careful not to offend. Because Cheryl's friends were a group of unknown kids, I was awfully shy around them. Cheryl didn't seem that way with her friends, constantly asking what was going on. But the funny thing is, when Cheryl and her family visited me a year later, I took her to a friend's house where many girls gathered, and she was so shy that she never said a single word. Our circumstances and behavior had completely reversed!

When I reunited with Diane at the graduation ceremony, I wondered how she'd be able to handle the hearing world after spending so many years in special education. I feared that the change was going to be much too drastic a change for Diane as a sixteen-year-old. However, I managed to keep these feelings to myself and gave her my congratulatory support. Then I stayed with her at the family cottage on the lake. Laura, another Clarke student who had graduated with Diane and who was also my roommate long ago, lived close by, so we walked over there a lot. I admit it, the whole visit was awkward, but not because of the Karases. It was because of *friends*. Diane and I were at an age where we

struggled to fit in. I could see that Diane was anxious to keep up with Laura and other deaf friends despite the fact that they would now go to separate schools.

When we sat in Laura's den facing the lake, I couldn't escape the feeling of isolation. Yes, they were the same friends I had at Clarke, with whom I had once felt comfortable and happy. But it had been five years since I left them, so I felt more immersed in the hearing world in spite of its obstacles. I should've been more delighted to be with friends of the old world but I was sixteen, a young emotionally immature sixteen, and had a serious boyfriend constantly on my mind. And I worried about who my friends were.

I struck up a conversation in a lighthearted way to break the ice and used some of the old hand signals, fondly remembering how we communicated in the past. To my chagrin, they looked at me weird and then questioningly at Diane who didn't say anything. As I sat there embarrassed, I realized that these hand signals were a thing of the past, now considered "baby talk." I got up to go to the bathroom just to escape the tension. Worse yet, I felt isolated from Diane, my old best friend, and she seemed to feel the same way about me.

On the way home I was disheartened at the possibility of drifting away from Diane. But then her letter came. Diane wrote like she did before, describing her summer activities, and asked *twice* if I had a good time. It was a worried question. Obviously, she didn't want to drift away either. Wanting to be an honest friend, I wrote Diane back and explained why I felt uncomfortable with the deaf friends after spending five years in the hearing world. I also wrote of my desire to keep our friendship intact, no matter what. Diane responded with understanding and promised to keep me posted on how she was faring in regular school. Needless to say, I knew that her first entry into the hearing world would start out overwhelming and painful. So I prayed hard that she would be able to handle it okay.

Social life was becoming more difficult for me. My friends and I had outgrown neighborhood activities such as climbing trees. Our bodies had reached full adolescence, and our energy levels had become more passive, except when we engaged in sports. We were now mid-teenagers who cherished only a few activities, one of which was to sit around and talk. Talk, talk, talk—imagine how hard it was for a deaf

teenager in the hearing world. Of course, I hated it, but there was nothing I could do about it, and I kept quiet, seething inside.

I remember tearfully complaining to Mom that I felt like everyone was ignoring me. With a heartfelt embrace, she explained that they may have not intended to because I was usually so quiet that they forgot I was there. Mom was probably right, but in a group of less than three girls, well, I wouldn't think so. Not everyone was patient enough to talk slowly to me; they could manage only to say "Hi" with a quick grin before walking away.

For anyone, growing up involves pain. Everyone tries to fit in, and self-esteem quivers like a fragile leaf, going up and down and sideways—the movement of insecurity. I had seen in high school that teenagers do a lot of backstabbing. Even good friends backstab one another. Whispering and snickering negative things behind backs are even more hurtful than a knife; the cruel words you hear (if by unfortunate chance) can creep to every part of your body and linger there longer than a flesh wound.

The threat of backstabbing had me worried all the time, paranoid. I couldn't hear what people said behind me, and I kept thinking they were talking about me. Maybe they were. Maybe they weren't. All the way through high school and college I became testy whenever people walked or stood behind my back. The paranoid feeling was difficult to avoid. My psychologist friend has told me that foreigners who know little or none of the English language react the same way. As a matter of fact, deaf people and foreigners are very much alike, both having to learn the language and not understanding the jabbering around them.

My teenage phase wasn't horrible; it had its normal ups and downs. I did make wonderful friends who have stuck with me to this day. Back then, they helped tremendously, letting me copy their school notes and explaining what went on in the movie we had just seen. But I have to admit that my friendship with them wasn't the confiding type because I built a wall around myself, not expressing my feelings in the hearing world to anyone. Because I didn't want sympathy, I harbored the occasional blues, put up a smiling face, and pretended to blend with the hearing world while there was an invisible wall around me.

At the time of my eighteenth birthday I flew up to Clarke for two weeks of speech therapy, and it was indeed productive. Beth the therapist

and I worked for a couple hours twice daily, and each time was like military training. If you spend two hours repeatedly coordinating the movements of your tongue, lips, cheeks, and jaws for just one word, you will just about crash. Your brain will seem to weigh a ton from the intense concentration on making perfect vowels and consonants. Sure enough, I was dead to the world by the end of each session, my jaws aching like crazy, but I managed to bounce back after lunch or a good night's sleep.

I had developed a habit of talking through my unmoving jaw since attending regular school. After years of communicating with deaf friends, I began to realize that I didn't have to talk slowly and deliberately around hearing people. Hence, I relaxed my mouth just a bit too much, not bothering to move my jaws wide enough as I tried to talk like a hearing person. Eventually, I was often running my sentences in a blur, all through my unmoving jaw. No wonder people asked if I had broken my jaw. I needed to learn to articulate the vowels coming out of my mouth. If I said, "Bob," it sounded like "Beb," with my mouth hardly moving a centimeter. This intensive speech therapy was providing a challenging workout for my jaw muscles that had gotten so far out of shape!

I also learned of my other speech impediments; one was the way I held my breath until I finished talking, letting out excess breath at the end of the sentence. When Beth told me what I was doing, it certainly didn't sound like an attractive speaking style. Beth taught me to inhale before talking and exhale along the way, so I would be more audible. Most deaf people tend to hold their breath while talking because they cannot hear how consonants are supposed to be exhaled. In fact, young deaf children have to be taught to blow, even to blow out their birthday candles. They do know to round their lips but they don't realize when blowing is supposed to occur. The sight of a feather fluttering from being blown can help.

Because many deaf people do not breath correctly when they speak, they end up having weak diaphragms, which inhibits their ability to project their voices across a distance. I was once sitting in a school bus as it waited at a red light and happened to see my mother walking down the street. Opening the window, I yelled, "Hey, Mom!" But she didn't hear, even though I was only thirty feet away. A hearing friend sitting next to me watched me try a few more times with my voice raised at

the highest volume. She then leaned over and yelled, "Hey Mom!" My mother turned her head, puzzled because she didn't recognize the voice. I sank in my seat, my face bright red!

As I worked with Beth, I also did relaxation exercises with my often restricted voice. I tended to tense my throat during speaking, which Beth suspected had been happening nearly all my life. The habit would be impossible to eliminate during only two weeks of speech therapy, so Beth made me promise to continue relaxation exercises after I had gone back home. Relaxing my throat was still difficult to do all the way through college where I often felt insecure and uptight. Now, I can relax my voice, but only when I'm in a pleasant mood. You don't want to hear how my voice sounds when I want to strangle someone or kick a trash can.

In addition, Beth informed me that I was still omitting some consonant sounds like the *NG* sound and a final *G*. Beth also had to teach me what to do with my tongue to produce a perfect *CH* and *J*, which wasn't easy. I had trouble making a correct *S* sound when another consonant followed immediately, for example *ST, SK,* and other blends; however, Beth had an S indicator, a device the size of a cigarette pack that blinked its red light when I correctly made the sound, which was an enormous help. Somehow, we managed to squeeze in work on all these errors during our therapy, and Beth really did work hard to motivate me. In fact, a speech therapy career might even be more laborious than one hauling sacks of cement mix.

Harvey and Nash had moved back home after graduating from their colleges. The house had been awfully quiet with only me and my parents for a long time, so I was delighted to have my brothers again under the roof. Lindsay was about five miles away in his tiny apartment; however, he came over frequently to catch up with the family. Mom and Dad had been great company during my bad days, but I had long ached for a sibling to share secrets, to tell dirty jokes, and most of all, to laugh with. I just wanted a lively atmosphere to get rid of the blues and needed my brothers for a good laugh.

Even in his mid-twenties, Harvey never tired of beating me up or pulling jokes on me. But fortunately, I had either Nash or Lindsay running to protect me. They would pound on Harvey, rattling the

My family in 1978. From left to right: Harvey, Nash, Lindsay, Mom, me, and Dad.

whole house. I'd never forget the clever trick Lindsay did to protect me. One night, Harvey seemed bored around the house, so he decided to prey on me while I was doing homework in my room. Knowing that I could not hear him come in, he sneaked up behind me and said "Boo!" My shriek was loud enough to alert Lindsay who came running in and tossed Harvey out of the room. Lindsay and I then cast worried looks at each other, knowing that Harvey could sneak back in, since we all knew I couldn't hear the doorknob turning.

A quick thinker, Lindsay grabbed a ball of string and tied one end to the lamp on my desk and the other to the doorknob. My room looked like some old yard with a clothesline running across. Lindsay hung a folded paper over the string close to my lamp and told me to holler when the paper went down. After he left, I kept my eyes open for the movement. As you would expect, the paper collapsed and I hollered. Harvey stood there shocked, his hand on the doorknob. Then came a loud *Thud!* There was Lindsay, crashing headlong into Harvey, and they slid ten feet across the floor.

With my brothers around, my social life had more good days than bad because I was able to turn to them for advice. I had a good junior year not

only because of the social life but also because I had made good grades and it was now time to start thinking about college. I already knew what kind of career I wanted in the future: landscape design. This type of job, I assumed, would be beneficial for me because it required sight but not necessarily hearing. When I was eleven, a landscape designer drew up a plan for my mother's backyard. I was fascinated with this large blueprint full of lines and shapes. My eyes studied it inch by inch.

I was all geared up for college hunting, but something worried me sick: my low score on the scholastic aptitude test, which could have quashed my dreams of going to a good college. That SAT had been a four-hour nightmare while I racked my brain and chewed on pencils. I would never take it again, even if someone put a gun to my head. All the other aptitude tests I had taken at Garrison-Williams and Collegiate were a nightmare, too.

That's because these tests contained mostly verbal content. V-e-r-b-a-l: Something that seems impossible for deaf people. I had gotten extremely low scores on every one of the aptitude tests, which had never surprised me. I took my SAT score with a Oh-well-what-can-I-do? attitude, but even so, my low score shocked me. I didn't even make it to 800, half of the standard score. Anyone who scores 1600 on a SAT must have very good ears!

Mom and Dad told me not to dwell so much on the SAT score and be optimistic because of my school grades, so we took off for a weekend of college-hunting as soon as I started my senior year. We had been told that Virginia Tech had disability services and could possibly help me out with expenses. And more important, this school had one of the top five horticultural education programs in the country.

After visiting a few other universities that seemed reluctant to accept a deaf person, I was deeply worried when we arrived at Virginia Tech, and I prayed that this place would accept me. We were given directions to the Equal Opportunity-Affirmative Action office on the edge of the huge campus. A brunette lady greeted us at the front desk and introduced herself as an assistant for the Handicap Concerns Officer who was not in at that time. Every time I think about her these days, my mind replays the powerful scene in which she really buoyed my hopes for the future.

After apologizing for her boss's absence, the lady offered to look at my grade report. She took one look and raised her hands in absolution

and said, "You will be accepted." My heart suddenly leaped. She repeated this sentence in an adamant way, even though I had not applied to this university yet. She also assured me that there was no need to worry about my SAT score and that I would receive plenty of help here through note takers and private tutors, all paid by the university. The lady had said it so forthrightly that I had to believe it. And she was right!

A Different World

Before even setting foot in college, I was preoccupied with the exciting future of independence awaiting me. But when I arrived on Virginia Tech campus with all my luggage, my excitement turned to fear. Strangers were everywhere, strangers who obviously did not have any experience with a deaf person. I wasn't prepared for this part—being away from home, the place where everyone understood my deafness. I wanted to cling to Mom and Nash who were helping loading things into my dorm room. Relieved to have my oldest brother during our brief campus walk, I listened to Nash's warning that college life could be reckless with tons of alcohol and one-night stands.

When Mom and Nash turned to leave, I felt an instant pang of homesickness, a wrench in my stomach, so sharp that I nearly keeled over. And the lump in my throat was so big that I couldn't swallow. I sure as hell didn't want Mom and Nash to leave; I even considered grabbing my luggage and fleeing back home from my new room. But then I quickly reminded myself that I was an adult, old enough to cope with this rite of passage on my own. My body tensed, trying to resist from running after my family, and I reluctantly waved good-bye to them. It was the worst homesick feeling I had ever had. Being left at Clarke School at the age of five might have been worse, but I don't remember that at all. That departure at Virginia Tech, yes, my memory is so strong that I can still feel my stomach rip.

Wayne, the Handicap Concerns Officer, offered to find me a tutor for every one of my classes, but I declined, assuming that lecture notes and textbooks would help me pull through. But it helped to have a fellow classmate hand me the notes after each class so I could take them to Wayne's building for free copies. Wayne and I would then discuss my progress in each class. Acting like a concerned parent, he wrote up a list

of my classes on the blackboard and asked about the updates. After listening to my reports, he'd tell me that I needed to study harder. Although he didn't have much experience with deafness, I always felt confident with Wayne and considered him a great friend. Before I left his office each time, we swapped tales and shared interests like outdoor adventures.

Despite help from the note takers, college was difficult because it demanded so many things in a short time. I never thought I'd have to read at least five chapters for each test; therefore, my reading pace had to increase for me to keep up. The demands gave me little time to reread and understand the meaning of a sentence or an entire paragraph. And college required so many papers to write. I'd have to turn in a paper almost every week, especially in that loathsome English composition class. My writing skills were still far below average, which was something I tried to hide from others on campus. I had no family to turn to for help and was too embarrassed to ask my dormmates for fear I'd be considered not so smart. They had no idea that deafness caused such difficulty in language development. So I struggled to write papers on my own, cautious not to plagiarize. Sometimes it took me a whole night to finish the first paragraph, and I'd become so frustrated that I'd throw a pencil across the room—only when I was alone—creating a line on the wall.

I was nervous about sharing a room with someone totally unfamiliar with deafness, which I had never done before. I knew that, to the majority, deafness was one of the most intolerable of all disabilities. But my roommate didn't appear to be bothered by my deafness. She was always out working or marching in the school band, which suited me fine.

Always looking for fun and companionship, I turned to the girls in my hall and tried to be like a regular girl. We ate meals at the cafeteria, walked to class together, and checked out bars during happy hour. I usually had a great time with these girls but, still, often felt lonely on the inside. More of a wallflower than a participant, I normally kept quiet around the group. I told myself that I was used to standing back anyway.

As I had expected, none of the girls tried to become real close with me, although they treated me with great kindness. I wasn't angry with them because they didn't grow up with me and were unaware of so many aspects of deafness. That's why my college friends were different from those back at home. It was no surprise to me that the invisible wall I had

built around myself got thicker. It would take me years to push it down, making myself more available emotionally and not worrying about what kind of friend I was. Today, however, the college friends with whom I've kept in touch are no different than my hometown friends.

Social life was even harder because Blacksburg was all parties, at somebody's apartment or at a fraternity house. With the rock music blaring at 115 decibels, I couldn't communicate, and my unmonitored voice was often drowned out. I usually clammed up and entertained my talk-devoid mind by staring at people and studying their body language. It was an interesting diversion; however, I tried not to stare too long. I knew it would irritate people and it'd be an invasion of privacy. But hey, it was fun to watch how people conversed with physical language. Looking sideways with a lowered gaze, I could tell when a couple was arguing; their heaving chests and tightened lips revealed the clues.

The ear-splitting parties were not always fun, but I figured it'd be better to hang out with friends than stay alone in my room. I started drinking a lot, way too much at a time. I drank more than I talked. I took too many sips without pausing to say something. It wouldn't be worth trying to converse in a loud atmosphere. It did make me angry not being able to communicate, so I thought five or six beers would lessen my frustration or even totally wipe it out. Then the next morning I'd wake up in my own bed (if luck would have it) and wonder why the ceiling lamp moved like an amoeba. When I'd sit up, a massive hangover would hit me, shooting a jab of pain through the side of my head. Gosh, I hated that feeling. But it happened again and again. As a matter of fact, I turned to alcohol to avoid not only the communication hassles but also the blues that were becoming more and more frequent.

I joined a sorority called Delta Delta Delta, looking forward to interacting with a variety of girls. Fortunately, my hometown friend Mary Park was in my pledge class, and it was a relief to have someone who understood deafness. Mary had been one of my best friends since I came home from Clarke, and we attended the same schools, playing basketball together. She would eventually become my roommate for eight years after college until I tied the knot with Steve.

During my pledge period I grew comfortable with the sisters, especially when speaking on a one-on-one basis. But still, I remained painfully shy in a group. While introducing ourselves at the first meeting, I was scared

to death of speaking in front of these girls. My whole body trembled inside, nerves jabbing each other like lightning bolts. I was so self-conscious of my deaf voice, I even thought about escaping the room. When it was my turn to speak, I inhaled to calm my frazzled nerves and talked so fast that it went like a blur. I just wanted to get it over with, and I didn't worry whether or not the girls understood me. I didn't have the guts to look the girls in the eye when speaking.

Then I met my big sister Faith Rios and immediately liked her elaborate way of teaching me about the sorority—its bylaws, purposes, symbols, and all that. Faith was, and is, one of the easiest people to speechread; she's got incredibly readable lips that would break into a cute smile. As my pledge period proceeded, Faith came by my room with sentimental cards and presents before lecturing on whatever I was supposed to learn.

I received a letter from Cheryl saying she had also joined a sorority at National Technical Institute for the Deaf in New York. It took me by surprise because she was in a deaf college after spending a decade in regular school. I fearfully wondered if she had returned to the deaf world, but let it go because Cheryl sounded happy in her letters, especially compared to her high school days when she expressed her frustration in writing.

For the past few years I had not heard much from Diane and wondered how she was handling the hearing world. She responded to my letters but never really elaborated on this issue. Switching from deaf school to regular school at the age of sixteen was certainly not a breeze. Not wanting to pester, I continued writing to Diane—and to Cheryl—just to say hello and tell them about my struggle in the hearing world. We had always written to each other when we felt the blues, sharing hearing-world experiences. I wanted to tell my deaf friends what I had here was definitely no piece of cake.

Because pledging took so much time, my grades started slipping and I was down in the dumps. This period was one of the hardest times of my life. I can't blame it on the sorority; it was my whole self. I was lacking motivation, and there was no family to kick my butt. Here in college I had no discipline and didn't study as much as I should have. I was skipping many classes, although I knew it was a dumb thing to do. Still, I believed

it would be a waste of time to go to class and not understand anything. So I stayed in my room reading magazines or walking downtown; my mind just drifted lazily, not worrying about what I was missing.

I made a mistake by putting social life ahead of school. It had been the top priority from day one. I knew it was wrong, but I had this disability that required a battle for acceptance. I desperately wanted to fit in. I had some close friends, both at home and in college, and I knew they cared about me. And, I cared about them, too. But here, I considered myself a loner, feeling different from everyone around me. I felt completely insecure, and I constantly worried about what people thought of me. Yet, I tried hard to fit in—sometimes too hard.

Not wanting any sympathy, I hid my moodiness and put on a smiling face. Sometimes I felt good about myself when passing a test or having dinner with a friend. But other times, more often than not, I had no self-esteem. Most of all, my deafness made me feel like a ten-year-old around hearing people because I usually got upset over stupid little things and made a big deal out of something that no one else would really pay attention to. I was emotionally immature. Perhaps if I had heard how people reacted to things in a mature way, I wouldn't have dwelled so much on things not worth worrying about.

Even when in a good mood, I still felt immature. I know I had made some people mad without meaning to, or I must have hurt their feelings when I really didn't mean to. Once I made some remarks to a friend, which I thought was just playful verbal teasing; my heart sank when she gave an offended look. Even as a twenty-one-year-old, I had not yet learned those verbal rights and wrongs.

Constant worrying about social life, I continued to do poorly in school and drink heavily at parties. Alone in my room, I'd break down in tears, cursing my own disability. When friends noticed my anguish, I'd just tell them it was because of my academic difficulties. I avoided mentioning my insecurity as a deaf person. Obviously, some of my friends worried about me and my drinking, yet seemed afraid to say anything.

One night, I received a call from Faith who expressed her concern about my grades. As my big sister warned, I would not be initiated in the sorority if I didn't make good grades. Her call scared me into wanting to change my studying habits. At about the same time, Wayne beckoned

me to his office and asked why I was having a hard time. I wept and confessed cutting classes, explaining the reason for it. He gently pressed that I still needed to go to class even if I didn't understand because not going at all would take away more motivation. A few professors had called him, expressing concern about my frequent absences, so that meant they cared, Wayne told me.

Wayne once again suggested that I get a tutor for every class. He explained that most professors hardly paid attention to textbooks, depending on their own lectures. And the students didn't always jot down everything, so that's why I had missed quite a bit. To my realization, college was mostly verbal, different from high school where textbooks were usually dependable. However, Wayne advised reading textbooks for the sake of information. As I listened, I thought about my parents who had sent me a heartfelt letter of encouragement. Just then, I felt a jolt of motivation, realizing everyone wanted me to do well here at Virginia Tech. There would be support all the way to graduation. I finally agreed on tutors and promised Wayne to do better, taking the last tissue from his Kleenex™ box.

My grades had improved after I started working with Martha, a fellow horticulture major, who deliberately explained the notes with enthusiasm. She was an excellent tutor and also a great friend. We decided to take elective classes together, one of which was, well, a very popular one: Human Sexual Development. Martha didn't have to tutor a whole lot on that one because most of the material came from the textbook and of course, "X-rated" videos.

To my mother's horror, I was taking another sinful course at the same time: Wines and Vines. Yes, Martha had to teach me all the complicated wine-making stuff while we were in a lab mashing grapes. When I came home, Dad said I had better learn a lot about wine and sex because he had paid for it. I hadn't told my parents about registering for those courses until they started.

Whenever I showed Wayne my test grades, he crossed his arms and gave me that big I-told-you-so grin. Okay, I learned a lesson, I admitted, and asked him to get me more tutors. School was moving right along, and I had made the grade to join the TriDelta sisterhood. With better grades and a sorority membership, I was beginning to feel more settled at Virginia Tech, although I still occasionally felt blue when my

social life would take a turn downward. But now, the number one priority was school, not how I could fit in.

People asked me "What is your major?" over-emphasizing the last word with questioning faces. To me, it seemed as though they were asking what I, a deaf person, was doing here in college. One half of me felt offended and the other half felt proud. The proud half could prove that I was just like them, able to strive for a college degree. Imagine what they would say if I replied, "Physics."

If I hadn't joined the sorority, I don't know what my life would be like at this moment. TriDelta really changed my life in many positive ways, giving me a chance to cope better with deafness. I had an opportunity to learn to deal with all kinds of personalities—and to read lips of all shapes and movements. With my good hearing aids, I learned to understand who was speaking, especially at meetings, by the different tones of each person's voice; I could hear the voice better than words. In fact, watching others speak prepared me for the future in the working world.

It took me a while to have the guts to speak in front of a large audience. I remember the first time I did it. Normally, my sisters and I formed a large circle at the end of a meeting to announce or say whatever we wanted. If we wanted to say something, we would hold the gavel until we were finished and then pass it on. For a long time, I had been mute and had treated the gavel like burning firewood, passing it along as fast as I could. But that night, I wanted to tell my sisters about the strange dream I had about a sorority event. I held the gavel, ready to speak, and that just about shocked everybody's pants off. They stared at me in disbelief, mouths half-open. I told about my dream, feeling nervous and trying not to talk too fast. To my enormous relief, everyone laughed and hooted. After that, I no longer stood there like a standup board figure.

When it was time for me to take on the responsibility for a little sister, I wondered with concern how I could handle the advising as a deaf person. I was relieved when I was paired with a little sister named Kathy Hyland because she was sweet and patient. I tried to teach her the same way Faith taught me. It was completely weird to teach someone because, all my life, I had been the one who was taught. For the first

time, I had responsibilities for another human being; that gave me a shot of self-esteem. I wanted to be worthy and dependable to someone, and I loved it!

My sorority occasionally gave low-key parties in the daytime, and these helped me to learn to monitor my voice and talk with less difficulty. The sun's rays shining through the room also made it easier to speechread, but I could never understand people with the window or lamp behind them. They looked like silhouettes in front of the glare, making speechreading impossible. Most often, I'd have to ask people to step away from the window or lamp, but sometimes, I'd sneak around to have my back to the light.

Speechreading is definitely more laborious than hearing. Some people are hard to speechread. I have to watch the movements of lips, teeth, tongue, and cheeks, and decipher every word that is spoken. It wears me out, and before too long, I can feel my brain turning into mush. That's why I envy hearing people who are able to understand words without relying on their eyes. Some hearing friends tell me that listening can be difficult, too. I'm sure it is—at times. But for me, every day is filled with trying to speechread all the look-alike sounds and maneuvering to see everything that is spoken—trivial or not—while piecing together information and trying to keep up with a communication flow that continuously races ahead. And that constant challenge can take its toll.

At first, I was frustrated for not being able to understand what people said and went home to discuss it with Mom. She advised that I just smile and nod, even if words zoomed over my head. So then I went back to school and grinned, bobbing my head like a jack-in-the-box. Finally, a friend had the heart to tell me not to do that. She warned, what if a guy asked you to sleep with him and you grinned, your head bouncing? I gasped in horror and went home to tell Mom that her advice was the worst advice she had ever given. As I later realized, hearing people also just smile and nod to deaf people because they are afraid to hurt feelings if they ask for a repetition. (Often, deaf people sense that and repeat anyway.) So both deaf and hearing people can sometimes look like fools.

I learned from sorority parties that I could get away with not understanding someone without having to grin and nod. I learned how to

handle a blabbermouth by looking interested while words flew over my head. Whenever that person paused, I'd raise my eyebrows and say, "Oh really?" or tilt my head back with a low "Eh-heh." I still do that; it helps me look polite, not bored or plain worn out.

During my sorority days, I learned to love round tables. You guessed it, a round table gives me a chance to see everybody's lips. A small square table is okay, much better than a rectangular one. I avoid sitting in the middle of a long rectangular table because my neck and muscles become stiff from switching back and forth like a water sprinkler. Instead, I try to take a seat next to or at the head of the table where I can keep my neck at a comfortable angle and move only my eyes around.

❧

As a Handicap Concerns Officer, Wayne's primary goal was to make students and faculty more aware of the disabled population on campus, so he decided to sponsor Virginia Tech's first "Handicap Awareness Day." During my four years at Tech, I watched Wayne struggle to make the campus more disabled-friendly by building wheelchair ramps and curb cuts. His work was driven by subsection 504 of the Rehabilitation Act of 1973, which forbade discrimination against disabled individuals in any program using federal money.

On "Handicap Awareness Day," I attended a luncheon where there was a panel discussion on accessibility problems in Blacksburg; then later, I watched a wheelchair basketball game in which a men's wheelchair basketball team played against Tech's regular women's team. Much to my surprise, several of my sorority sisters showed up at the game because of me. I didn't tell them anything about this special event; they just came. I was deeply moved and appreciated my sisters for coming to support.

But it was a depressing day for me because everyone was looking at me as a handicapped person. To tell the truth, the terms *handicapped* or *disabled* always haunted me. Although I did have a disability, I just couldn't imagine myself in the same category as those in wheelchairs. I badly wanted to be considered a regular girl, that's all. That's why I was tearfully bummed out that night, lying to concerned friends that I was upset because of a poor test grade. (It wasn't Wayne's fault for holding a handicapped awareness day. It was me, just young and emotionally

immature. I would've felt proud today, since I have grown to accept my disability.)

I never told anyone about my real feelings as a deaf person, not even my mother, not even when I broke down in front of someone every once in a while. I expressed only my frustration, but never how I fully felt as a deaf person. Nobody suspected any conflict because I was normally a happy-looking person and readily admitted my deafness, even joking about it. But the truth is, I was often ashamed of my disability.

I was embarrassed enough to avoid the other two deaf students on campus, trying to blend in with the majority. One was a really shy girl, and the other was a handsome bodybuilder; they both could talk and speechread. I wonder how the girl felt about being one of the three deaf students at this large university; she was so shy and reserved that I couldn't guess. But the bodybuilder, I could see how he felt—exactly the same way I did; he tried to avoid me, too. The bodybuilder and I somehow knew the same people and occasionally ended up at the same parties. Whenever he saw me, he'd quickly avert his eyes and walk away into his crowd. That didn't offend me because I understood. We were both trying to blend with the hearing people.

No one knew, but I was often angry about having this disability and struggled to keep it to myself. I'd sometimes explode alone in my room, throwing things and smacking my fist into my hand and whispering a string of obscenities—all in silence because I didn't want anyone to know. When I watched people conversing with such ease at a loud party, I'd get so livid that I thought about finding a baseball bat or a heavy tree branch and smashing the blaring speakers into smithereens. I even came close to it a few times.

I envied hearing people for their easy abilities to communicate with one another. I admit, it was intense envy. It bothered me to watch people carry on conversation a hundred feet apart or from different rooms, without having to look at each other. And these people didn't have to struggle to be patient as I always did—most of the time without luck. Unhappy about having this much-ignored disability, I often wondered what it would be like to be hearing—so nice and easy.

Honest to say, I sometimes felt a spark of anger toward God, but that never lasted more than a few seconds. I tried hard not to blame Him for

my disadvantages and this difficult disability. I tried to remind myself of good things He had done for me: giving me a loving, supportive family, especially my wonderful mother, who couldn't prevent the disability from occurring during her pregnancy. I was extremely grateful for my good functional family and loved them with all my heart.

But my family didn't know what it was like being deaf. That's why I sometimes felt isolated from them. I never told them of my feelings. Years later, my parents and I talked about how I had "successfully" pulled through as a deaf person. When I finally told them it wasn't all that rosy in the past, Mom disagreed, saying I was just fine with hardly a sign of distress. So I showed her a part of my unpublished novel, based on deafness, in which all the deep feelings spilled out. After reading it, Mom looked at me in surprise and remarked, "I didn't know you were depressed."

Not everyone in my family was always patient with me, and I wasn't always patient with them either. We have had screaming fights, not speaking to each other for days. However, there is an incredibly powerful bond between us; we just forgive and forget. We try to help each other get over hard times and look to the future. If I had told my family about my feelings as a deaf person, they would have offered emotional support but also would have firmly persuaded me to quit moping around and try to make the best of it.

After four years of muddling through parties and books, I managed to earn a bachelor's degree in landscape horticulture. During my last year, I had a variety of tutors for my horticulture classes. I less frequently came bursting into Wayne's office in tears to complain about a test or some hard-nosed professor. With all his caring, Wayne had made the college graduation possible, and I was grateful enough to give him and his wife a farewell gift.

With a college degree, I vowed to change myself as a person and cut down on my drinking, learning when to stop. I'd had enough of watching the ceiling lamp move like an amoeba every weekend morning. Now that I was back in my hometown where everyone was understanding of my handicap, I determined to stop worrying so much about fitting in and try to maintain a high level of self-esteem. Most of all, I

wanted to be more emotionally stable, and if anything went wrong, I'd go to my family.

Three Paths

Once settled at home, I decided to take a vacation before my job search. My idea was to drive up to Massachusetts and visit Cheryl and Diane whom I hadn't seen for six years. Although that time was the longest we had been separated, we had managed to keep in touch by mail. But letters hadn't been enough. I had to see them.

Solitude was something I had long grown accustomed to, even with great pleasure; therefore, I wouldn't mind driving by myself. Equipped with the AAA maps, I convinced my worried parents that I would handle the road trip by staying with several friends along the way. After contacting these friends by phone, I had my two-week vacation mapped out day by day.

First I stopped in Philadelphia to see Faith who had moved there for her job. Another sorority girl Susan joined us for a weekend visit. That wasn't the first time the three of us had visited together far from our hometowns. We had once traveled in Spain where I had to grapple with a foreign language, but Faith and Susan, with their good ability to speak Spanish, had alleviated the situation by teaching me one sentence: No hablo Español. Sure enough, that sentence, (which translated, "I don't know Spanish"), quieted the fast-talking natives every time I said it. Although I had been to Philadelphia a hundred times before, I had never gotten beyond the airport where I had changed flights between Clarke School and home. So in a sense, I once more visited a new place with them and was delighted to see the Liberty Bell for the first time.

Next I drove up to Massachusetts, cutting through New York City and listening to the Rolling Stones at full blast. I stopped in Boston to visit my high school friend Elizabeth who had decided to settle there after college. Still fancy-free and footloose, we spent a few days shopping and barhopping. From Boston, I drove west to Greenfield to reunite with Cheryl and her family. When I pulled into their driveway, I felt like a long-departed seaman coming home. Mr. Robbins stood there with his eyes watering; it really choked me up to see a grown man that way. Then I met Cheryl's fiancé Rick and couldn't get over the fact that

one of my earliest best friends was getting married. Rick was also deaf and hailed from Ohio. He had attended NTID with Cheryl and her brother Chuck.

We spent days looking at old photo albums in that same yellow house where I still felt pretty much at home. Chuck brought his year-old daughter Sarah, and it was touching to see Mrs. Robbins, a new grandmother, play with her granddaughter on the grass. Mr. Robbins had not changed; he was still always doing something around the house, whether it was chopping firewood at ten degrees below or hacking tall weeds at above one hundred degrees.

Cheryl and Rick followed me to the Karases' place in Springfield where we reunited with hugs and kisses. It was a captivating moment, and again, I felt welcomed home after a long, long time away. Diane, now married, introduced me to her three-year-old son Artie. I was overwhelmed by Diane's progress to motherhood. We were *old*.

After spending an afternoon with us, Cheryl gave me a sentimental good-bye with the I-love-you sign, which choked me up. We would always care deeply for each other. But I also felt sad, and even worried, about our friendship because we were now in totally different worlds. Cheryl had switched to the deaf signing world, using sign language with her college friends. Fortunately, she hadn't given up oralism completely; we could still speechread together. Nevertheless, the last time I had seen her, she had hearing friends; now there were none, it seemed to me. And she was going to marry a deaf guy which would bring her deeper into the deaf world. At that time, I didn't understand the term *Deaf community*. Without my realizing it, however, Cheryl had joined a world with its own language and culture.

I managed to brush off the situation and savored my time with Diane and her family, once again devouring Mrs. Karas's Polish sausage and sharing jokes with Mr. Karas. With Diane's brothers joining us, we spent a day on the lake, waterskiing and barbecuing. I had a chance to talk with Diane's husband Butch whom she had met in high school. I felt comfortable with Butch and liked him as a person.

When Diane and I settled to talk at her apartment, I expressed my bafflement about Cheryl joining the deaf world. Diane assumed that, because Cheryl's brother had gone to NTID, she had decided to follow in his footsteps. Little sister following big brother was what we

concluded. After trading our concerns, Diane and I shrugged helplessly and figured we'd have to just let it go. Deep down in my heart, I still felt let down because Cheryl and I had spent years writing letters about hearing-world experiences. But now, we could no longer do that.

Back at home, I told Mom about Cheryl and about my fearing that our long friendship could possibly dwindle. Mom assured me that it would not happen if Cheryl and I kept writing to each other like old times, as if nothing had happened. She made the point that Cheryl may have decided to give up the hearing culture because she was profoundly deaf, not hard of hearing like me and Diane. The hearing world must have been much more difficult for Cheryl, Mom said. Realizing that Cheryl was too important a friend to relinquish, I vowed to keep writing and visiting her. I told Mom how grateful I was for the talk; Mom told me to stop worrying about Cheryl—and find a job.

As I planned for job hunting, I braced myself for introducing myself to strangers on the phone, which I had never done before. Now that I was a college graduate off to independence, I declined my mother's offer to contact landscaping companies for me. I wanted to try it myself and practice expanding my voice to a professional tone without quivering. Over the years, I had always been afraid to talk too loud and, therefore, was a low talker, which caused people to lean over or tell me to speak up.

The other concern, of course, involved my ability to understand what strangers were saying. On the phone, I've had to struggle to hear, not speechread. I can hear on the phone for two reasons: first, it's closer to my ear, and second, there is no sound feedback. Without feedback, I can easily recognize people's voices as well as their laughs most of the time. But still, I have trouble distinguishing vowel and consonant sounds on the phone.

When I started talking on the phone, Mom had an amplifier installed in our kitchen phone. Most of the time I had the amplifier turned all the way up and forgot to turn it off when finished. Then some poor member of the family would pick up the ringing phone and hear the caller's blasting hello in the receiver. To my dismay, I had seen every one of my family, at one time or another, suddenly fling the phone at arm's length and look at me as if they were about to wring my neck.

It's funny how some people relate the term *deaf* or even *hard of hearing* to no hearing at all—nothing, zero, zilch. They don't realize that many deaf people can be helped by amplification and that every deaf person has a different degree of hearing loss. So anyway, I've had people look at me in total shock when I talk on the phone or hear a jumbo jet zooming overhead. They ask me, amazed, how I can hear, and I politely tell them that I'm not stone deaf, pointing to my hearing aid.

My job-hunting phone calls led me to a small landscaping company where, relying on my eyes, I learned to design and plant. I was pleased that my landscape design career was enabling me to deal with clients on a one-on-one basis. Fortunately, I was able to communicate well with most clients, except some elderly people who often presented special challenges. Once, I had a ninety-five-year-old client who was so hunched over when walking that she talked with her head down. Well, I had to walk that way, too, holding a clipboard to my side, so I would be able to look at her lips. We looked like a pair of question marks moving very slowly through her rose garden.

Two of my long-time friends and I found an apartment in Ghent, a popular section of Norfolk, Virginia. I was delighted to room with Mary Park and Molly Hubard since we had grown up together in the same neighborhood. Back in high school, we drove around doing pranks like flying our brassieres on the antenna. And Mary was the one who had pledged with me in the sorority at Tech. I certainly looked forward to pure entertainment from those two girls after a long day's work.

Our den had a fake furnace, shaped like a funnel extending to the ceiling, and we wondered why the landlord had stuck it there. One hot summer night, Molly and I figured out what to do with the furnace, so we dragged it to Mary's bedroom while she was out. We taped a note on it saying that a cold front was coming and we wanted her to stay warm, signing the note with "Your considerate loving roommates." Imagine how Mary felt when she walked in and saw that monstrous black thing next to her bed!

Another night after Molly had gone out, Mary and I stuffed a pair of jeans and connected boots to them. We placed this partial dummy under Molly's bed so it would look like a dead man with his legs poking out. Mary heard the door open, and we dove into her bedroom next to Molly's. We sat waiting in the pitch dark, trying not to make any

sound. I tapped Mary, turning my palms in puzzlement. At first, Mary tried to whisper into my ear, but it was no use. So she flung her hands in the air, making some kind of gesture. Once, again, I tapped Mary, again flipping up my palms. She repeated all her indecipherable gestures over her head. It turned out that Molly had not yet seen the "dead person" because she went straight to the shower. When we emerged from the bedroom, Mary exhaled in exhaustion and declared, "I'm not ever going to talk to you in the dark again."

Now that I had a closed caption decoder, given to me by my parents, it helped that my roommates liked to watch the same TV shows as me. That decoder really changed my life, providing a much broader view of the everyday world. Seeing dialogue word by word greatly improved my language. I could also understand jokes better. Now, I understood the jokes and didn't have to fake a laugh.

In my new home, I was pretty well equipped with special devices for the hearing impaired. I had a phone amplifier and a digital alarm clock with a small flash, even more powerful than a camera flash. Now that I had this clock, I was thrilled about not having my roommates wake me up. My brother Harvey had found it at the Gallaudet bookstore and gave it to me for Christmas. When he came across this clock, an excited signing clerk explained how it worked by widening her eyes and exploding her hands outward. Yes, it was blindingly bright!

All of my brothers and I lived within only one mile of one another, and my parents had moved to a townhouse within walking distance. We regularly met at Lindsay's raw bar for a few drinks or a birthday party. I felt blessed to have the whole family close together in the same area. Nash and his wife Vickie often had a cookout where we gathered on the deck until sunset, sharing jokes and current events.

One night, Lindsay took me to watch *It's a Wonderful Life*. My brother explained the movie plot (I knew he had rehearsed doing it) while we waited for it to begin. I watched how George Bailey was led by the angel Clarence through a totally different setting. That movie left me profoundly touched and became one of my favorites. If it weren't for Lindsay's consideration, I wouldn't have any idea why Clarence popped out of the blue, much less understand his angel identity or why the town suddenly turned harsh with all the brooding people amid those Christmas decorations.

My social life in the hearing world had improved because I had more emotional security and no longer worried what people thought of me. And I no longer tried to please impatient or mean people. Most of all, I'd learned to be myself instead of trying to blend in. I feel fortunate to have kept, even to this day, both new and old close friends with whom I can dine, mostly on a one-on-one basis. But I always enjoy a trio lunch with my childhood friends Nancy Nusbaum and Helen Roberts, who always have the patience to talk slowly throughout the whole meal. There has never been a lunch without us teasing one another; no wonder Nancy, Helen, and I are usually the rowdiest customers at every quiet restaurant.

＊

As I remember it, almost perfectly, March 1988 was a dramatic month because so many things happened—all having to do with deafness. The first event was thoroughly encouraging for my self-esteem; the second, shocking yet later successful; and the third, extremely discouraging. It's just a crazy coincidence that all these events occurred in a short time but at least it helps me remember them well.

With saved money, I decided to buy a small pickup truck that I could use to carry plants. Dad offered to go with me, but I wanted to try buying the truck myself. Of course, I was edgy about buying a vehicle on my own, especially deciding how to make installments, signing contracts, and all that—and most important, handling all the communication. But it helped to collect advice from friends beforehand so I was prepared not to have any misunderstanding with car salesmen, some of whom could be pushy for a young single woman like myself.

It took me about a week to narrow my search down to one dealership that offered the best price on a new Chevy truck. In truth, I had trouble understanding everything the salesman said from the start because he talked pretty fast. That's why I was set to review every single bit of the contract and see what options such as AC were included and, of course, what type of monthly payment I would have to make. After reading the contract several times, I felt confident to sign and make a down payment. In a few days I brought home a new truck, equipped with everything I asked for. The whole thing gave me a huge notch of self-esteem because I had handled it without help from anybody. As a

deaf person, I felt buoyant for signing a big contract for the first time, instead of depending on others.

Then Gallaudet University became the focus of the world. Watching the news, I was amazed by the marching deaf students with big banners emblazoned with DEAF PRESIDENT NOW! At first, I wondered how would a deaf college president be able to handle such a huge responsibility? Communication would be the main issue. I thought these marching students were unrealistic until I learned that Gallaudet had hired a woman president who had no experience with deaf people. A president who knew absolutely nothing about deafness, much less how to communicate? I could not believe it. Despite her good resume, she did not belong at Gallaudet. As I watched the news of her unwelcome entry to Gallaudet, I felt sorry for her, but I could feel my heart marching with the students.

Caught up in the headlines, I realized that Gallaudet consisted of a deaf community with its own culture and language. The student body and some faculty members had been waiting for a deaf president for years. Under enormous pressure, the mostly hearing board of directors finally dismissed the new president, turning the job over to Irving King Jordan, Jr., a deaf man who had worked there as dean of the college of arts and sciences. I began to believe that he would work out because Dr. Jordan knew what it was like having this disability and would be able to respond to the students' needs. Those marching students certainly got what they wanted, and this showed the true confidence of the deaf community.

As soon as the Gallaudet hype lessened, my grandmother began to have difficulty breathing and was rushed to the emergency room. While waiting in the lobby, I was approached by a nurse who informed me that the doctors had told her of my hearing impairment. She explained that there was a deaf AIDS patient in the other room who was trying to tell them about the medicine he had been taking, but no one could understand him. The nurse asked if I knew sign language. Feeling uncertain, I admitted knowing only fingerspelling, which wouldn't help much because of its slow pace and complicated method. Then with a flicker of hope, I suggested a notepad but was crushed when the nurse replied she already tried that, only to find that this AIDS patient was illiterate.

After regretfully explaining to the nurse that I wouldn't be of any use, I plopped down in the chair and buried my head in my hands. I had never felt so guilty before and was mad at myself for not knowing sign language. But moments later, my feeling of guilt was replaced by shock and anger. Why didn't the hospital have an interpreter? I looked around, disgusted. The hospital should've thought of identifying one or two staff members to learn sign language so an interpreter would be available at all times. I was pretty sure that some of those hospital staff had learned to speak French or Spanish for the sake of communicating with foreign patients. It wouldn't hurt to learn sign language, although it may require daily practice for fluency, even if the person didn't become a certified interpreter.

I still feel contrite whenever I think about that deaf AIDS patient and wonder what became of him. Although I never saw him, I often picture him as a desperate, gaunt man with curly black hair. The thought of the hospital staff, desperate because of the communication problem, giving him the wrong medication or even none at all makes me tremble. I want to say my prayers are with him, although I don't know his fate. Today, that emergency-room scene would have turned out differently because I now know sign language.

❧

Mary and I continued living together after Molly got married and moved away. So another friend Barbara moved in with us. Soon, we all had to move out because the new landlord wanted to convert our place into a condo, so we settled in our second apartment just across the street. A while later, Barbara married her long-time beau Than and moved out. Mary and I couldn't find another roommate, so we moved a mile away to our third apartment for better rent. I had all of my brothers move the furniture every time we relocated, providing pizza to keep them happy, although they still cussed like sailors as they hauled our massive sofa up stairs and through narrow doorways.

A few months into our third apartment, Mary heard something right above her bedroom. It was the couple who lived above us enjoying their bed, if you know what I mean. When Mary first described the noises to me, we fell to the floor in laughter. But then the sounds became too frequent, much to Mary's irritation. When we were sitting in

the den, she'd suddenly drop a magazine on her lap and growl, "Here they go again." I felt bad for her having to listen to all this and even apologized for my deafness. Glaring at me in envy, Mary had me stand in her bedroom and told me to turn my hearing aid all the way up. Sure enough, I heard it, loud and clear, but only if I stood in that spot. Considering my hearing roommate's lack of sleep, I offered to trade my bedroom, but Mary assumed that the honeymoon would soon be over. And she was right. The noises eventually turned to loud bickering and then silence. It was good to see Mary smile again in the mornings.

Mary occasionally went away for several days, and I had to adjust to being alone in the apartment. I wasn't too concerned about safety. But the problem was, I yearned to hear something in this lonely place. I had been taught to hear things with pleasure. So I'd talk to my cat Ernie, just to hear my own voice. I'd say to him, "So! How was your day? Slept and ate all day? Look at you, you've got a wonderful life sitting on your butt and not having to work." If Ernie could understand what I was telling him, he'd agree and never change that kind of life.

I know I could have turned on the stereo just to hear something, but I was always afraid to miss an expected phone call or a warning sound such as the disposal being accidentally left on—which I had done before. The disposal in this apartment ran with such little sound that I didn't know it was on. I had brought my landlord in to check the stalled disposal, too embarrassed to give the reason for it. To my relief, he found a lever under the disposal and clicked it back on.

These days, I walk out the door and then pause, unsure if I've left the water running. So I check every sink on all floors because I've always had an enormous fear of turning my place into a raging flood. Even with powerful amplification, I can never hear the low sound of water running. So I check every single faucet, sometimes two or three times—and not by just looking at it. I place my hand under the faucet. I just don't trust my eyes when it comes to clear water, which seems invisible to me.

❧

Cheryl's father died unexpectedly of a heart attack, and the family was quite devastated. Mom contacted Mrs. Robbins by phone to offer our condolences and to invite her and Cheryl to come down for a mother-daughter getaway at our beach cottage in Sandbridge. A few months after

the death, Cheryl and her mother flew down and spent a few days alone watching the sunrise and listening to waves as they tried to recover from shock and devastation. My parents and I drove over to treat them to a seafood restaurant where we talked openly about Mr. Robbins's death.

During that visit, I had a better chance to talk with Cheryl, and for the first time, I came to accept her decision to join the deaf community. While we walked on the beach, Cheryl described all the activities with her deaf friends, expressing satisfaction with her social life because she had joined a circle of those with the same disability. It had been four years since she married her deaf husband Rick; Cheryl appeared to be happy with this union. So why should I be upset with Cheryl's decision to join the deaf community if that was what made her happy? By the end of her and her mother's visit to Sandbridge, I felt ecstatic that Cheryl and I could still remain great friends and that I no longer felt awkward about her choice of lifestyle. I finally respected it.

A few months later, I flew to Massachusetts for a respite after going through a horrible breakup with a hearing boyfriend that devastated me to the point where I thought I would never date again. I hadn't often been asked out before I had met this guy; therefore, I was thrilled to date somebody seriously for the first time in a long time. But then, after a year, it wasn't working, and I severed the relationship.

At first, I visited my high school friend Elizabeth who had become Mrs. David Wadman the previous fall. She cheered me up by taking me around Boston for a few days and chatting endlessly about our old days. And then I pitched my tent with Cheryl and Rick, sharing a meaningful conversation through speechreading and some hand gestures. I grew to respect Rick as the guy one of my best friends chose to marry. When we talked about my bad breakup, Rick asked a question that has stuck in my mind for years: "Is it because of deafness?"

That was a good question because most hearing-deaf relationships don't work. They just don't. As shocking as it may sound, hearing-blind relationships work better. You don't need to talk slowly or sign to a blind person, so communication is pretty normal. But with a deaf person, you need patience and tolerance—which didn't exist in my relationship with that guy. He just complained and complained, saying that the problem was much harder for him. Now I look back derisively and say, "Oh, please," while I play an invisible fiddle.

After my stay with Cheryl and Rick, Diane brought me to her house, having invited a few of our Clarke friends for the evening. Before they came, Diane sat me down and said she didn't want me to feel isolated like I did when we were sixteen. Knowing that I was more absorbed in the hearing world than she was, Diane gently explained that she had decided to go "both ways," meaning that she belonged to the hearing world yet had mostly deaf friends she could sign with. If that's what makes her happy, I thought to myself, it's great, go for it. I thanked Diane for the talk and vowed to have a good time no matter what.

That night turned out to be one of the best times I'd ever had in my life. Communication was no problem, really, because I could speechread these friends and vice versa. Despite my lack of signing skills, it was certainly good to be with my deaf friends again. Throughout the evening, Diane kept asking me if I felt out of place to which I answered absolutely not.

I flew home feeling refreshed; visiting old friends certainly was therapeutic. Cheryl was now in the deaf community, and Diane was in between, and I was totally in the hearing world; but they could still remain great friends of mine. No more feelings of isolation or awkwardness. The path we had all started on had eventually separated, slowly but surely, into three paths as we began leading different lives. But our paths would still entwine, and we would always support one another.

A get-together with old friends. From left to right: Me, Cheryl, and Diane.

The Reunion

The next drama wouldn't have ensued if Mom had not returned a box of Clarke memorabilia to me. For a couple nights I dug into the cardboard box at my apartment and spread each item on the floor, amazed at how all the items—Miss Miller's weekly letters, my dad's drawings, and all the Polaroids—had stayed in excellent condition, after nearly three decades.

At Mom's suggestion, I wrote an update letter to Clarke, and they responded with the announcement of an upcoming reunion. So I asked Diane and Cheryl by mail if they were coming to this special event. Yes, they were. That prompted my plan to drive up north alone, to visit friends along the way, explore famous gardens to expand my horticultural knowledge, and at last, attend the reunion. So off I went in my little pickup truck at dawn, the rock'n'roll music blaring for the next 700 miles.

I first visited the National Arboretum in Washington, D.C., admiring ancient bonsai and taking notes. My next stop was definitely memorable. It was Gallaudet University, the place I had desperately wanted to visit since the Deaf President Now movement. I parked in front of Chapel Hall, feeling odd, as if I were about to enter a deaf world unlike the one at Clarke. Expecting to see flying hands all around, I braced myself as the lone oralist on this campus. It was such a weird sensation when I entered the open area where summer-school students sat signing on the manicured lawn—all silence. I felt like I'd been dropped from outer space. Even though we all had the same disability, I didn't feel a sense of belonging here. But still, it fascinated me. Why not explore a world I knew absolutely nothing about?

Walking into the bookstore, I noticed the jewelry counter where items depicting the I LOVE YOU and FRIEND hand signs dominated the display. Each gold earring had the thumb, index finger, and pinky extended, showing a manual alphabet combination of I, L, and Y—the I LOVE YOU sign. Other jewelry had the FRIEND sign in which right and left index fingers interlocked, a perfect sign for closeness.

In the book section, while flipping through a book drawn in sign language, I heard loud grunts and looked over to the next aisle where a couple argued, their hands darting in and out at high speed. I watched

sideways with my head down, amazed by the sight of such ferocious signing. And something else struck me: the grunting and hissing sounds the couple made as if they were lifting fifty-pound crates. Why the couple dared to make these grotesque sounds in public was something most hearing people would not understand. I understood. It was because this profoundly deaf couple could not hear themselves and did not know it.

I settled in with coffee at a slow-paced cafeteria and watched a group of students signing across the room. With a small smile, I thought about my past at Clarke where we waved our hands and tapped on shoulders. That's how these Gallaudet students were trying to catch attention, the same way my friends and I did years ago. But here, their signing looked official, unlike the homemade signs at Clarke.

Once in the library, I noticed the door signs saying Classroom on the first floor. Eager to see a deaf college classroom, I sneaked behind a book shelf and watched a small class through an open door. Yes, there was a semicircular pattern of desks, just like at Clarke. But there was no headphone, just hands flying in the air. And the whole atmosphere was dead quiet, not a single voice present. That silence still seemed eerie to me.

The exhibit at the Edward Miner Gallaudet Memorial Building was the most interesting of all. After first admiring historic pictures depicting deaf athletics and early sign language in the hall, I then walked into a room that looked like a hands-on museum. Because this exhibit looked new, I assumed it was set up after the Deaf President Now movement four years earlier.

The next twenty minutes would teach me more about deafness than I had learned in my lifetime. Just standing in this exhibit made me realize there was a *real* deaf culture, something I had never taken seriously before. To my total surprise, I had known very little about my own disability.

I pressed a button on the wall TV and watched thousands of people walking on a New York City sidewalk. The closed caption lines began rolling, "All these people look the same. Do you see any deaf person? You can never tell. Deafness is a hidden handicap." The video continued, explaining that much of the world did not know the complexity of this disability and had trouble understanding it. Absolutely true, I thought with a nod.

Then I turned to the other wall, which bore a large caption: MIS-CONCEPTIONS ABOUT DEAFNESS. The myths listed below it read

> Deaf people can only do certain jobs.
> Deaf people are less intelligent than hearing people.
> Deaf people have similar abilities, ideas, and outlooks.
> All deaf people use sign language.
> All hearing losses are the same.
> All deaf people read lips.
> Noisy environments don't bother deaf people.
> Deaf people can't talk.
> Hearing aids restore hearing.

Impressed by this list, I wished I could grab every single soul on earth and bring them in to look at these short yet meaningful misconceptions. This myth wall could totally change the world's perception of deafness in sixty seconds.

Several biographical posters on the other wall caught my eye, since they showed Gallaudet graduates who had achieved high success in the working world. I was awestruck by one poster showing a female lawyer and another showing a male stockbroker and many more. Indeed, deaf people can climb to success just like hearing people.

Later, I met my brother Lindsay at a Baltimore hotel as planned, since he had gone there to attend a Grateful Dead concert the following night, just as he had a million times. His dear wife Koggie, who was no fan of this long-lasting band, had put up with Lindsay's globetrotting but always busied herself with social activities at home to avoid having to go with him. Lindsay had even missed a family picnic for the sake of listening to Jerry Garcia. We had gotten tickets to the Orioles game that night, so Lindsay and I met with his friends for a ride to the game. In the car, I recounted my Gallaudet tour, and one of these friends said he had seen some deaf kids, possibly Gallaudet students, at a Grateful Dead concert, dancing behind the stage with some special vibrating device in their hands.

Years later, I was touched by the movie *Mr. Holland's Opus* in which there was a profoundly deaf boy named Cole. The scene of Cole sitting atop a stereo speaker and shoulder-dancing proved that deaf people,

even those who cannot be helped by amplification, *do* love music. Feeling the rhythm of vibrations motivates you to waltz away. Like I've said before, I love music despite incomprehensible lyrics; the instrumental sounds are what attract me. I wonder what it would be like to hold that special device in my hands at a concert. I've learned that hugging a big, sturdy balloon is another way to feel vibrations.

After my visit with Lindsay, I headed northward, and midway, I had to face the anxiety of driving through the Bronx to reach the New York Botanical Gardens. You can't be distracted for a single millisecond on a New York City street because so many cars are swerving in front of you. And the persistent honking! If I ever had to live in this world's noisiest city, my hearing aids would end up in a dumpster! Anyway, I spent all afternoon exploring this amazing garden before continuing the road trip to Boston to visit my high school friend Elizabeth for a few days.

Elizabeth and I brought her baby Caroline to Boston Common where we met with Cheryl and her deaf baby Stephanie. With a smile, I figured that those two new mothers would have plenty to talk about. Caroline and Stephanie were only four months apart and there I found something absorbing about these two babies, one hearing and one deaf. I watched how they acted, showing a vast difference in their behaviors. Because she could hear all the environmental sounds, Caroline was much more vigorous than Stephanie, who just stared ahead in a pensive way. With chirping birds and yakking pedestrians around her, Caroline continued thrashing around in her stroller as if she wondered what all these sounds were, unlike Stephanie who didn't even know they existed. I added this interesting observation to all the others I had collected on this trip.

After saying good-bye to Elizabeth, I followed Cheryl to her apartment where she showed me all the special devices that would alert her to Stephanie's crying or whatever the baby was doing. Cheryl pointed to a monitor on the wall behind Stephanie's crib and intentionally made a sound. Sure enough, the hall light flicked on and so did the one in the master bedroom. Cheryl informed me that these lights would also turn on to the sounds of the phone ringing, the doorbell buzzing, and the smoke detector squealing. This deaf family certainly wouldn't miss anything important or dangerous.

Cheryl announced that Diane would call that evening to make plans for the reunion and that I would use a TTY for the first time. I'd seen a picture of this device in a magazine so I wasn't surprised by its resemblance to a typewriter. Cheryl explained that the red signal light would flash slowly, indicating the ringing of the other line. The typed conversation would appear in green-lighted words across the screen. Typing could cause the conversation to drag, so Cheryl told me I should use abbreviations or just single letters such as *u* for *you* and *q* for a question mark or for the word *question*. She explained two commonly used abbreviations that would help the other person know whether I had finished talking or was prepared to hang up: "GA" for "Go ahead" and "SK" for "Stop keying."

As promised, Diane phoned, and I was so frazzled with excitement that Cheryl had to keep reminding me how to use the TTY. I just couldn't believe I was actually "talking" to a deaf friend as I typed with shaking hands. I remember one part of our conversation perfectly. It went like this:

"WHERE CAN I MEET U ON FRIDAYQ THE SCHEDULE SAYS THERE WILL BE AN AFTERNOON RECEPTION. GA," I asked Diane regarding the reunion.

"I'LL JUST MEET U THERE. SHOULD BE AROUND 4 OR 5. DONT WAIT FOR ME CUZ THERE WILL BE OLD FRIENDS YOU HAVENT SEEN IN AGES. GA," Diane typed back rapidly, causing the words to zoom across the screen.

"OKIEDOKIE. TTY IS GREAT!!!!! WILL HAVE TO BUY ONE. SEE U AT THE RECEPTION. BYE BYE SK." I stopped with a grin while Cheryl patted me on the shoulder.

"BYE BYE OXOXO SKSK." The TTY's red, unblinking light then signaled that Diane had hung up. I made a promise to buy one for myself, ecstatic about the possibility of contacting Cheryl and Diane more frequently, rather than by mail.

Before my departure, Cheryl and I made plans on where to meet at the reunion. Just then, she told me not to get too excited about seeing our old friends because a majority of them were now signing. I felt my heart slump at her direct-eye warning that they could be hostile to me for maintaining oralism. Cheryl went on to tell me not to let them hurt my feelings and just to have a good time. Belonging now to the Deaf

community (*Deaf* with a capital *D* to represent deaf culture and language), she could've acted the same way these friends would, but our friendship was too special to dissolve on account of different worlds.

But still, I was totally perplexed while driving to Northampton. All those friends were now signing? Why would they give up oralism if they had attended Clarke for years? Were they really in the Deaf community? I tried to imagine the possible difference between our past and present times. I cringed at the thought of my old friends looking at me in disgrace and asking, "Why are you still oral?" I had known that some people in the Deaf community could be quite harsh on those who chose to speak. They could be so fanatical about sign language that moving lips repulsed or even infuriated them—a total reverse of how the majority world had perceived sign language before 1960s, treating it then as taboo.

Thinking about all this, I became deeply concerned about seeing my old friends at the reunion. I'd be hurt like hell if they avoided me once they learned I had remained an oralist. After moments of pondering, I vowed to tell my friends immediately why I hadn't learned to sign. I'd just tell the truth: I was from Virginia where there weren't many deaf people for me to meet, not as many as in Massachusetts. And I had my hearing family help me through regular school, so I ended up fully immersed in the hearing world.

I also tried to understand why people, after learning oral methods for years, suddenly switched to sign. My mind turned to Cheryl who claimed that she had long felt miserably isolated in the hearing world and that she didn't learn much until her first year at NTID. She was, and is, profoundly deaf with approximately 88 percent hearing loss, compared to my 75 percent loss. There is an enormous difference between these two figures, even with powerful amplification. Cheryl cannot hear a teacup shattering on the floor like I can. She cannot talk on the phone with hearing friends like I can. No wonder Cheryl had to constantly struggle in the hearing world, only to find herself even more isolated. I just didn't understand all this when I first learned she had joined the Deaf community. Now I had grown to respect her choice of lifestyle if that was the reason she no longer felt lonely.

So maybe that's why many of my old friends had made the same choice—because they were profoundly deaf, not hard of hearing like

me and Diane. But some profoundly deaf people actually belong to the hearing world with great success. Mark my word, every single deaf person is different, regardless of his or her degree of hearing loss. Some hard of hearing people even belong to the Deaf community, but only after they become fluent in American Sign Language.

On the first night of the reunion, we had a kickoff party where I reunited with some of my old classmates. Later, I joined them at a downtown bar and couldn't help feeling isolated when everyone was signing, although they could still speechread. One guy turned to me with a sheepish shrug and said that he wished I could sign. I must have looked chagrined when he told me not to be upset and reminded me of our capability to speechread. His words reassured me but I couldn't handle staying much longer and announced that I was heading back to the hotel.

Feeling letdown, I sat at the edge of the bed and wondered if I would have a good time with nearly everyone signing. I had realized that these old friends didn't really speechread those who signed to them, even though they still mouthed words. So maybe I could still communicate with them by using a combination of speechreading and hand gestures, even if my gestures weren't official sign language. It was better than nothing. I was not going to let myself sulk throughout the reunion.

Fortunately, the next day was better because more people who still speechread showed up, and I had long intense conversations with some of them. My explanation for not knowing sign language must have worked because many of my old friends were still super friendly and even taught me a few signs. Diane showed up later, afterward staying at the hotel with me, and Cheryl came for the day. Their presence made the reunion much more pleasant for me.

I found that, after graduating from Clarke, many of my friends were miserable or unsuccessful in the hearing world and therefore rejoined their deaf counterparts for a sense of belonging, somehow blending in with those who never went to Clarke, possibly at NTID or Gallaudet. After recognizing sign language as a definite remedy for miscommunication, these friends angrily felt that they had wasted time on oralism. That's the big reason several of them expressed resentment toward Clarke, calling it "too strict" or "unfair." These were the words I repeatedly heard during the reunion. A few of these friends even declared they would never forgive their hearing parents for sending them to the wrong school.

Honestly, if I were in their shoes, I would not be angry with my parents. Mom and Dad were the parents of the '60s, a time when sign language was considered repulsive. I would forgive my parents if they unintentionally deprived me of the most suitable communication method, not knowing how difficult the future would become. Cheryl, now in the Deaf community, had always been a realistic person and therefore knew that her parents were only trying to do the best for her.

When I came home and told people about how many of my friends had turned against Clarke, detesting its strict oral program, they each asked me the same question: Why did those people go to the reunion? My response was that they came because of friends. At the reunion, I watched how everyone expressed strong affection toward each other, giving bear hugs. The bonds, despite all the communication issues, were still strong.

I have to remind myself that every deaf person is different, no matter what the degree of hearing loss is. The truth is, not all deaf children can learn to speak well. That's what happened with many of my profoundly deaf friends. So I don't blame them for being angry that the early part of their lives had been wasted on oralism because that's the phase when language development is most significant. I can see why these friends feel they had missed a great deal of language through time-consuming oralism.

In spite of all this, I strongly support Clarke as an oral school. Although it could be extremely strict in the past, it was just doing its job teaching children to speak. I can understand why it didn't want the interference of sign language if its goal was to prepare students for the hearing world. Oralism was big during the 1960s and 1970s, but now it has changed. At the time of the reunion, Clarke's enrollment had been cut in half. But this school is still very much alive today because it now offers a wide variety of educational sessions throughout the country.

While driving home, I thought about all the events I had encountered over the last two weeks on this incredible trip. I was pleased with how the Clarke reunion had turned out, although I sorely wished that I had known sign language. The deaf world out there was totally different, something I did not expect at all. I felt a pang of desire to learn more about my own disability. Could there be so much about deafness that I still didn't know? It was definitely a mysterious disability, one of the most misunderstood disabilities to everyone, even myself.

Finally, I made two plans before arriving home, the first of which was to learn more about deafness by reading books, maybe meet local people associated with deafness and get their modern ideas, which had to be more flexible than those during the 1960s. And the second plan—to learn sign language seriously so I would be able to communicate with deaf people—would not affect my oral skills one single bit. I could not wait to put these plans into action, pushing my foot a little further down on the pedal.

At Ease

I had purchased a TTY and was now able to communicate with Cheryl and Diane through the phone lines. I also had purchased an American Sign Language book, trying to follow each picture of a signer with my awkward hands. I began to realize the liveliness and beauty of sign language, which motivated me to ask my audiologist Angela Sheppard about sign language classes. Angela, who has been a great lunch friend of mine all these years, has had to repair my broken tubes or listen to my complaints that manufacturers should invent sweat-proof hearing aids. (Oh, how nice those would be for playing competitive tennis!)

When I first met Angela, I was taken aback by her young age and even thought she was an earmold maker. My retiring audiologist had referred me to Angela's firm, saying "Ms. Sheppard" would help me. I had set up an appointment, assuming that my new audiologist would be about forty-five, slightly grey haired, and maybe pleasantly plump. That was what all the Clarke teachers had looked like, I remembered with fondness.

When I arrived at Ms. Sheppard's office, an attractive girl in her mid-twenties greeted me with a smile and asked what she could do for my hearing aid. After I hesitantly explained that the tube needed a replacement, she took my aid and disappeared. I sat there wondering where Ms. Sheppard was. Then the girl returned with a new tube and I asked very politely about my new audiologist. She looked at me in surprise and said she was the one. Caught off guard, I stared at her, thinking, That's *her*? Nah! I mean, this person was a *girl*, not the forty-five-year-old lady I expected. I realized that, despite my stereotyped expectations, anybody could be associated with deafness.

Anyway, Angela gave me a brochure of TAHIC (Tidewater Association for Hearing Impaired Children), a local deaf organization, so I could get information on sign language classes. I decided to join TAHIC just to meet interesting people, hearing or deaf. Since the Clarke reunion, I had a strong desire to learn more about deafness and believed that any TAHIC event would help broaden my knowledge of viewpoints.

I attended a Christmas party for deaf children and spoke with many hearing parents, most of whom could sign fluently. A majority of those children had cochlear implants and I couldn't keep my eyes off the steering-wheel magnet behind their ears. It was the first time I had seen a cochlear implant up close. Years before, Mom and I went to my ear doctor to discuss the possibility of a cochlear implant. It was so new at the time that we wondered if it was going to be a miracle for me. After giving me a hearing test, the doctor concluded that I wouldn't need an implant if I had enough help from my hearing aid. He explained that cochlear implants were particularly designed for those who could not be helped by amplification.

It turned out that most of the children at that party were in mainstream programs, attending regular schools that provided sign language interpreters and special classes. Regardless of their education methods, some of them could speak while others chose not to. I was elated with the atmosphere of mixed communication: sign language, oralism, and Cued Speech. The scene was a clear picture of diversity where everyone seemed happy with the chosen method of communication. There were people of all races: White, Black, Asian, Hispanic, and so on. I was psyched to learn sign and maybe Cued Speech, not just to develop the ability to communicate but also to broaden my perception of a disability with numerous controversial and sensitive issues.

✖

While taking a sign language class, I learned that the two common signed languages in the United States were American Sign Language (ASL) and Signed Exact English (SEE). ASL, the number one signed language in the Deaf community, is actually a cultural language rich with beauty and fascination. It differs from SEE by having its own grammar and syntax. ASL uses signs, facial expressions, and body position to communicate concepts, defining objects, actions, and ideas with

hand pictures and gestures. Sometimes, one ASL sign can express an entire sentence. ASL is a lot like French; in this sign language, an action or object comes first and a person comes last: TODAY STORE GO ME or PARTY GIVE SHE. SEE, on the other hand, takes the English language, every bit of it, including all the little verb endings like *ing* and *ed*, and literally translates it into manual gestures.

Deaf people prefer ASL over English because it is much quicker and flows smoothly. The sign order of ASL allows them to rapidly form pictures or thoughts in their minds. It is difficult to be patient with the exact word order of Signed English where every small word must be included. I've heard negative comments from some deaf people and even interpreters, calling this method "slow" and "boring." Undoubtedly, deaf people feel more motivated with ASL, enjoying its speedy pace for social conversations.

But ASL is not without controversy. Opponents claim that this language prevents normal development in reading and writing skills and that ASL does not help with education. No book or closed captions are written in ASL. And very few hearing people actually use ASL. Therefore, opponents believe ASL causes deeper isolation of deaf people in the larger world.

Because of its quick and colorful way to communicate, I strongly support ASL, but I also believe that the English language should be a part of deaf culture. Understanding the English language's word order would enhance the ability to read warnings, instructions, and closed captions as well as books and magazines. Personally, I would hate for deaf people to miss things they could easily learn with their perfectly normal minds.

Fortunately, there is a solution; it is a bilingual and bicultural system in which ASL is considered the first language and English the second. I strongly support this education method for deaf children if they are going to be raised in ASL. It is difficult to teach deaf toddlers the English language. However, with ASL, you can teach them their first words and help them identify pictures and people—all in a heartbeat. Then, these children can learn English through ASL. When they write, they can translate from ASL to English. When they read, they can translate from English to ASL. Most people can learn two different languages and cultures at the same time, for example, immigrants

who speak English at school yet maintain their native tongues at home. The same is true with the bilingual-bicultural education involving ASL and English. Most important of all, this system helps build a bridge between deaf and hearing people.

I'm still not fluent in American Sign Language because its syntax is complicated. However, I use a combination of ASL and SEE; that's called Pidgin Sign English (PSE) in which you basically follow English word order but make shortcuts by eliminating small words such as *the* or *to*. And, like in ASL, I usually show physical language; for example, for the question mark, I raise my eyebrows or shrug my shoulders in a curious fashion. In fact, facial and body expressions are an absolute must for deaf people, whether speaking or signing, because they can't vary tones when using their voices to express feelings. Americans are more reserved with these physical aspects of language than Europeans; that's why Americans usually recoil or stare at deaf people who sign with one another using a variety of facial expressions. Deaf people just have to be that way, always making faces. Archie Bunker or Lucille Ball would have understood.

Now heavily involved in TAHIC, I realized that 90 percent of deaf children come from hearing families. And unfortunately, not all of these parents have the patience or "the time" to learn sign language or even to talk slowly to their deaf children; they just send them off to be mainstreamed at elementary schools, expecting the teachers to take care of everything. Sometimes, they send them to the closest deaf school, expecting the same of teachers there. It's true that deaf children often feel isolated in their families, unable to communicate with their parents and siblings who don't even try to understand anything about deafness.

Considering the 90 percent of deaf children coming from hearing families, only a handful of their parents are attentive enough to improve the mainstreaming education by meeting with school officials. I got to know these TAHIC parents personally, admiring them for their caring, even though raising a deaf child is not so easy.

In spite of all their immersion in deafness, it is unlikely that the hearing parents know what it is like being deaf. At one meeting, I spoke with a young mother whose deaf son kept interrupting our conversation. After he ran off, the mother apologized for his behavior. I brushed it off with understanding and asked if she had figured out why deaf

children usually interrupt conversation. To my surprise, she had not. Of course, I had to explain that, because deaf children don't hear low conversation, they figure no one is talking. It's just a simple thing anyone can figure out about deafness.

One time, I was the only deaf person serving on the TAHIC board and had trouble understanding, despite the interpreter. I was so confused when the other members threw an assignment on my lap, giving the name of speaker to contact by phone. I didn't even know who that person was or what I was supposed to say to him. So I stormed out of the meeting, throwing up my arms. One of the members came out to ask what was wrong. I expressed my anger and frustration for not understanding what was going on. She nodded and admitted that she and the board members were not always deaf-friendly, especially during intense discussions. With a weary smile from the corner of my mouth, I told her they all *had* to be because of their deaf children. My point is, even excellent hearing professionals and parents of deaf children make thoughtless communication mistakes because they are not deaf.

If it weren't for TAHIC, I wouldn't have been able to collect all the astounding details about deafness. In truth, I had known very little about my own disability. I began to read numerous books on deafness, some medical and others biographical. Much to my surprise, I finally learned why my voice had always sounded foreign, even though I knew my vocal cords were normal. And I learned why my language development had taken so long to catch up. The more I learned, the more I appreciated my own life as a deaf person. I was finally at ease with my disability.

TAHIC had an annual weekend camp in which people came for workshops and the kids came for fun. Parents, educators, and interpreters took courses on topics such as child psychology and the individual education plan (or IEP). As a volunteer for children's activities, I took these kids canoeing and rope climbing. Because most families who attended brought all their members, there were hearing siblings interacting with deaf children in all age groups. It was a wonderful connection because all these kids could communicate in sign language.

One time, I attended a Cued Speech camp, just to learn this unusual type of communication. Cued Speech is a simple, sound-based system, using eight hand shapes in four different positions that combine with the motions of the lips to make visible and clearly understandable all

the sounds of the English language. So the reader of Cued Speech would be able to distinguish "man," "bat," and "pad," even if he or she were completely deaf. In fact, this method, along with speechreading, enables a deaf person to see exactly what a hearing person hears.

At camps, I learned a great deal about the Deaf community, which is really diverse. Not everyone has the same views and outlooks. There are indeed different groups of deaf people. Some speak; others don't. Some read well; others don't. Some support Total Communication; others don't. Some are understanding of hearing people; others are not. But still, the Deaf community is like a big family absorbed in one language, American Sign Language.

From what I had witnessed at camps, the Deaf community is a close-knit group full of love and friendship. Unlike the hearing culture, these deaf people form strong bonds, expressing affection with hugs and long good-byes. Because they live in the midst of a larger world with all kinds of people, Deaf people tend to linger on at a social gathering, hesitant to leave where they feel they most belong. In fact, the Deaf culture is so unusual and unpretentious that the larger world doesn't even know it exists.

People are often puzzled with the fierceness of the Deaf community. That fierceness has developed because the community desperately wants to save its diminishing culture and is especially upset with the cochlear implant, perceiving it as a clash with its culture. As a matter of fact, the Deaf community wants to prove that many people are perfectly happy without hearing aids. These people declare that the cochlear implant won't work for everyone. They aren't the only ones with this viewpoint, however. Even some doctors and professionals admit that the implant is not for every deaf person; hearing losses can vary in so many complex ways. The implant does work for some people, especially the older ones who want their hearing back, although the sounds coming from it are indeed different from the normal ear. And some prelingually deaf children grow up successfully with the cochlear implant, happy to hear only environmental sounds, while others just throw it away, declaring that they do not need to hear. That's why the cochlear implant poses a huge dilemma for most hearing parents of deaf newborns.

Meeting several of the signing people at meetings and camps, I learned that the Deaf community supports its own members better than the hearing world supports those who are deaf within it. Deaf children raised by

deaf parents don't feel inferior when facing the harsh reality of the every-day world. In addition, these children, often attending deaf schools, are able to learn warnings early through signed language, so they're likely to be less naive than the deaf children relying on the hearing world. (Tell me about it!) That's because deaf families can communicate with each other more completely.

However, that richer communication happens not only in deaf fam-ilies but also in families with deaf parents and hearing children. Two in-teresting people I met at one of the camps were Yvonne and April: a deaf mother and her hearing daughter. Yvonne, immersed in the Deaf community heart and soul, told me how she taught her daughter to stand up to neighborhood bullies. She signed "STAND UP [for] YOUR-SELF!" by standing two fingertips in a V—two legs standing proudly—on her upturned palm (Stand up!) and then, with her thumb rising from a fist, thrusting her hand toward April with great force (Yourself). Obviously, it had worked because April was as tough as her mother was, though they didn't belong in the same worlds.

While April volunteered with me at the camp, she told me about her past experiences fiercely protecting her deaf mother, even as a little girl. She proudly regaled her stories of getting into physical fights with kids who ridiculed her deaf mother. Awestruck by her courage, I asked April if she ever felt embarrassed about having a deaf mother. She replied no because Yvonne's strong character taught her that deaf people were real human beings and didn't deserve such ignorance and mockery.

Some hearing people don't realize deaf people can feel and think like them. They often think deaf people are merely hollow statues. No, no, no. Deaf people's feelings and thoughts run deep. If they are supported and encouraged early, deaf children can grow up to be confident and curious, testing things around them and exploring what others think.

My husband Steve once underwent outpatient knee surgery and waited at the door with a hospital nurse while I went to pick up our car. When I pulled up, the nurse frowned at Steve and asked, "Your wife can drive?" Well, of course! And I remember playing badminton years ago and someone approached, looking me up and down skeptically and asking how I could play. I mean, really. All you have to do is whack that little birdie over the net. Well, I have a message for those who think deaf people don't know how to do things. Let me put it this way: I'll be

polite, but I want to let you know that we deaf people are not stupid. We know how to drink tequila the right way, using lemon and salt. We know how to smoke a fat cigar and roll the dice across the poker table—and even win the pot. We know how to sneak into a neighbor's pool at midnight for a marvelous nude swim. We know how to neck all night on the beach before going much further. We can be as resourceful and clever as anybody. Please note that deaf people are normal-minded human beings. Thank you.

I was amazed to learn how controversial this disability really is, possibly the most controversial of all. I cannot think of any other disability that is as intense: Oralism versus Sign Language, American Sign Language versus Signed Exact English, Cochlear Implant versus Deaf Culture, Mainstreaming versus Special Education. Learning more about deafness had made me less ashamed of what I'd experienced since birth. The wall around me had now crumbled down and I was willing to reveal all the deep feelings about being deaf in a hearing world, especially in the past.

❧

Not too long after a terrible breakup with another guy, I went to dinner at a restaurant with a small group of friends and met the man who would become my husband. As we mingled within this small group, it became clear that we were obviously attracted to each other. After chatting with him for a few hours, I assumed that Steve knew about my deafness. But he didn't; he later asked one of our friends why I kept looking at his teeth. The friend gaped at Steve and exclaimed, "She is deaf! She was reading your lips!" On our second date, Steve shared that, on that first night, he had been so worried that he had some green vegetable stuck between his teeth.

Now we have been married eleven years, and we often marvel at our successful hearing-deaf relationship. I believe that our four years of dating helped foster patience and understanding on Steve's part. Since I knew most hearing-deaf marriages did not work, I asked Steve four or five times with a cautious look on my face if he was absolutely positive that he would tolerate living with a deaf person. Each time, Steve explained that he knew all along that he would be the one who needed to adjust to my disability; that's why I felt confident about marrying

him. When we first started dating, we took the necessary time and had the needed patience to develop a trusting relationship, especially one involving a hearing impaired person. Most important, Steve and I knew that love and respect would grow, not just pop out of the blue. That love and respect did grow for us, and it was worth the wait and the patience.

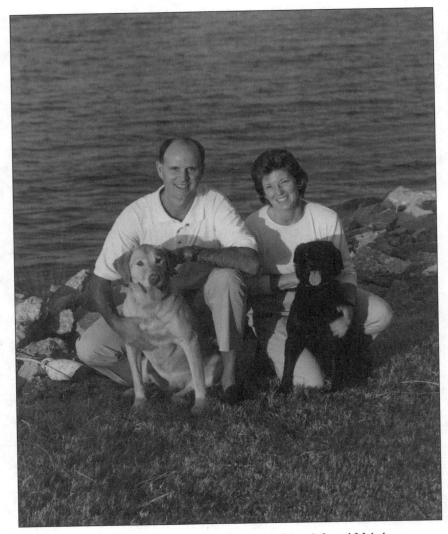

With my husband Steve and our two dogs Olive, left, and Mabel.

Soon after Steve and I settled in at his house, newly married, he became perplexed about how I detected sounds around the house. Shortly after our honeymoon, I was boiling eggs and eventually forgot about them while cleaning the house. Before long, the smoke detector seemed to emit a high-pitched sound, which I heard off and on. What I mean by "off and on" is a tricky characteristic of nerve deafness. I couldn't tell whether the high-pitched alarm was an actual sound or just an echoing in my head. Fortunately, there was no fire, and I threw the scorched pot, along with the scalded eggs, out the door.

But then, I was uncertain about the sound of a smoke detector, so I grabbed a chair and stood on it and fiddled with the device, trying to turn off the red light. Being terribly naive about alarm systems, I wasn't sure if that light was supposed to stay on. Increasingly unsettled, I phoned Steve at work and told him to listen carefully. He did not reply. As he was listening, the red light on the smoke detector finally went off, perhaps because of my excess fiddling, and I said never mind, hanging up. Later in the evening, Steve came home, still puzzled, asking for my explanation. He then told me that he had heard no sound on the phone. These days he likes telling the story about how I stood up on a chair, holding the phone up to the soundless smoke detector.

It didn't take Steve long to understand that I can neither hear high-pitched sounds very well nor pinpoint where sounds come from. Every time he calls me from the other room, I hear him, but head the wrong way. At times, we go around and around inside the house until poor Steve stops his pursuit and wails, "I'm right here!" Sometimes, I stop in frustration and holler that he has to come over to me. We both know that, because of my little twisted auditory nerve, there is no way we can talk or holler to each other from different rooms as most married couples do. Back in college, my roommate was tapping her wet hairbrush on the edge of our little sink and I turned to the door in a light inviting tone, "Come in." That's nerve deafness for you!

One night, Steve and I took our yellow lab Olive for a walk, and our dog disappeared into the bushes yards away. After waiting, I wondered aloud if Olive had already done her business. Steve insisted that was what she was doing right at this moment. I stared at him doubtfully and asked, "Well, then how do you know if you can't see Olive taking a poop fifty feet away in the total dark?" With a huge grin, he explained

that once our dog's tags stopped jiggling and the leaves stopped rustling, it was happening right there. I tell you, hearing people's hearing never ceases to amaze me.

Always a caring person, Steve has showed me how to ignore hurtful remarks and stand up to insensitive people. Once, we were in Boston, meeting with Cheryl and her family for a deaf walkathon along the Charles River. Hundreds of deaf people took over the whole pathway, but cyclists, runners, and rollerbladers were also flying by. One big guy yelled for everyone to scoot out of his way, "Hey, (bleep)! Get the (bleep) out of my way! Move! (Bleep)! Are they deaf or what? (Bleep)!" My dear husband shot back, "Yes, you dumb (bleep)! They are deaf, (bleep)! This is a deaf walkathon! Why don't *you* move the (bleep) of the way!" Sure enough, the rollerblader slowed down with a surprised look and then tucked his head and rolled away.

Being married to Steve has given me a true identity in the hearing world. Before meeting him, I wasn't sure about belonging to the hearing culture 100 percent because I was rarely asked out by hearing guys and had such a difficult time finding a tolerant mate. Because I had spent years fighting so hard for acceptance and finally found happiness with work and social life in the hearing world, I didn't want to throw it all away by marrying a deaf guy. In truth, I was fully set to marry a hearing guy and would wait forever if I had to. Maybe it was my relationship with my three brothers that prompted me to choose this kind of union; I was so familiar with hearing males. But I often worried that the man I would fall in love with would not get used to me as a deaf person. It was a disturbing feeling.

It is important for a deaf person to have a true identity, either in the Deaf community or in the hearing world. Unfortunately, many deaf and hard of hearing people feel torn between those opposite cultures, uncertain where they really belong. That conflict leads to zero self-esteem and severe depression, causing one to feel like a nobody. It is the worst feeling ever. The Deaf community does not accept those who don't know ASL fluently. And the hearing world does not readily accept all deaf and hard of hearing people. Therefore, many of these people are left in the middle without a sense of belonging. That's what happened to me when I was twenty-one. My sense of belonging was an off-and-on situation that gave me a roller-coaster

emotional ride. One day was bad enough; a lifetime would be too hard to bear.

Hard of hearing people are likely to take the most abuse from both the Deaf community and the hearing world. The former shuns them, believing that they are not really "Deaf." And the hearing world either ignores them or expects too much of them while it tends to be more sympathetic with those who are profoundly deaf. You see, most hard of hearing people can speak and hear with amplification, so they are expected to be like hearing people. I've been through that before. The truth is, I can sometimes hear fully and clearly what is said behind my back, and other times, I can't. It just depends on the sound feedback or just my concentration. So really, people need to be more gentle on hard of hearing people, most of whom are miserably struggling for a true identity, torn between the hearing world and the Deaf community. Actually it's even more difficult and more depressing to be hard of hearing than totally deaf.

While doing research, I was shocked to read that only 3 percent of hearing-deaf marriages actually work. But other books said 5 percent, 10 percent, and other small figures, so the exact percentage may never be known. (I'd be shocked if 25 percent of hearing-deaf marriages did work!) Anyway, I showed the book to Steve, pointing to the 3 percent in astonishment. He didn't react much, but the next day he came home with a dozen red roses and announced that he was delighted and proud "to be in the 3 percent." You can imagine tears in my eyes.

Because deafness is emotional and intense, I plan to become a counselor for deaf people and their hearing families, as I expect to receive my master's degree in counseling in December 2004. When I counsel deaf clients, I will never give advice on which type of communication or lifestyle to choose; I will try only to encourage these clients to make the best of their disability and to lead productive, healthy lives. I would also like to help reduce friction between deaf children and their hearing families—and yes, even between deaf and hearing spouses. After designing landscapes for twenty years and trying unsuccessfully to have children, I decided to opt for a more fulfilling career, that is, counseling people with a disability similar to mine.

My main goal in writing this memoir is to build a bridge between hearing and deaf people. It is badly needed. Those two different groups

can help one another understand their worlds. The Deaf community needs to be recognized for its own culture and language; therefore, it should not be eliminated altogether. The hearing culture needs to understand that deaf people are unlike them only in terms of their ears. Hearing and deaf people need to share. Hearing people shouldn't ignore deaf people, and deaf people shouldn't resent hearing people.

It's time to break ground and get to work. We need to build a bridge and cross it soon. It has been too long.

Making Sense of It All

The Battle of Britain Through
a Jewish Deaf Girl's Eyes

Eileen Katz and Celeste Cheyney

The first time that something seemed different was one morning in September 1938, when I was six years old. We had been back only a few days from our summer holiday and were in our little red brick house, 46 Wormholt Road, Shepherds Bush, London W2, having breakfast at our square wooden table by the window. Outside, it was gloomy and damp, but as always, our dinette with the flowered wallpaper felt cozy and warm. On the mantel, next to a photograph of my Uncle Jacob and his family, who lived in Paris, was one of Leslie and me taken recently on Leslie's third birthday. In that photograph, we were dressed up for his party in outfits Daddy had made in his shop—Leslie in a cute little sailor suit and I in a lovely frock embroidered with small, bright blue flowers that matched my eyes. Mummy had carefully combed Leslie's silky brown hair, and she had brushed my blonde curls until they were perfect. She loved dressing us up in fancy clothes and always beamed when the neighbours pointed at us and smiled. On the mantel next to the photographs were our brass menorah and a clock that Daddy had to wind up every night. On the table, were stainless cutlery, white cloth

Leslie and I in the back garden at our home in London.

servettes, and my mother's maroon and white dishes with the Chinese design. I could smell soft-cooked eggs in their egg cups, toasted bread with sweet orange marmalade, and English Breakfast Tea brewing in our potbellied teapot.

The day had begun in its normal way, with Daddy giving me a good-morning hug and loving pat on the face. Now that he, Leslie, and I were seated at the table, we could see, through the sheer white curtains,

that the lights were on next door, where my Auntie Hewitt lived. She was a tall, thin woman who was a spinster, which is what you called an unmarried woman in those days, and she wasn't really my aunt, but my mother's close friend. As always, Daddy was hiding behind his *Daily Express*, trying to avoid Leslie and me. Whenever Mummy ran back into the kitchen, we stuffed ourselves with toast smothered with marmalade, banged our spoons on the table, giggled, and kicked each other. Nobody noticed when we broke off pieces of toast and hid them in our pockets for the birds. Later, we would sneak out to the garden through the kitchen door and scatter the crumbs behind the coal shed. It was my idea, but Leslie was always happy to follow along.

That morning in September 1938, my father was somehow different. He was usually a warm, easygoing man, although these days, whenever he glanced at the photograph of Uncle Jacob and his family, he frowned. That morning, when he closed his *Daily Express* and placed it on the table, my father looked ready to cry. He was dressed for work, in his grey wool suit with the two rows of buttons, carefully pressed white shirt, and wide tie with stripes. Now Daddy was staring at something on the front page of the newspaper. It was a large photograph of an angry man with a dark moustache and wild eyes. Around him were lots of smiling people, and every one of them had an arm raised. Something about that photo made me feel afraid.

My mother, who had never been easygoing, looked ready to cry, too. As always, she was smartly dressed, a white apron over her pale green frock with the matching lace collar and her lisle stockings and polished black-and-white shoes with little heels. Mummy was rushing back and forth through the open door between the dinette and the kitchen, which she closed only when she was frying fish. She hurried past the gas stove to the larder, the small storage room where we kept tinned foods. Like most British families, we had no refrigerator, so we stored butter, milk, fish, and meat in enamel bowls on the floor of the larder. Mummy dashed in with some milk for our porridge, then saw that we had finished the marmalade and ran back to the larder for more. In her mind, if you didn't eat a proper breakfast, you would be weak all day. My mother always found something to fuss about, which only made us laugh and do more things to upset her. Still, that look was even worse than usual. What could be worrying Mummy now?

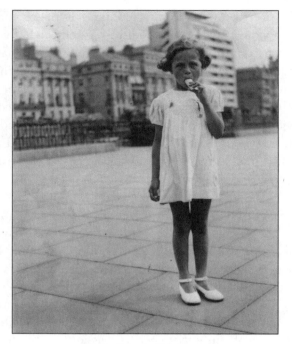

On holiday in Brighton.

Our summer holiday had lasted a fortnight—one week at a boarding house in Brighton and the other week with Grandpa Sam and Auntie Julie in Hove. Mummy, Leslie, and I stayed all week, and Daddy came down on Sundays, when the shop was closed.

Now that we were home, my mother had taken out my summer uniforms—pale blue frocks with navy blue collars that were worn with ugly black oxford shoes and white socks. Soon, it would be time to return to school, where I stayed except for weekends and holidays at home. I had been going to school for two years—first at a day school, Fulham Palace School for the Deaf, and last year at the Residential School for Jewish Deaf Children. Finally, I was beginning to read, write, speechread, and even say some words.

At home, I was the only one who couldn't hear, and that made it hard for everyone. We weren't sure what had made me totally deaf, but my mother said it was my own fault. Leslie was quiet and calm, but I had

always been active, and my mother thought that, as a small child, I had rolled out of bed and hit my head. She tried to teach me the names of things, always pointing and making silly movements with her mouth, but it made no sense at all. At first, all I was able to do was point to things and make faces and use gestures; sometimes, I grabbed, hit, kicked, or bit, and everyone looked horrified. Now that I was beginning to read, write, speechread, and say some words, I was better at understanding and getting my message across, but being deaf in a hearing family was still difficult.

That morning after breakfast in September 1938, Daddy went back to his normal routine. He finished his tea, stood up, walked over, hugged Leslie and me, smiled, and patted our faces. He glanced at his wristwatch, looked shocked, grabbed his newspaper, umbrella, and hat, and waved as he rushed out the door. We stood outside and watched him race down Wormholt Road to catch the bus to his shop, which was in Askew Road.

Leslie and I played on the kitchen floor while my mother cleared the table, washed and dried the dishes, and stacked them neatly in the cupboard. We raced upstairs to our small, square bedroom where we always felt so private and safe. It was in the rear of the house, overlooking our long garden with the picket fence. The room had white wallpaper with tiny yellow flowers and sheer white curtains that waved when there was a breeze. Our beds were on opposite sides, each with a yellow blanket and a soft, goosefeather pillow. On my cupboard dresser, on the wall opposite from Leslie's, were a doll and some stuffed animals. My favourite was a soft, furry, white dog.

I had the bed next to the window, with a lovely view of the garden, and for a while, Leslie and I sat on my bed stroking each other's hair and looking out. If we glanced to the left, we could see the area near the kitchen where the mint and spinach were growing. My mother had those plants near the door, so if we picked them when it rained, we wouldn't have to step on the grass. She was sure that, if we got our feet wet, we would catch colds. To the right was the latched door to the lavatory, where we pulled a chain to make it flush. Straight ahead was a large plot of grass, and in the middle, a ceramic stand stood filled with geraniums. On both sides were pathways leading all the way back

to the tomato plants, the rhubarb, the dark red cherry tree, and the blackcurrant and gooseberry bushes. The red and yellow cherry trees and the flowers Daddy had planted all around the edge of the grass— dahlias, snapdragons, lilies of the valley, hydrangeas—all looked so lovely.

That morning, because it was gloomy and damp outside, we stayed up in our room, and I taught Leslie some signs. Being the only one in the family who was deaf, I was the only one who knew how to sign well. Leslie thought I was quite clever, and once when we were signing out in front of the house, he proudly told the neighbours we were speaking French! Of course, I thought Leslie was the clever one. After all, I was just beginning to understand Mummy and Daddy's words when they were speaking. Leslie understood everything, even when he wasn't looking at them, and he was only three.

Later, when the sun came out and it was a bit warmer, my mother strapped Leslie into his pushchair and we strolled to Wormholt Park. It was fun racing up the climbing bars on two ladders that were side by side. Later, Mummy pushed us on the swings, and we pumped as hard as we could to make ourselves go up high.

On the way home, Mummy stopped at the greengrocer, the dairy, and the sweets shop. Then we went on to the kosher butcher. Leslie and I were always happy to see the butcher, Mr. Cohen, a tiny man with a bald head and a bushy black beard. The shop was disgusting—full of dead chickens, huge chunks of meat, and an awful smell, and Mr. Cohen's white apron was always covered with blood. He was terribly nice, though, and whenever we came in, he smiled. Best of all, once he had given us a shilling each for Chanukah *gelt*.

That afternoon, Mr. Cohen was standing behind the counter staring at a newspaper, and he didn't smile at all. He looked just the way my father had. Mr. Cohen shuffled away and brought back a dead chicken, then called my mother over and pointed at the newspaper. It was that same photograph of the angry man with the dark moustache and the wild eyes. Right away, Mummy was ready to cry. Why did she have that look again?

When we arrived home, it was sunny and warm, and Leslie and I ran out to the garden. My father was already there, and he was watering the geraniums in the ceramic stand. When he saw us, he smiled and handed

me the metal watering pail with the long spout, and I watered all the flowers. Then, I knelt down and crawled around the grass and scooped up some slimy worms, which I dumped in the rain-filled beer keg near the kitchen door. Leslie just stood and watched; he was less curious and never touched anything slimy. We played catch with our little rubber ball, and when it landed in one of Daddy's flower beds, we fetched it quickly so he wouldn't notice. Playing together at home was great fun. Our little red brick house with the garden was the most wonderful place in the world, and that was never going to change.

After a while, my father shuffled over to the kitchen door and stepped inside. When he came back out, he was carrying his *Daily Express*. He sat down on a garden chair and kept staring at that photograph on the front page. Why was he doing that again? And why had Mr. Cohen and my mother looked worried, too? Who was that man in the newspaper and why did he make everyone feel so bad? It was a pity I didn't know how to ask here at home, but perhaps I could ask someone at school.

Of course, I had no idea what had been happening in Germany since Adolf Hitler and the Nazi party had come to power in 1933. I was not aware that, by 1938, Jews were losing their homes, their businesses, their jobs, as well as the right to attend certain schools and to move about freely.

I also didn't know that, according to the Nazis, people with mental or physical disabilities were "imperfect," and their lives were "not worth living," and that included deaf people. Soon, thousands who were disabled would have involuntary treatments that would make them unable to have children. Under the so-called "Euthanasia program," many disabled people would be killed. So wherever the Nazis were in power, someone like me had two reasons to be afraid.

Our Own Special Place

A few days later, it was time to take the double-decker bus to school. It was nice to be going back. I couldn't wait to be once again with other children like me and to tell my dear friend Catherine about our stay at the seaside. It would be fun to share the jellydrops from the sweets shop and the butter biscuits Mummy had baked.

That morning when we trudged down Wormholt Road to the bus stop, it was cloudy and cool with a light breeze. Daddy was carrying a large brown case filled with my belongings. When the bus stopped, we all jumped on and climbed the narrow winding staircase to the upper deck. Soon, we were sitting down, and Leslie and I were on our knees looking out the window. We passed the church, the kosher butcher, the dairy, the park, and rows of red brick houses. My mother kept tapping me on the shoulder to get my attention and pointing at everything. She was making those silly movements with her mouth, which made people stare, and I hated it. Also, because it was breezy, she buttoned my cardigan so I wouldn't catch a cold. I moved the buttons out of their holes, one by one, just to annoy her.

After a while, we were jumping off the bus and Leslie and I were skipping along. That part of London was pretty, with more open space and trees than our neighbourhood. Soon we were running along next to a stone wall, and ahead were three high stone posts and one large metal gate and another gate that was smaller. Behind the wall was a red brick building with long windows and lots of tall chimneys. We were back at the Residential School for Jewish Deaf Children (RSJDC).

The Residential School for Jewish Deaf Children.

We trudged through the smaller gate and along the narrow cobble-stone path, surrounded by a garden full of leafy trees. We climbed a few steps to two huge wooden doors and soon were in the entrance hall with its winding staircase and a table made of dark wood that always held a large vase of fresh flowers.

Mummy and Daddy strolled down the corridor, and Leslie and I skipped along next to them. Other families were hanging about, and everyone smiled. A tall, slim man with white hair and a bushy white moustache was standing with some parents, and when he saw us, he waved. He was someone we all loved—the principal, Mr. Hart. Soon he strutted over, smiled, patted me on the head, and chatted with Mummy and Daddy. He always did that, and it made us feel important and wel-come. However, this time, Mr. Hart did something he had never done before. He stopped smiling, looked serious, and spoke to my parents, and they nodded in agreement. It was all a bit odd.

Mummy, Daddy, Leslie, and I climbed the stairs to the second storey, and before long, we were in the dorm. It was a large, long, narrow room with pale green walls and about twenty metal beds with their head-boards against the walls. Most of the beds were grownup size, but at the far end were some smaller ones. Between all the beds were large, square boxes that we kept our belongings in. Lots of girls were there, and it was quite lively. They were signing, fingerspelling with both hands, wink-ing, smiling, frowning, laughing, tapping each other, pointing at things, and moving their mouths. Sign language was forbidden in the class-room and the dining room, but it was allowed in the playgrounds and the dorms, and it felt so good to see it again. It was not formal British Sign Language, but the school's own version, which had always been passed down from older students to younger ones. It was a clear and easy way to talk to one another and to build concepts, and it made us feel we had something special that was our own.

At the far end of the dorm, on one of the small beds, was a slim girl my age with straight brown hair, brown eyes, and the friendliest smile. It was my dear friend, Catherine, whom I had met last year on the very first day of school. When she saw me, she jumped up and ran over and we cuddled.

Before long, the families were starting to leave, and Mummy, Daddy, and Leslie were kissing me good-bye and strolling toward the door. My

father would pick me up on Friday to go home for the weekend and bring me back on Sunday, so this was like any other week. However, just as Mummy, Daddy, and Leslie were reaching the door, something happened that had never happened before. Mr. Hart popped in and waved to all the mums and dads, and they shuffled over to a corner and huddled there. Over in the corner, looking quite grim, Mr. Hart and the parents talked on and on, and their meeting seemed to last forever. Finally, when Mummy and Daddy waved good-bye, they were frowning. I didn't like it at all.

Soon, all the parents were gone and we sat down on Catherine's bed and caught up on all the news. She had spent the fortnight at home with her parents and her older brother, who was deaf and attended our school, too. Catherine was fortunate because, even though her Mum and Dad were hearing, she always had someone she could sign to. Also, they lived in Southend-on-Sea, so they must have felt they were always on holiday.

I was happy to be here at school. That hadn't been true at all last year. Last autumn, when the family left me at school for the first time one Sunday morning and didn't come back until Friday afternoon, I was terrified. I wasn't sure I would ever see them again. "Why me?" I kept asking myself. "Why me?" For a long time, I had missed everyone at home and was miserable. Sometimes, when it was time for Daddy to take me back to school on Sunday, I would crawl under my bed and hide, and he had to crawl under and pull me out. Now I was comfortable here at school. Because we were able to sign, I could understand what others were saying, and they could understand me. For children like us, it was our own special place.

RSJDC was beautiful, both inside and outside. The rooms had high ceilings and some, like the staff dining room, had walls of shiny dark wood. The building had places like the assembly room—used for religious services, parties, and shows—and the gymnasium, which had ropes we could climb all the way to the ceiling and long narrow boards that we could balance on. Outside, behind the building, were a garden for the staff, a large grassy area that the boys used for sport, and a playground on each side. At the end of the garden were cottages that were used as classrooms and one that was an infirmary, and there was even an outdoor swimming pool that had just opened this summer. Someone must have known how much I loved to splash about.

Because it was Sunday, we wouldn't be going to our classroom, which was in the main building on the first storey. The room was full of picture books and toys, but we only touched them when our teacher, Mrs. Hånnah Benham, allowed it. She was a tall, chunky young woman with short brown hair and glasses who was quite strict and greatly respected at the school. Mrs. Benham was a strong believer in the oral method, with its focus on speechreading and speech—the recommended method of instruction at schools for the deaf in Britain before the war. Every morning, the four girls—me, Catherine, Sylvia, and Shirley—and the four boys—Jack, Isadore, Harry, and Sam—had to sit on little chairs in a semicircle and keep our eyes glued to Mrs. Benham. The first lesson was always the News of the Day, when we looked at the calendar and talked about the weather and Mrs. Benham wrote everything on a chart. We spent lots of time on speech, when we had to use our eyes, hands, lips, tongue, and throat, and our hearing if we had any. We also spent lots of time on speechreading. Mrs. Benham had a chart that always had five words, and when she said one, we pointed to it, and that was confusing because different words looked the same. Mrs. Benham expected us to be able to spell, too. During reading class, we had to copy those five words and learn to match them with pictures, and after a while, she would hold up the pictures and we had to write the words properly. It was all very hard work. Why did school have to be this way? Why couldn't we just come to class and play?

Before the war, the major goals of RSJDC were to train deaf children to earn their living and to instruct them in religion. When they came of age, the girls were trained in domestic science, to prepare them to work as laundresses or dressmakers. Boys were taught woodworking, gardening, boot repairing, shoemaking, tailoring, and bookbinding. Our religious training consisted of a brief service every day after breakfast. Most of us spent weekends and holidays with our families, so the *shabbos* and most Jewish holidays were observed at home.

Now that we were here in the dorm, I began putting things away in the box next to my bed. I grabbed my toothbrush, toothpaste, soap, and towel, carried them into the bathroom, and placed them under my number, which was 43.

Before long, something wonderful was coming from the corridor—the smell of everyone's favourite—shepherd's pie. It was time to go

The staff at school. Mrs. Benham is the woman with the glasses and her husband is standing behind her in a suit.

down to the dining room for our midday meal. RSJDC paid close attention to the menu. Both Jewish and British dishes were served, and we often had both kinds of food at one meal. Whatever its style, the food was always kosher, which would be true even during the worst days of the war. The other girls in the class had arrived: Sylvia, who was chubby and had curly red hair and freckles, and Shirley, who was skinny and had straight blonde hair. I didn't really like those two, but I was careful to smile at them. Later, they might have some biscuits or sweets to share.

We queued up and marched downstairs to the huge dining room, with its rows of long tables set with white crockery and stainless cutlery. Then we filed in and sat down on the long bench, and Mrs. Benham went to fetch our tray of food. When she returned, we passed our plates and she filled them with shepherd's pie. Later, for dessert, we feasted on soft, sweet macaroons. Mrs. Benham pointed at the food, moving her mouth that silly way my mother did. She watched everything we did and expected us to finish our portions and to say "please" and "thank you." We didn't dare bang our spoons, kick each other, reach across the table, or grab or spill anything. If we did anything improper, Mrs. Benham pointed

at us and scowled, and sometimes, she even took away our food. We were expected to have perfect table manners, even though we were only six years old.

In the evening, our dorm matron from before the summer, Miss Grey, was back with us. She was a small, thin woman with white hair tied back in a bun, and we loved her. When we made our beds, she always helped us and the older girls lift our mattresses to make it easier to tuck in the sheets. When our boxes were untidy, she helped us tidy them up. If we sneezed or coughed, she asked the kitchen help to bring up some juice or some hot tea with honey. After the lights were out, if she came in and found us awake, she scolded us, but she never actually got cross.

That first evening back from holiday, when Miss Grey had turned out the lights and shuffled out, the four girls from our class sat on Catherine's bed. I brought out my torch (smuggled from home) and turned it on and we pulled out our biscuits and sweets. We had brought from our homes all kinds of biscuits—oatmeal, shortcake, sweetmeal, wafers, arrowroot, cinnamon sugar, butter, assorted creme. As for the sweets, we had brought plenty of those, too. I had my toffees and jelly-drops, Shirley had some chocolates, and Sylvia had mints—which were white with a smooth, peppermint filling. It had been a good idea to be nice to those two. Soon we were passing everything around and tasting it. It was so much fun being back at school that I forgot to ask about the angry man with the dark moustache and the wild eyes.

Attending RSJDC would do more than affect how I prepared for the world of work, learned about my religion, and acquired language and social skills. It would also play a huge role in how I experienced the terrible war that was ahead.

A Sudden Change

Soon, we were back in our school routine, and our days were busy. When we awoke, Miss Grey and the older girls came over to help us make our beds and get dressed. Then we had breakfast, which was porridge with milk and a slice of buttered bread. After that was a short religious service in the assembly room, where we sang "God Save the King," then said The Sh'ma (Hear, O Israel).

In the classroom, we started every morning with the news, and we were learning the days of the week by saying, speechreading, reading, and writing them. In speech, we were working on the difference between sounds that were breathed, voiced, and nasal. We started with *p*, *b*, and *m*, and we had to put our hands in front of our mouths or on our throats or under our noses to tell the difference. Sometimes, we used feathers when we did the *p* sound, and when the breath came out, the feathers ended up flying around the room. When we made a *b* sound, we could feel our throats move, but if we made an *m* sound, we could feel it under our noses. It was confusing, but after a while, we began to know the difference. Sometimes, we worked alone with Mrs. Benham in front of her speech mirror. It was nice to be able to look into it and smile, but when she put her hands on my face and I had to put mine on hers, I hated it. In speechreading, we often had to guess because different words look the same. Sometimes, we got it wrong and Mrs. Benham frowned at us. For reading, we were using a silly book about a boy and girl and their dog and cat. It was mostly pictures, but it had a few words, and Mrs. Benham wrote them on a chart so we could all read them together. For spelling, instead of writing five new words each week, we now had to do ten. For penmanship, we practiced writing letters on the blackboard and in our notebooks, and that was nice because I didn't have to think too much.

Everyone loved recess, when the boys played over in their playground and we played in ours or when we all stayed in the gymnasium. After that, we marched into the dining room for the midday meal, like shepherd's pie. Then came the best time in the classroom, when we looked at picture books or played. Later in the afternoon we had high tea—a light meal of salad or soup and some muffins, biscuits, or scones. After tea, we played in the dorm and the older girls came over to help us get ready to retire. Then at seven o'clock, Miss Grey checked to see if we were in bed. Of course, the best time of all was after she turned off the lights and we could share our biscuits and sweets.

Every Friday after high tea, my father arrived to take me home, and I stayed with the family until Sunday after the midday meal. Everything at home was the same, except for one thing—a big change at the bottom of Wormholt Road. There, before we came to the row of shops, a long, narrow trench had been dug in the street, and it went on in both

directions as far as we could see. To get across, we had to walk on a wooden plank with rails on both sides, and it shook a lot. I held on to the rail, but I was afraid of falling off anyway. I didn't know it was one of many trenches being dug in London's streets and parks to hold back the Germans if they landed there. Daddy still frowned when he glanced at the photograph of Uncle Jacob and looked ready to cry when he read his *Daily Express*. I was going to ask about that angry man when I got back to school, but I always forgot.

One morning when we had been back at school for a while, there was a sudden change. Miss Grey usually shuffled from bed to bed and woke us with a gentle tap and a smile. That morning, her tap was more like a jab, and rather than shuffling, she was dashing about. She didn't seem cross, but she was in a big hurry.

It was dark in the dorm and dreadfully cold and I wanted to stay under the covers because I was shivering and my throat was sore. Outside the window, huge grey clouds swelled, the trees swayed, and rain beat down. This was a day for staying indoors, and nothing could get me to go outside! A glass of juice would make my throat feel better, so I coughed a few times to get Miss Grey's attention, but she didn't even turn around.

By then, most of the girls were sitting on their beds, waiting for Miss Grey to flick the lights—the signal to queue up and march to the bathroom—but this time, she ignored us. She dashed over to each bed, bent down, and pulled out the case that was stored underneath. Before long, my brown case was there on the floor next to my bed, wide open. Catherine and I glanced at each other and shrugged our shoulders, and soon, everyone else was shrugging, too.

Miss Grey rushed from box to box, pulling out our clothing and anything else that was there. She didn't fold things and place them carefully, the way my mother always did. She just threw them into our cases as if tidiness didn't matter at all. We ran to the bathroom and wrapped our toothbrushes, toothpaste, washcloths, and soap in our towels and ran back and threw them in, too. When the older girls arrived to help us get dressed, they took out our blouses, overalls, and cardigans instead of our uniforms—very strange indeed because it was a school day. I didn't like this rushing about at all. I never liked it when things happened too quickly. We must be going somewhere, but where could it be?

We all trudged down to the dining room. Breakfast was the usual lumpy porridge with milk and a slice of buttered bread, but it was different in one way. Mrs. Benham, who usually sat with the class, was up and rushing about. For once, it wasn't necessary to say "please" or "thank you" or to finish the food if we didn't want to. I left most of the porridge in the bowl and smothered a slice of bread with butter, wolfed it down, licked my fingers, and banged my spoon and giggled until Mrs. Benham glowered at me from another table. After breakfast, we filed into the assembly room to sing "God Save the King" and recite The Sh'ma, but this time, we did it fast.

When we returned upstairs, our cases weren't there, and when I looked inside my box, it was empty. I bent down and poked my head under the bed, but I saw only some dust. Mummy thought that dust caused breathing problems, so this sight would make her very unhappy! On every bed were mackintoshes, umbrellas, and Wellington boots.

When Miss Grey pointed at the boots, I stuck out my tongue and threw my pair across the floor. Nobody was forcing me to put them on and go outside in the rain! One of the big girls held me down, and soon, the boots were on and I was in a queue. When I threw myself down on the floor and screamed, nobody paid attention.

Mrs. Benham was standing behind the doors at the front entrance with the boys in our class, and she was carrying a large black umbrella. We all huddled around her and she pointed at the doors and we stepped outside under the umbrella and tramped toward the front gate. Mrs. Benham tried her best to keep us dry, but soon our faces were dripping with rain. It was muddy, even on the cobblestone path, and our boots soon became filthy.

Outside the front gates, several cars were lined up. The first car belonged to Mr. Benham, who opened the rear door and lifted all eight of us into the back seat. He was a tall, stocky man with light brown hair and was gentle and kind. The Benhams had a lovely little girl who was always smiling, but she wasn't with them now. Mr. Benham checked that our hands were safe and carefully closed the door, then climbed in and sat behind the wheel while Mrs. Benham climbed into the front seat. She turned around and watched us, and when my nose began to run, she handed me a handkerchief. The car started with a jolt, and we

were on our way. It was hard to see through the windows with all that rain pouring down. Where could we possibly be going?

I don't know how long we were in the car, but I felt dizzy and was blowing my nose a lot. It was crowded in the back seat, my legs felt cramped, and Jack was kicking me. I kept kicking him back until Mrs. Benham gave us one of her looks. When she turned back around, I waved my dirty handkerchief in his face with one hand and gave him a poke with the other. After a while, I leaned my head on Catherine's shoulder and fell asleep.

Suddenly the car was slowing down. It was even harder to see through the windows because it was raining more heavily than before. The car stopped, and Mr. Benham stepped outside. He held the door open and grabbed our hands as we climbed out onto the muddy road. Mrs. Benham was waiting with an umbrella, but it didn't keep us dry.

The scene around us wasn't like London at all. In front of us were fields full of horses and cows. Next to us on the road, a wagon filled with hay, pulled by a brown horse, had stopped. We held our noses to block a dreadful smell, and when we looked under the horse, we knew where it was coming from. Across the road was a row of small shops. On our side of the road was a large building made of red brick, and then a small stone church with colourful windows and a tall, square-shaped tower. Next to the church was a narrow river that gushed over rocks as the rain poured down. Many thoughts that I couldn't put into words began to race through my head. What was this strange place, and why were we here? Were we on holiday? When would we be going back to school? And when would I see Leslie, Mummy, and Daddy again?

Soon, other cars from the school pulled up, and we waved to the children as they climbed out. Mrs. Benham marched us up a few stairs and into the red brick building, then into a huge room. It was warm there and we could smell something cooking, but it was hard to tell what it was. It felt good to be inside. Some women wearing aprons smiled at us, then led us into a cloakroom, helped us take off our wet clothes, and hung them on hooks. This place even had indoor toilets, and soon there was a long queue.

By now, everyone had filed into the huge room, and before long, a group of older boys began playing catch over in a corner while other children settled themselves on the floor to play jacks or draw or look at

picture books. This place wasn't so bad, actually, as long as we could do things that were fun. It was better than sitting on a chair with my eyes glued to Mrs. Benham, hoping she wouldn't call on me. I should be quite happy if school were always like this.

The teachers carried a long table into the room and brought in some large pots of soup. We were instructed to queue up, and when it was our turn, we were to grab a bowl and spoon and let a teacher ladle some soup into the bowl. The soup tasted awful, but it made my throat feel better.

Mr. Benham flicked the lights to get our attention and had the eight of us in our group queue up against the wall. We trudged into the cloakroom and put on our mackintoshes and boots, then marched outside. The rain had stopped, but it was still gloomy, muddy, and damp. We looked both ways, then crossed the road to where the shops were. We passed one place that looked like fun. It had a hanging sign with a picture of a mug, and inside, people were having a party. What a pity I was feeling ill.

Where the shops ended we turned onto a narrow dirt road with a row of houses. Mrs. Benham knocked on a door, and a man and woman who were both chubby answered. We wiped our muddy boots on a straw mat and stepped inside. Something good was baking, and it smelled like Mummy's scones. We removed our mackintoshes and boots and trudged up a narrow winding staircase. At the top, Mr. Benham showed the boys into one bedroom and we followed Mrs. Benham into another. It was quite cozy, with a wide, high bed that had a floral bedspread, and there were matching curtains and a cupboard dresser, desk, and chair all made of dark wood. Four cases, including my brown one, were at the foot of the bed, and when I opened the case, a photograph of the family taken in Brighton was there. It was good to see their faces, but when would I actually be with them again?

Tea was served at a long table with benches, in front of a roaring fire. The man and woman kept grinning at us and I kept looking the other way. A huge plate of scones sat in front of us, but I had no appetite. My nose was feeling stuffy and my throat was sore again. Mrs. Benham noticed when I pushed the food away, but this time, she didn't force me to eat. She walked over and felt my forehead, then picked me up and carried me up to bed. She brought some hot tea with lemon and honey and

Our family on holiday in Brighton.

stayed while I sipped it down. Then she turned out the light and I fell asleep.

The next morning it was raining again, and I felt dreadful. Catherine, Shirley, and Sylvia were out most of the day, but I just stayed in bed, and the chubby woman brought up some soup that I didn't eat. Most of the time I slept, but otherwise, I just stared out the window at horses and cows. I was missing the family so much. If only Mummy could be fussing over me now!

The following day, I felt better but still didn't go outside. I coloured, looked at picture books, and slept a lot, and the woman brought up goat's milk, which tasted horrid. Finally, the next morning, I felt well again. Every day, we slept in the house and had breakfast and high tea there. We played and had our midday meal in the large, red brick building, and when it wasn't raining, we took walks in the town. Being in this

strange new place was fine, except when I thought about Mummy, Daddy, and Leslie. When would I see them again?

Then one cloudy morning, the older girls came running into our room. They told us to throw everything into our cases and hurry downstairs. After a hasty breakfast, we trudged over to the large building. The cars were lining up, and teachers were loading cases into the boots. Mr. Benham lifted us into his car, checked that our hands were safe, and closed the door. Soon, he was at the wheel with Mrs. Benham next to him and the car was speeding away. Catherine and I just shrugged our shoulders and rolled our eyes. Where could we be going now? After a while, I put my head on Catherine's shoulder and fell asleep.

Before long, we were pulling up in front of three high posts and two metal gates. We were back at the Residential School for Jewish Deaf Children. Our stay in that strange new place was over. One question kept racing through my mind. Why had we gone there?

Our stay in the village of Speen, near Newbury, took place Wednesday, September 28, to Thursday, October 6, 1938. It was one small part of the first evacuation of British children to the countryside that was related to World War II. Our school had been advised to leave London because of a problem brewing in the Sudetenland—a large area of Czechoslovakia that Adolf Hitler wanted to control. The British and the French, in an attempt to avoid war, were urging the Czechs to hand over the area to Germany, but the Czechs refused. By September 23, war seemed inevitable, and preparation for our move began. On September 29, one day after we arrived in Speen, leaders from Britain, France, Italy, and Germany met in Munich. Through the agreement called the Munich Pact, they carved up Czechoslovakia until there was almost nothing left and, thus, avoided war. By Monday, October 3, it was safe for us to return to London, and a lorry came down and took back most of the goods. However, the school followed Jewish laws concerning diet and holidays. Because of the Yom Kippur holiday that was taking place, Jewish law prohibited bringing us back on the following day or the next, so we remained in Speen until Thursday.

That evacuation in the autumn of 1938 proved unnecessary, but it would not be long before Germany was attacking Britain. We would have to move from place to place to survive.

More Changes

Now that we were back in London, we were working hard again. We were learning more and more words—speechreading them, saying them, and reading them over and over. Every morning after the news, we copied the numbers from the calendar. We were speechreading short commands such as "Take out your notebooks" or "Stop that" or "Queue up, please," and there was a list of them on a chart. In speech, Mrs. Benham made us repeat everything again and again, and we had to think about how we moved our lips and our tongues and how our throats felt. She also wanted us to develop listening skills, but that was hard even for those who had some hearing. We had no hearing aids of our own. The school owned only one large, clumsy group aid, and it was kept in its own room and our class didn't get to use it. The book we were reading about the boy and girl and their dog and cat was boring, and I didn't pay much attention. (What a pity that school wasn't the way it had been in that village, where we could play all day.)

Soon, changes began to take place, and the first was in the dorm. One evening when we were getting ready to retire, Mrs. Benham popped in and announced that Miss Grey was no longer our dorm matron. A bit later, she marched in with our new matron, and right away we all wanted to crawl under our beds and hide. The woman was enormous, with black hair cut short like a man's, a long face, and the teeth of a horse. Even when she smiled, she looked mean. Mrs. Benham held up a card with her name, MISS STERN, and we had to stand up and say "Good evening." After a while, Mrs. Benham left and Miss Stern began storming around the room with her brows creased and her huge mouth open wide. She glowered at anyone who was sitting up and everyone crawled under the covers. Miss Stern turned off the lights and flashed her torch around the room, and we closed our eyes and pretended we were asleep. If we opened our eyes a bit, we could see her storming out and slamming the door, but just when we were ready to take out the biscuits and sweets, she would come storming back in. Right away, we had a sign for her: HORSE TEETH.

The next change took place the following morning, in the classroom. When we filed in, I got a clear feeling that we were going to do some

work we had never done before. I don't know why, but I had a feeling it was going to be important. Now I would pay attention.

Mrs. Benham turned around and wrote something on the blackboard:

Who has the book?
_____ has the book.

I looked at it carefully and was able to read the word "book," but what was that funny looking mark at the end? Next to the blackboard, on the chart rack, was a chart with WHO at the top. Mrs. Benham waved at Sylvia, who was directed to stand up, march over, and hold a book. Mrs. Benham took her stick and pointed to the sentence on top and then to the one under it, writing Sylvia's name on the line and again on the chart under WHO. Then Shirley marched up and held the book, and Mrs. Benham erased Sylvia and added Shirley's name to the line and the chart. Next, it was Catherine's turn, then mine, and then the boys marched up. They made silly faces, and Sam put the book on his head and it fell on the floor, and we couldn't stop laughing.

I wanted to know what that funny looking mark was, so I raised my hand. When Mrs. Benham nodded, I ran up to the blackboard and pointed to it, and she wrote the words *question mark*. She circled the word *question* and pointed to the word on the chart: WHO. *Question* was a hard word to read because it had more letters than we were used to, but it clearly had to do with wanting to know something. When we had all had a turn, every one of our names was on the chart, and we had to copy the list in our notebooks. It was becoming clear that WHO meant us. For the first time ever, we had seen how to ask and answer a question, and that was exciting.

For a few days, we went over our work on WHO, and everyone marched up and held something. It might be a book, but it could also be a pencil, a ruler, or a doll. For a while, it seemed as if WHO only meant us, but then one morning, Mr. Benham and Mr. Hart popped in, and Mrs. Benham added their names to the chart. WHO didn't only mean us. It meant people outside the class, too. After a while, Mrs. Benham added a separate WHO chart with words like boy, girl, man, woman, teacher, and matron. WHO wasn't only individuals but also groups of people. This new information really was exciting.

As for Miss Stern, she wasn't going to keep us from having a good time. Every evening when the lights went out, we still crawled into one another's beds with our torches, biscuits, and sweets. Miss Stern loved it when she caught us doing something naughty, and it was great fun trying to outsmart her. In fact, with my talent for mischief, I was becoming quite the ringleader, even though I was only six. At home, I could be in a room with a closed door and know when someone was about to come in. That ability made my mother think that I could hear, but actually, I could tell because of the shadow under the door. I told all the girls to watch for Miss Stern's shadow, and we took turns being on guard to warn when she was on her way. If we moved quickly, we could hide everything and get back to our own beds on time. Those who were caught might be dragged by Miss Stern into Mr. Hart's office. There they would have to stand against a wall, and he would hit their bottoms again and again with a cane. It hurt a lot, but our mischief was worth the risk.

One morning when we filed into the classroom, we saw something different on the blackboard:

What does Sylvia have?
Sylvia has a _____.

Could this be another important lesson? There was that funny looking mark, so perhaps these words were also about questions. Questions were important because they helped us ask about things. It would be a good idea to pay attention. Next to the board sat a new chart, and at the top it said WHAT. Mrs. Benham handed Sylvia a book, pointed to the first sentence on the board, and then wrote "book" on the line, quickly rubbing it off, and listing it on the WHAT chart. Then Mrs. Benham gave Sylvia a ruler, a puzzle, and a pen and listed them. Then Catherine came up and held a ball, a cup, and a doll. Clearly, WHAT meant things. Now we were able to answer two kinds of questions: WHO and WHAT. This information was very exciting indeed.

Although school was stimulating, I looked forward to weekends, especially playing in the garden with Leslie. Now that it was autumn, we loved kicking the fallen leaves and watching them fly up into the air,

and the bonfire at the rear of the garden smelled so good when Daddy burned the leaves. The cooler weather gave me a chance to wear my new pixie hood, which framed the face, buttoned under the chin, and came to a small point at the top of the head. That year, *Snow White,* the Disney cartoon, was the rage, and every child in London had one of those hoods. Occasionally when I didn't get my way, I still kicked and screamed, but Mummy and I were getting on better. It got dark early, which made it feel cozy inside, and we toasted bread over the fire in the dinette and sometimes Mummy served latkes or blintzes. She fussed too much about silly things, but she was a jolly good cook.

On Saturday afternoons, my mother took Leslie and me to play in Wormholt Park. Because it was the *shabbos,* we couldn't see Mr. Cohen on the way home, but we did visit the sweets shop and I saved most of the sweets for school. Coming home from the park was the most fun of all. Now that Leslie was older and we didn't have to bring his pushchair, we could run far ahead of my mother. With her bags of groceries, she could never keep up with us. That wooden plank was still at the bottom of Wormholt Road and it shook a lot when we walked across it, but everything else was the same as before.

Back at school, we encountered another new sight. Our class was out on one of our strolls through Wandsworth Common, which we had once a week. We typically talked about those walks when we got back to the classroom, Mrs. Benham writing related words and sentences and us copying them. It was a lovely autumn day, a bit chilly but with lots of sunshine, and we were skipping along the path. Suddenly, a group of boys about our age came marching along with their teacher, and their faces were covered with something that was horrid. It had a strap going over the head in the center and a strap going around over the ears to the back of the head. It had goggles, so you could see the boys' eyes and noses, but each of their mouths was hidden under a round nozzle with small holes. At first, we were terrified and ran over to Mrs. Benham. When she smiled, patted our heads, and shrugged her shoulders, we felt a little better. Those boys looked odd, but they must be playing a game and those masks must be part of their costumes. We looked back at them once, then skipped along again.

One weekend when I arrived home, I noticed another change. On a chair in a corner of the dinette were more of those strange masks—two

large ones and two small. My mother walked over to the chair, smiled, and picked up one of the large ones and put it on. She looked rather silly, but Leslie was frightened and crawled under the table to hide. My father strutted over and picked up a mask and put it on, looking silly, too. He picked up the two small masks and pointed to Leslie and me. I was curious, so I allowed Mummy to put one over my face and to fasten the buckle in the back. Right from the start, wearing that mask was horrid. The rubber smelled bad, and it was difficult to breathe. Even worse, Mummy and Daddy couldn't see most of my face and I couldn't see most of theirs. The mask made me feel terribly helpless. I was surprised when Leslie tried on his mask and pulled it off right away. After all, he didn't need to see faces. Years later, I asked my mother if people could hear a person speaking who had a mask on and if that person could hear others. Her answer to both questions was "Yes, love, but not very well." Perhaps Leslie didn't feel helpless but was a bit confused.

One rainy Saturday afternoon, yet another change took place. Because it was raining, Leslie and I stayed in the house. In the late afternoon, when my father arrived home from the shop, he and my mother rushed over to that large wooden box with knobs that stood against a wall in the parlour. It was the radio and, like the telephone, it made people do things that were strange. Sometimes, my parents sat next to it and looked serious. At other times, they laughed or mouthed words and bobbed their heads, and sometimes, they even got up and danced. Now, my parents looked shocked, as if something terrible were going on.

That evening, when I was supposed to be asleep, I crawled out of bed and tiptoed to the top of the stairs. I saw my father sitting next to the radio, sobbing, and in his hand was the photograph of my Uncle Jacob and his family. On the floor was a newspaper, and on the front page was a huge photograph. It was a large building with a dome and it was on fire. It looked a lot like our synagogue, where we sometimes attended services. After a while, I tiptoed back into the bedroom and crawled into bed, but it was hard to fall asleep. Why did the newspaper and the radio make Mummy and Daddy sad? And why was that building on fire?

The next day, when I was back at school, I decided that it was time to ask someone about all of these changes taking place. I had to try to

make sense of it all. That angry man was a person, so he was a WHO. Now that I knew that, I could ask about him. Those masks were things, so they came under WHAT. I wasn't sure about the burning building because it was a bit large, but it must go under WHAT, too.

In the evening, when two of the older girls came over to help us get ready for bed, I stood in front of them and signed "BAD MAN—WHO?" Then I placed two fingers sideways above my mouth and, keeping the other arm straight, raised it until it was almost touching my head. Surely that would remind them of that man in the newspaper and all those people with their arms raised. I kept staring at those girls and all they did was glare back at me as if I were daft. Perhaps they didn't know about that man, but they must know about that building on fire. I knew how to fingerspell F-I-R-E, and they showed me the sign, but when I signed back "FIRE—WHAT?" the girls just glared at me again. They were older and were supposed to know more than I did. Hadn't they seen the photographs in the *Daily Express*?

Those girls were not aware that, on November 9, 1938, organized acts of violence occurred against the Jews and Jewish property all over Germany. They didn't know that more than 7,000 Jewish businesses were destroyed and that nearly 200 synagogues were burned and 76 razed to the ground. Almost 100 Jews were killed and 36 severely wounded, and more than 36,000 were sent away from their homes and held. This was *Kristallnacht*—literally, "Crystal Night," or "Night of Broken Glass."

Well, those older girls must have seen gas masks, so I grabbed a piece of paper and tried to draw one. When they just shrugged their shoulders, I wanted to fall down and scream. I glanced around, hoping to see a newspaper so I could point to some photographs, but nobody had one. I wanted so much to make sense of it all, but that would have to wait until some other time.

One cold winter day, we queued up and marched into the assembly room. It was already filled with children, and standing behind a long table was Mr. Hart. On that table were lots and lots of those strange looking masks, both large and small, and written in large letters was a sign saying GAS MASKS. Mr. Hart flicked the lights to get our attention, and then an unusual kind of speechreading lesson began. The lesson was a simple one. He called out names and each child called was supposed to stand up. Those children then marched over to the table,

picked up one of the small masks, and marched back to their places. If someone missed his or her name Mr. Hart looked cross and everyone stared, so it was important to watch carefully. When all of us children had masks, the teachers helped us put them on and buckle them. The boys in our class thought it was a game and marched around with them on, but most of us hated the masks and pulled them off. Catherine and I looked at each other through the goggles, pulled ours off, and held our noses. Thank goodness Mr. Hart handed everyone a square box with a long string, and we could put our masks inside them, queue up, and put them back on the table.

Nobody had told us why these masks were showing up here at school, so I decided again to ask the older girls. Perhaps this time, someone would be able to help. I ran over to one of the girls and pointed at the table, signing "MASK—WHAT?" Surely she would know something about these dreadful things. All the girl did was shrug her shoulders and fingerspell "g-a-s-m-a-s-k-s." I had seen that sign on the table, so it didn't tell me anything new.

Gas masks were there to protect us from the large-scale gas attacks that everyone feared. By the spring of 1939, when it was clear that war was inevitable, millions of them would be issued throughout Britain. They were carried everywhere in cardboard boxes that hung from the shoulder on a strap. There were full-sized masks for adults, smaller red rubber children's "Mickey Mouse" gas masks that were less frightening, and special ones for infants that were almost as big as they were. There were even models that were designed for pets.

I kept staring at the older girl and, finally, in a mixture of signing and fingerspelling, she came up with something that was very strange indeed. It didn't seem to have anything to do with the masks at all. BAD G-E-R-M-A-N-S was what she said. What did that mean? Who were the G-E-R-M-A-N-S? And what were they doing that was bad?

More and More Odd

These days, my father often looked worried or sad, but there were two places where he still seemed happy—in the garden and in his shop. In the garden, Daddy loved digging up the earth, scattering the seeds, and pouring water on them with his metal watering can with the huge spout.

In his shop, he was happy when he was folding a cuff or stitching a hem or making a buttonhole.

Lately, even in the two places where he normally was happy, my father was doing things that were more and more odd. One weekend in March 1939, he acted oddly in both places on the same day.

In the morning, my father did something peculiar in the garden. The family had been sitting at the table in the dinette having our breakfast of scones and gooseberry jam. When my mother shuffled toward the larder to fetch some more milk, Daddy winked at us, stood up, and signaled to follow him. Right away Leslie and I sprang up, and we all tiptoed toward the kitchen. We waited until Mummy had gone into the larder, then hurried through the kitchen and slipped outside. We had no winter coats on, even though it was cloudy, chilly, and damp and there was still some snow on the ground. The earth did have a new kind of smell, though, which meant that spring would be here soon, and Daddy had a huge smile. He pointed toward the rear of the garden and we all tramped over there. Next to the white picket fence was the reason he was happy; a few tiny crocuses were poking up through the snow. Then, without warning, Daddy leaned his head back, looked up at the sky, followed something that was moving, and began to frown. Leslie and I leaned back and looked up, too. We were expecting to see storm clouds, but we saw only a passing aeroplane. Aeroplanes flew over us all the time, so why should seeing one now make Daddy frown?

I glanced toward the house and there was Mummy, rushing toward us and carrying our winter coats. She was rolling her eyes at my father and pointing her finger at us. We all scooted past her and ran back into the house, rushed into the dinette, and sat down at the table. Soon Leslie and I were stuffing ourselves with scones smothered with gooseberry jam. Still, I kept thinking about that look on Daddy's face. Why had he looked up and frowned like that? I didn't know the Germans had been building up the Luftwaffe—their Air Force—since 1934 and that the coming war would largely be fought in the skies.

When Daddy finished eating, he was back to his usual ways. He finished his tea, then stood up, walked over, hugged Leslie and me, smiled, and patted our faces. He glanced at his wristwatch, looked shocked, grabbed his newspaper, umbrella, and hat, and waved as he rushed out the door. Leslie and I sat on the kitchen floor and looked at picture

books while Mummy washed and dried the dishes and stacked them neatly in the cupboard.

In the afternoon, we expected to go to the park, but found ourselves at the bus stop. When the bus arrived, we climbed the winding stairs to the upper level, and Leslie and I turned around, got on our knees, and looked out the window. When we reached an area with narrow streets, we knew where we were going—to Daddy's shop in Askew Road.

When we climbed off the bus, we turned onto one of those narrow streets. Lots of people milled about, and most of them looked odd. The men wore long black coats and tall black hats and had beards; some had long curly sideburns. Most of the women wore long frocks and scarves that tied under the chin. We had come to the East End, a mostly Jewish quarter that was full of immigrants from Eastern Europe. Like my father, who came from Poland and was on his way to America, many tradesmen and workers settled in the East End and found work in the needle trades.

I signaled to Leslie, and we ran ahead while my mother chased after us. It was crowded, so we had to be careful not to bump into anyone. When we reached the wooden door to the shop, we waited for Mummy, who was shaking her finger at us and panting as she approached. Soon, she was opening the door and we were all stepping inside.

My father was a tailor who ran his own outfitter's shop for men. Not surprisingly, we found him at his sewing machine. Here in the shop was where his other odd behaviour took place that day. Daddy was making stitches along the top of some fabric that had never been there before. It was plain black and was quite different from all the other cloth. When he saw us, my father looked up, then went right back to his work. He seemed to be in a big hurry—which was odd because, usually when we came in, he stopped and smiled.

Leslie and I loved visiting Daddy's shop in Askew Road. It smelled a bit musty and it was crowded, with a long, high table for cutting cloth and floor-to-ceiling rows of shelves against the walls. Everywhere were bolts of fabric and piles of small, square pieces of cloth that were made of wool—in pinstripes, herringbones, and tweeds, and dark drab colours like navy blue, brown, or grey. Except for some smooth pieces of suede for elbow patches, most of the cloth felt rough. Three mannequins stood among the fabrics, and they were good to hide behind when we played hide-and-seek.

My father had a wonderful collection of buttons, which he kept in tin boxes. There were shiny gold ones with sailing ships, brass buttons with crossed swords, silver ones with waving flags, small bone-coloured buttons with four holes, larger black ones with two holes, and lots of others. My favourites were the gold ones with the sailing ships. The designs on some of the buttons were raised a bit, which I could feel if I ran my fingers over them. Sometimes Leslie and I sorted the buttons according to colour, size, or the number of holes. Other times we played a game where we made a pile of mixed-up buttons on the table. One player closed his or her eyes and the other gave him or her one button to feel. Then that player would throw the button back in the pile and, with opened eyes, would have to identify which one it was. Leslie usually had to guess a few times before he got it right. When it was my turn, I thought about how big the button was, how many holes it had, and whether it had a raised design, and I usually got it right on the first try.

Leslie and I always got to sit up on the table and be Daddy's helpers. First we helped him roll out the bolt of cloth. We didn't help him cut it because the shears were too big and heavy. However, we did get to measure the cloth with his yardstick, to mark it with white chalk, and to take the straight pins out of the box and hand them to him. My mother always stood there and watched because she was afraid we would fall off the table. Daddy's shop also had a long mirror on a stand, which gave us a chance to see ourselves all the way down to our shoes. Sometimes, we pranced around in front of it and made silly faces. At the rear of the shop was a small area behind a curtain where men were measured for their new outfits. To be measured correctly, they had to take off some of their clothes, and once in a while, Leslie and I peaked in and spotted someone in his drawers. One day, a portly man had come into the shop, and he stared at me as if I was strange, so I decided to get even with him. My father had shuffled out to get some fabric, and the man had gone behind the curtain to get undressed. When his trousers fell to the floor, I reached under and pulled them out. Leslie and I were going to hide them, but my father came back and caught us.

The best times were when Daddy allowed me to use his sewing machine. First, I would point to a piece of cloth and a matching spool of thread. Then, my father would roll out the cloth on the table and cut off a piece with those huge, heavy shears. He would sit down at the

sewing machine and point to his lap, my signal to climb on. Together, we would thread the needle, and it often took several tries to get the thread to go through the tiny hole. We would guide the needle along the cloth trying to keep it straight, which was difficult, too. Sometimes I even did it myself, while Daddy pushed the treadle with his foot. He always looked at my work with great care, and most of the time he smiled.

My father was not the only person in the family who had worked in the needle trades. Grandpa Sam also had been a tailor. Years after the war, at the moment when he died in good health at the age of ninety-two, he was still sewing. He was in the bathroom, changing the feathers from an old mattress cover to a new one he was making for my bed. The feathers flew up and filled the room, and some went up his nose. He died right there in the bathroom because he wasn't able to breathe. My mother, too, had been a seamstress. She left school at fourteen and went to work behind Grandpa Sam's shop in a windowless room with a hanging light. She sat alone in that room all day, making buttonholes for men's custom-made suits, and she stayed there until she married Daddy. (She was supposed to marry a man from a wealthy family that made kosher cream cheese, but when Grandpa Sam visited the family, he couldn't stand the smell of cheese, so he called off the marriage.)

On that day in March 1939, Leslie and I stood there and watched Daddy finish stitching along the top of the black cloth. It seemed to take him forever. Then, finally, we went over to the table and helped him measure some navy blue cloth and watched as he cut off a piece with his shears. That day, my father spent much less time with us than usual, rushing back to his sewing machine. It was odd, but Leslie and I shrugged our shoulders, grabbed a box of buttons, and sat down on the floor to play the button game. Later, we played hide-and-seek, with one of the mannequins as base.

After our game, I ran over to Daddy because I wanted so much to sit down with him at the sewing machine. This time when I pointed at it, he shook his head no and went on working. I looked down at what he was sewing, and it was very peculiar indeed. That black fabric was still there, and he had stitched it along the top. The bottom was turned up, and I saw something odd—that the fabric was attached to a sheer white curtain! Why would anyone stitch that black fabric to a curtain, which

was supposed to be pretty and let the sunlight in? And why was my father too busy to sit with me at the sewing machine?

After a while, my mother appeared at the door to the room behind the shop. It was time for the midday meal. I was hungry, so I forgot about Daddy and ran back there. The room was small and had a tiny window looking out on a dark alley. Next to the window was a sink, and in the center of the room was a little square table with four metal folding chairs. Before she let us sit down, my mother ran her finger over the back of a chair, then wiped it with a cloth, the way she did at home because she hated dust. On the table were some cheddar cheese sandwiches on brown bread, glasses of milk, and some sweetmeal biscuits. Mummy led us over to the sink, washed our hands with foul-smelling tan soap, and dried them with a towel. Then Leslie and I sat down and ate our sandwiches, gulped down our milk, and had a few biscuits. When Mummy had her back to us, we grabbed more biscuits and stuffed them into our pockets.

Afterward, Leslie and I grabbed a puzzle and sat down on the floor. There, against one wall, were bolts and bolts of that same black fabric my father had at his sewing machine—very strange indeed. Why did Daddy have all of that cloth in his shop? Perhaps he was going to make long coats for those men with the tall hats and the beards.

My father dashed into the room, and he looked stunned. He pointed at a small radio that was on a shelf, and my mother ran over and turned the knob. At first, they just stood there and stared at the radio. Then they started talking quickly, looking very serious. After a while, both of them lowered their heads and covered their faces with their hands. What was happening now to make them look that way?

That day must have been March 15, 1939, when German troops took control of what was left of Czechoslovakia after the Munich Pact. By then, even the British, who wanted so much to avoid war, knew that it would not be possible.

I glanced around the room to see where my father had left his *Daily Express*. By now I'd had lots of practice with WHO and WHAT. The shop was where Daddy always brought his newspaper. I would find a photograph of that man, one of a gas mask, and one of a building on fire and write the question words. I couldn't do that at school, but I could do it here. It was so important to try to make sense of all these

strange things that were happening. I glanced around the room, but Daddy's newspaper wasn't there. I dashed into the shop and looked everywhere, but it wasn't there either. My father always grabbed his *Daily Express* and carried it to work, so where could it be now?

Its absence was upsetting, but at least I could ask about the odd things my father had done today. I thought about him in the garden, then ran back to the little room and grabbed a pencil and a sheet of paper from the shelf. I ran over to the table and actually wrote a sentence: Who hates aeroplane? It didn't really make sense, but perhaps he would tell me something about why he had looked up at the sky that way. Daddy just stood there, stared at me, and looked confused. Perhaps if I asked him about something that was right here, he would answer. That would be easy. I tugged on Daddy's arm and pulled him over to the bolts of black fabric and pointed to them. I ran back, grabbed the pencil and paper, and wrote another sentence: What is black cloth? I really wanted to ask what it was for, but I didn't know how. This time, Daddy seemed to understand, and he rushed over to the table, took the pencil and paper, and began to write. I was excited because he had never done that before. Perhaps now, finally, I would know why these strange things were happening. I looked at the paper and there was his sentence: Black cloth is for windows. That didn't tell me anything new. I had already seen the curtain under that black cloth, and everyone knew that curtains are for windows. Didn't Daddy realize that? Didn't he understand that I wanted to know why he had all these bolts of cloth? Was he going to sew all of the cloth to curtains? And why would he do something silly like that?

I didn't know that the government had provided that black fabric for all citizens so they could follow the strict blackout rules. Everyone had been ordered to pull black curtains or shades over all windows in the evening to keep light from showing. Street lights and windows of public vehicles were also required to be covered over. Any light seen from the air would make it easier for pilots of night bombers to tell where their targets were, and the goal was to avoid detection as much as possible. For a small fee, my father lined people's curtains with the black cloth or made new ones for different-sized windows. That was why he was so busy.

My mother shuffled over and placed some cheddar cheese sandwiches and a glass of milk on the table and pointed to them. It was time

for my father to sit down and have his midday meal. He was tired, so I left him alone.

Well, at least Daddy had tried to answer my question, and that was rewarding indeed. Still, why were all these odd things happening?

A Strange New Family

All spring, we worked hard in the classroom. Our spelling and penmanship were getting better, and we practiced a lot of WHO and WHAT questions. To my disappointment though, when I tried a few more times to ask the older girls about the gas masks, they still didn't know anything.

Time passed quickly, and before long summer was here. It was July 12, 1939, the day of the annual garden fete at the school. Now it was time to forget about serious things and simply have a good time.

The afternoon was perfect—sunny and warm with a light breeze—and the roses were in full bloom. It was lovely to close your eyes and feel the warm sun and the cool breeze and to breathe in the sweet air. The girls were dressed in their best frocks, and the boys had on suits, white shirts, and ties. I was wearing a pink frock with white lace trim that Daddy had made in his shop, my white shoes with the ankle straps, and pink socks with white lace. Our families were there, strolling about and chatting. My parents were with Catherine's mother, and Leslie was playing tag with some boys.

The garden fete was held in the grassy area between the boys' and the girls' playgrounds where colourful balloons now were bobbing in the breeze. Some older boys were carrying folding chairs from the assembly room and setting them up in neat rows. Over in one corner were games that we would be allowed to play later. One of them involved throwing little balls at targets, and another involved rolling large balls to knock down pins. Winners might even be awarded a small prize—some playing cards, a game of jacks, or a colouring book. One older boy had set up a game of croquet, and another was putting in place a little stage where he would present a magic show. In addition, a Punch and Judy puppet show, like one we had seen on the boardwalk in Brighton, had been set up for our amusement.

Next to the games were some long tables, and Catherine and I sneaked over to see what was there. The first one held things for grownups:

neckties, aprons, small picture frames, and books. The next table displayed dolls and stuffed animals. Another table held puzzles, picture books, and toys such as small metal windup cars, little tea sets, wooden alphabet blocks, and windup toy soldiers that marched. Each item had a small sign next to it telling the price. Later, the teacher would give us a shilling, and we would queue up and walk over to the tables with our class to buy whatever we could. We were learning to add and subtract, and Mrs. Benham would help us add up the cost and determine how much money we had left. Of course, Catherine and I had our own idea. As soon as we had our coins, we were going to slip away and try to be the first ones over there, so we could have more choices.

Across the grassy area was a table full of delicious looking biscuits. Beside them were lemons cut in half, with candy sticks inside to suck the lemon juice through, and tall glasses of apple juice or lemonade.

We wouldn't be allowed to play games, buy anything, or eat for a while. First, in the middle of the grassy area, each class had to put on a little show, doing an English country dance, a song, or a poem. Some children were terrified, but Catherine and I just wanted to get it over with so we could get on with the fun.

Soon, the parents filed over to the folding chairs and sat down, and our class got ready to perform. Mrs. Benham helped us put on paper masks that we had made, which covered the top half of the face and had slits to see through and pointed cat ears. Then we put on our winter mittens. We skipped to the middle of the grassy area and stood side by side, the four boys on the left and the four girls on the right. With Mrs. Benham's help, we were going to recite "The Three Little Kittens."

Our show did not go smoothly. The bright sunshine made us squint, and the masks kept moving up and down, so it was hard to see Mrs. Benham. I was in the middle, next to Isadore, and he kept shoving me and I kept shoving him back. After we had recited the first line, Harry's mask fell off and he started to cry and Mrs. Benham stopped everything and helped him put it back on. That got everyone confused, and some of us started reciting and some didn't. When we were all ready to continue, a bee started to fly around and we kept swatting it, which confused us even more. We started the poem again, and when we were supposed to take off our mittens, some of us couldn't get them off. When, finally, our

show was over, we curtseyed and bowed while the audience applauded and smiled. Years later, my mother told me that we had sounded dreadful but that we were certainly funny. The next class skipped to the middle of the grassy area, wearing absurd looking bonnets, and did an English country dance. Catherine and I were ready to slip away and hide behind a hedge, but Mrs. Benham gave us one of her looks. As other classes continued to skip up and begin singing or dancing or saying their poems, she was still watching us.

Finally, that awful show was over and we queued up for our shillings and marched over to the tables. I found a yellow apron with ruffles for Mummy, a navy blue and red striped tie for Daddy, and a small red metal windup car for Leslie. Catherine chose a pair of gold clip-on earrings for her mother and a mystery book for her brother. When we ran over and gave them the presents, we were rewarded with cuddles and smiles.

We skipped the magic show because there was a crowd, but we did see the Punch and Judy show. The puppets were doing the silliest dance, and we couldn't stop laughing. We played the game where you threw a little ball at a target and then the one where you rolled the large ball to knock down the pins. We didn't win any prizes, but we came close.

Next, Catherine and I rushed over to the tables that had the food. Each of us grabbed a glass of cold lemonade and gulped it down. We helped ourselves to lemons with candy sticks, then snatched as many biscuits as we could, especially the macaroons. Catherine's frock had two pockets, and we hid them in there. Then we raced over to the climbing bars and worked our way up the ladders to the platform. There we sat, munching on biscuits, sucking the tart lemon juice, and basking in the warm sun. From up there, we could see clearly through the rear windows of the school, where children would usually be waving. Today, because everyone was at the garden fete, surely no one would be inside.

To our surprise, a man we had never seen before and a large group of children were trudging up the stairs to the dorms. They were carrying cases, and Mr. Benham was leading. It was odd because when new children came to the school, they usually arrived with their families. Catherine and I glanced at each other and shrugged our shoulders. Perhaps this was a large family and that man was their father or they were just some boys and girls who were visiting. Surely they would be coming down to

the garden fete. Once they had passed the windows we forgot about them. We stayed up on the platform and enjoyed the warm sun, the cool breeze, the sweet-smelling air, the soft, tasty macaroons, and the cold, tart lemon juice.

The teachers brought out large bowls of potato pudding and coleslaw, huge platters of breaded chicken, and some loaves of fresh challah and placed them on one table. On another table were pitchers of iced tea and assorted cakes. We joined our families and queued up to get our food, then sat down on folding chairs, which were arranged in clusters. It was cooler now, so when my mother insisted that I put on a cardigan, I was willing.

We played hide-and-seek and, before long, the sky began to get dark. Mrs. Benham came and fetched us and told the class to queue up, and our families rushed over and kissed us good-bye. No one made a big fuss because we saw our parents every weekend. We trudged inside and up the stairs. It was late for us to be awake, and we were tired.

When we arrived in the dorm, we got quite a surprise—a new girl in the bed next to mine. She was a bit younger and was fast asleep with her arm around a beautiful doll with blonde curls and an elegant black velvet frock. On the box next to her bed was a silver picture frame and inside was a photograph of her with a man and a woman. The girl must be part of that family that had climbed the stairs.

In the morning when Catherine and I awoke, the new girl was lying in her bed sobbing. When she saw that we were staring at her, she pulled the blanket over her head. Then, little by little, she pulled the blanket down, first below her eyes, then her nose, then her chin. Catherine tried to comfort her, first with smiles, then by sitting on her bed and stroking her hair. For a while my best friend seemed to forget that I was there. When I frowned, Catherine said it was important to make the new girl feel at home. When the others in the dorm awoke, she told them to be gentle, so they wouldn't frighten the new girl. I glanced around the room and there were two other girls who were new, but they were older. After a while, they came over and helped the little one get dressed.

Of course, she wasn't as pretty as I was, but the new girl was quite nice looking. She had pale skin, red lips, straight shiny black hair, and big brown eyes. Soon, she had on a lovely red and white plaid frock and had a large, shiny white bow in her hair. On her feet were white ankle-high,

laced-up shoes and white socks with lace. She looked like a queen, ready to pose in a photograph. The rest of us had to wear our summer uniforms with those ugly black oxford shoes and white socks, which was quite unfair! When it was time to eat, Catherine signed FOOD, then took the girl's hand and led her downstairs.

When we arrived in the dining room, we found another surprise—new boys, mostly older. When I counted all the new children, there were ten. Most of them were tasting the food and frowning (no surprise if you think about what there was for breakfast). All the new boys and girls used fingerspelling and signs, but they were different from ours. A few were chatting with some of our students, as if they already knew one another—very peculiar indeed.

Catherine led the new girl to our table and sat her down between us. When the girl saw the lumpy porridge with milk, she held her nose and shook her head no. I hoped that Catherine wouldn't volunteer to eat it for her. We were expected to eat our full portion, and when Mrs. Benham wasn't looking, I often passed food to Catherine and she finished it for me. If she ate the new girl's porridge, would she have room for mine? The new girl must have been hungry because, after a while, she wolfed hers down and had three slices of buttered bread.

After breakfast, we queued up and marched to the assembly room to sing "God Save the King" and to say The Sh'ma. At first, the new children seemed confused, but when we got to The Sh'ma, the older ones seemed to understand and they moved their mouths the right way.

When we marched into our classroom, the girl in the red and white dress was the only new child there. During calendar work, she kept looking down at the floor so Mrs. Benham wouldn't call on her. (We had all done that same thing when we were new.) When we went outside to play, the girl ran over to some of the new children and stayed with them, and I was glad.

That evening when we were back in the dorm, I decided to ask one of the older girls about the strange new family. I just had to know who they were. I rushed over to an older girl, pointed to the new girl, and signed NEW CHILDREN—WHO? I really wanted to ask why they were there, but I didn't know how. At first, the older girl just stood there and stared at me. Then she shrugged her shoulders and fingerspelled a word—the one I had seen before—G-E-R-M-A-N-S. However, before, the girl had said

BAD G-E-R-M-A-N-S, which was confusing now because neither the man with the beard nor any of the children looked bad.

Actually, the newcomers were a group of ten German Jewish children, ranging in age from three to eleven, who had just arrived from the Israelite School for the Deaf in East Berlin. The man with them was Dr. Felix Reich, headmaster of their school. The group had boarded a train from Germany to Holland on July 11 and had taken a boat across the English Channel. They had arrived at Liverpool Station on July 12, where they were met by Mr. Benham, who had been instrumental in getting them out of Germany. He had arranged to have them driven to the school in two cars. When the group arrived at four o'clock in the afternoon, the children were exhausted and went straight to bed. That was why we didn't see them at the garden fete. The pupils from our school with whom they chatted the next day were wealthy children who had been their classmates and had been able to get out of Germany earlier.

Dr. Felix Reich was an odd looking man. He had a long white beard, was skinny and bent over, walked with a cane, and seemed quite frail. At that time, we were not aware that he was willing to risk his life for deaf children! Dr. Reich was in poor health because he had been in prison in Poland, where the Nazis had tortured him. He and his wife and four children had visas to go to Palestine, as Israel was known at that time, but he wanted to stay and bring deaf children to England.

Those refugee children would become permanent members of the school, but Dr. Reich would not be with us for long. Like many people who hated the Nazis but spoke German, he was probably suspected of being a German spy. We think that he was arrested and sent to the internment camp on the Isle of Wight, a place where many suspects were being taken. In fact, a bit later, from May 12 to July 12, 1940, the British government decided that all citizens from countries at war with Britain should be held. Dr. Reich had wanted to return to Germany to rescue more children, but by the time he was known to be innocent, the war had begun and it was too late. After 1939, he lost contact with our school.

As for the pupils left behind at the Israelite School for the Deaf, Nazis would break in, take them away, and end their lives. All that remains of the school is a plaque. Written in German, it says, "From this house 146 deaf Jewish citizens were dragged by Fascist bandits and murdered in 1942. A memorial to the dead. A reminder to the living."

A Different City

It was late August 1939, and after a fortnight at home, I was glad to be back at school. Actually, the two weeks with the family had been a let-down because, for the first time ever, we hadn't gone to Brighton or to Hove. Being at home was nice, but it didn't compare with a fortnight at the seaside. Of course, I didn't realize why my parents wisely avoided the south coast of England. That was the area most likely to be attacked, and it was where the war in the air would begin.

All the girls had brought biscuits or sweets from home, except for the new girl, whose name was Ruth. She and the other new children had stayed at school with the Benhams and that odd looking man with the beard. Catherine felt bad for her and said she must be missing home. She kept smiling at Ruth and even offered her some jellybeans, which I didn't like at all. One good thing did happen, though. Before we had gone on holiday, Ruth had not worn a uniform to class. She had worn a different frock every day, and they had all been beautiful. Now on her bed was a uniform, and she was going to have to wear it. Now at least things were fair. Maybe having her there wouldn't be so bad after all.

The next morning when we filed into the classroom and sat down, we did something we had never done before. We had to march out of the room, down the corridor, and back into the dining room. We had just finished breakfast, so our backtracking was rather odd. Mrs. Benham had a chart with her with WHERE at the top, and she rested it on a table, pointed around the room, and wrote the words *dining room*. We tramped into the kitchen, and she rested the chart on a counter, pointed, and wrote another word—*kitchen*. Then we marched outside, and she held the chart against the climbing bars, pointed around, and wrote another word—*playground*. We tramped into the infirmary, then up to the dorm, and she wrote those words, too. When we were back in the classroom, Mrs. Benham wrote on the blackboard:

Where did we go?
We went to the _____.

That strange looking mark was there, so this must be another kind of question. Mrs. Benham put up her chart with the WHERE words. She took her stick and pointed to the first sentence and then to each word

on the chart and then to the line. WHERE was another kind of question, and it clearly meant a place. Now we were able to answer not only WHO and WHAT but also WHERE questions. This revelation was more and more exciting.

After our midday meal, it was time for our weekly stroll through Wandsworth Common. Now, of course, we each had dangling from our shoulders a box with a mask inside, but otherwise, our stroll was the same as it had always been. Actually, that wasn't quite true. In fact, we were seeing so many changes that London would soon feel like a different city.

When we stepped out onto the cobblestone path and marched down Nightingale Lane, the weather was lovely. The day was one of many beautiful late summer days that year that brought warm sunshine and a light breeze. However, changes were everywhere. Right away, Mrs. Benham stopped the class and pointed at one. Next to a small block of flats, a lorry was parked. Some men were lifting bags off of it, and others were carrying bags over and piling them against the building. From the way they were bending down and picking them up, I could tell that the bags were heavy. We had seen men lifting things off lorries before at construction sites. What was so special about it now? Why was Mrs. Benham pointing and moving her mouth in that silly way? That behaviour always meant that something would be part of a lesson when we returned to school. Why would a pile of bags be part of a lesson? We didn't know that those sandbags being packed snugly against the lower walls of buildings were there to cushion the force of exploding bombs!

We marched along toward the Common, and a bus was waiting on a corner. It was not a school bus, but there were children inside waving and others queuing up to get on. All the children had on winter coats, which was odd on such a warm day when we hadn't even brought our cardigans. Once, our class had been on a bus like that, on an excursion to the London Zoo. Today, all those children had pieces of paper attached to their coats, the way we did when taking a trip, so the papers must have their names on them. However, these children also had those boxes on strings, their coats, cases or backpacks, small blankets, and stuffed animals or dolls. Some were smiling while others (especially the younger ones) were sobbing and clinging to their mums. The scene was all very strange because most of those children should have been in

school. Mrs. Benham pointed at the boxes on their shoulders, then at ours, and moved her mouth in that silly way. Clearly, all of this would be part of a lesson, too.

By that summer of 1939, the masks were carried everywhere because bombing was expected any day. Those children were part of a major evacuation from the cities. They were still on vacation when told to report back to school in late August. In three days, one million children were removed from their homes in British cities and transported by bus, train, car, or other means to people's homes in the countryside. Children were told to wear their winter coats and were allowed one small backpack or case with a toothbrush, a comb, and some soap, along with clothes that could be worn, carried, or jammed into pockets. They were given little bags with sandwiches or tins of corned beef and some juice or condensed milk, so they wouldn't arrive hungry.

Soon, we entered the Common and tramped along a narrow path. The day was especially lovely, with the sun shining and rows of bright yellow and orange chrysanthemums on either side of the path. Then suddenly, when we turned a bend and came to a small field, we saw the most peculiar thing ever. It was an enormous grey balloon that was shaped something like an aeroplane, and some women were pulling on ropes to raise it into the sky. We all pointed at it, and Mrs. Benham pointed and moved her mouth. We tramped along a bit more, and when we reached a larger field, we saw balloons like that in every direction. What could they possibly be? Most days I didn't want to return to school for a lesson, but now I was curious. These, of course, were barrage balloons, whose purpose was to discourage low-flying enemy planes. An umbrella of them protected British cities from dive-bombing attacks by the German Air Force.

When we were back in the classroom, we sat down right away. Mrs. Benham drew some pictures on a chart, and next to each drawing was its name—sandbag, gas mask, barrage balloon. The drawing for the last one—evacuation—was a bus full of children. Those words were longer than most words we could read, even the ones on the WHERE chart. It was easy to match the first three words with their drawings, but that last word, *evacuation,* was hard to understand. Weren't those children just going to the zoo? Mrs. Benham had each of us come up and try to say the words, then showed how they looked on the mouth, so we could

speechread them. We had to read some sentences about what we had seen on our stroll and point to the drawings to show that we understood. It was nice to know the words, but, even now, we didn't know why all these strange things were happening.

About a week later, we did something we had never done before and had wanted to do for a long while. Mrs. Benham brought out a clock from the cupboard, and we had our first lesson on telling time. She moved the little hand around, and we had to tell her the number it was on. The big hand stayed on the twelve, so as the small hand moved, it was one o'clock, two o'clock, and so on. We knew the days of the week and the months of the year from discussing the news, and Mrs. Benham had a chart for each of them. Every day, we put a line through the number on the calendar telling which day of the month it was. Now, Mrs. Benham wrote WHEN on the blackboard and explained that days, months, years, and the time on the clock all came under it. That meant we were learning to use another kind of question. Soon we would be able to use four kinds—WHO, WHAT, WHERE, and WHEN. This lesson was getting better and better.

One thing still bothered me though. We knew all these question words, but we still didn't know why all those changes were taking place! I had to do something about that. I had to try to make sense of it all. It was clear that Mrs. Benham didn't want to tell us why, and if we asked, she wasn't going to like it. I was trembling a bit, but I raised my hand anyway. When Mrs. Benham nodded I stood up, rushed to the blackboard, and wrote something: "What is sandbag, mask, balloon?" I left out the word *evacuation* because it was hard to spell. I really wanted to add What are they for? or Why are they necessary? but I still didn't know how. Mrs. Benham understood, and, actually, she was quite kind. She turned around and wrote something, too: "Because of the Germans." What did she mean by that? We knew about the "bad Germans," but the new children were German, too. Were the new children the "good Germans"?

The door opened, and Mr. Benham was standing there. Mrs. Benham rushed over to him, and they stepped outside. When she stepped back in, she glanced at the clock and told us to queue up because it was time to go outside to play. I would have to wait until some other time to make sense of it all.

That Friday was cloudy and cool, and more changes became evident. After the midday meal when my father arrived, he was frowning again and seemed more uneasy than ever. On the way to the bus, he scurried along so quickly that it was hard to keep up with him. When the bus pulled up, it looked different; the windows were covered with something strange—heavy metal screens! When we climbed up the stairs and sat down, I felt all closed in. I sat down next to my father, then turned around, got up on my knees, and tried to look out. Except for a small hole in the middle of the screen, I couldn't see outside, and it was hard to tell what we were passing. Whenever Daddy had fetched me from school, seeing Wormholt Park, the dairy, the greengrocer, and the kosher butcher meant that we were almost home. Perhaps now we would go past our stop and be lost in some strange neighbourhood. Why were the windows suddenly covered? Was this "because of the Germans," too? Actually, the screens were there to prevent window glass from breaking and injuring passengers or passersby and to protect people on buses from debris flying outside.

We did get off the bus at the bottom of Wormholt Road, and when I skipped up to the house, Mummy was at the door, waving. When Daddy and I stepped inside, I could tell that chicken soup was cooking, and it smelled delicious. When I ran into the parlour, though, I encountered a musty odour, and in the corner next to the radio was something new—a huge table covered with an old white cloth. What was a table like that doing in the parlour? Were we going to stop eating in the dinette? That was odd because we had always eaten there, and it was very cozy. Was that table a playhouse for Leslie and me? Perhaps we could bring our toys down and play with them here. If we played hide-and-seek, it would be a good place to hide. I lifted the cloth, and under the table was another surprise—a mattress—and on it was a pile of blankets. That mattress, which had been stored out in the shed, was what smelled musty. Did that mean we were going to sleep here? Leslie and I had our comfortable beds upstairs, and they had yellow blankets and soft goosefeather pillows and they smelled nice and clean. My parents had a long wide bed that was clean, too, with a lovely pale blue bedspread. Why would anyone want to sleep down here? I didn't realize that the table was a Morrison shelter, which was made of wrought iron and was for hiding under during a bombing attack. Many who did

not want to go to public shelters at night slept under those tables, which is why a mattress was there. The blankets could be used for warmth, but they could also be stuffed under doors to keep out gas.

Mummy pointed upstairs, which meant that Leslie was there. I rushed up, and when I opened the door to our room, I found still another surprise—the room was so dark that I could barely see. On the window, behind our sheer white curtains that usually let the light shine in, were black curtains like the ones in Daddy's shop. Leslie was on his bed, flashing a torch on the wall and making shadow puppets. He clearly thought that having the room dark in the afternoon was fun. I hated being in the dark, so I opened the curtain and shook my finger at him. Didn't he know how important it was for me to see?

Before long, my mother's shadow was under the door, and it was time for some food. We followed her down the stairs, and I ran into the parlour to fetch my father. He was sitting next to the radio frowning, and when I pointed to the dinette, he shook his head no. What was wrong with Daddy? What could be worrying him now? I was hungry, so I left him and ran in and sat down with Leslie. Mummy brought in a large pot of chicken soup and ladled it into our bowls, then carried in some freshly baked challah that was still warm. For dessert, we had custard that was creamy and sweet. Mummy was trying to be cheerful, but now she was frowning, too.

After tea, my mother put an old sheet on the mattress under the new table and Leslie and I decided to play there. He ran upstairs and brought down a torch and some little cars. The cloth reached the floor, so it was like being in a tent, which made it feel like our own secret place.

After a while, we got tired of staying inside and ran out into the garden. It was gloomy out there, and it had become quite cool. Leslie kept pointing toward the rear of the garden, and he grabbed my hand and pulled me back there. When we reached the back part of the picket fence, he showed me a place where you could peak through to our neighbours' garden. There, right next to the fence, was the strangest little house. It had a curved roof, and part of the house seemed to be underground. Our neighbours had two little boys about our ages. Could it be a playhouse for them? When my father stepped out from the kitchen and saw us, he waved and pointed to the side gate. Soon we were marching out of our garden and through a gate that led to our neighbours'

property. There they were, crawling out of that strange little playhouse. When they saw us, they pointed to it and to us, and my father, Leslie, and I crawled inside. The house had only a dirt floor, and it was cold and damp. I had thought it would be fun, but it felt awful in there, and I couldn't wait to get out. I didn't know that this, too, was to protect us from German attacks.

It was an Anderson shelter, named for Home Secretary John Anderson, who promoted their use. The British government supplied the public with more than two million of those portable air-raid shelters. Made of corrugated steel, some were like small sheds whereas others were more like igloos, partly buried in the ground. They provided adequate safety, except from a direct bomb hit, and would save thousands of lives. However, though they offered protection from bombs, Anderson shelters were extremely damp and cold in winter, and they were a perfect place for insects and rats. This strange little house was one of so many peculiar transformations that were happening in London. Why were all these changes showing up everywhere?

Later, when we were supposed to be asleep, I wasn't tired, so I tiptoed out of our room to the landing. My parents were looking at the newspaper, and now they were both sobbing. I couldn't read most of the words in the *Daily Express*, but I could read some of them. In enormous capital letters across the page was a word that I didn't know yet, but I can still remember exactly how it looked. It is something I shall never forget. That word was *WAR*.

That day was Friday, September 1, 1939. At dawn, German troops had stormed into Poland. Then German planes began to bomb the capital city, Warsaw. According to my mother, all that weekend, everyone in Britain stayed near the radio, terrified, but eager to hear what would happen next. At eleven o'clock in the morning on Sunday, September 3, the prime minister announced that Britain was at war with Germany. At six o'clock in the evening, King George VI was on the radio. He warned that war would not be limited to the battlefields and that British cities were likely to be bombed.

Meanwhile, wherever the Nazis were in power, attacks on Jews and other "undesirables" continued. For people with disabilities, things had taken a new turn for the worse. Those who were in institutions and considered "incurable"—both children and adults—were to be killed in gas

chambers. The program practiced everything that would be used later for the mass murder of European Jews and other groups: a stated intention to kill, people who were specially trained to carry it out, gas chambers, and the use of language that hid the fact that these killings were really crimes. For so many people in Europe, it was a terrible time, and it was going to get worse.

Eyes on the Sky

The autumn of 1939 brought many lovely warm sunny days, so it was odd that people kept looking up as if it were going to rain. Whenever an aeroplane passed over, they followed it and frowned, the way Daddy had done in the garden. They acted as though something terrible were going to fall from the sky. Now I was realizing that their behaviour clearly had something to do with that word *WAR*.

Winter arrived quite cold and bringing a lot of snow and ice. Some days were gloomy, with snow falling from morning to night. Sometimes none fell at all, but it stayed cloudy anyway. Other days were crisp and bright outside, and the snow on the ground, like the sky, was a beautiful bright blue. Snow made everything look softer, and it always felt like magic. It was lovely to wake up and find a fresh, white blanket on the ground and small clusters on the branches of the trees near the window.

In the classroom, Mrs. Benham kept us busy, and we worked a lot on our speech. Thinking about how the sounds looked and felt and having to control my lips, tongue, and throat were so hard to do. I still hated it when Mrs. Benham put her hands on my face and I had to put mine on hers, and it was even worse when she made me say a sound again and again. Mrs. Benham taught us the names of various foods and expected us to ask for them at the table. If we didn't try, we didn't eat, so we learned those words right away! We added more people under WHO—like mother, father, sister, brother, aunt, uncle, grandpa, and grandma. We added more under WHAT—like soap, towel, toothbrush, toothpaste, and cup. For WHERE, we added more places around the school—like larder, garden, and swimming pool. Mrs. Benham drew a map of the building and the grounds, and we began to understand that a map is a drawing of a place, looking down. She put a book in different places around a table to show us on, under, and next to. She wrote

sentences that were missing these words, and we had to find the right word and put it in the sentence. For WHEN, we worked on telling time and learned *now, soon, later, before,* and *after.* We did a lot of arithmetic, counting up to fifty and starting to add and subtract small numbers. In class, we used speech, speechreading, reading, and writing all together to help us learn new words. In the dorm, we asked the older girls to fingerspell and sign the words, which helped us understand and remember them better.

One cold, snowy evening when we filed into class, it was clear that we were going to do something different. Mrs. Benham had a new chart, and at the top of it was the word WHY. I had a feeling this lesson was what I had been waiting for. Perhaps, finally, we were going to work on the most important question of all.

On one part of the blackboard were two sentences:

Why is the boy wearing boots?
The boy is wearing boots because there is snow.

Mrs. Benham showed us two pictures. One was a picture of a street, and snow was coming down. In the other, a boy was looking out a window at the snow and holding a pair of boots. Mrs. Benham pointed to the sentence with the question mark. She pointed at the pictures and asked us which came first. Harry raised his hand and pointed at the one of the street and Mrs. Benham smiled.

On another part of the blackboard were two other sentences:

Why is the girl crying?
The girl is crying because the boy took her doll.

Mrs. Benham showed us two pictures. In one of them, a girl was crying. In the other, a boy was pulling away her doll. Mrs. Benham pointed to the sentence with the question mark. Then she pointed to the pictures and asked which one came first. When Sam pointed to the one with the boy pulling away the doll, Mrs. Benham smiled again.

Mrs. Benham showed us some other pictures, and each time we had to tell her which came first. WHY was clearly about something making something else happen. It could tell us the reason things were happening. It was truly the most exciting question of all. Also, that word *because* was in "because of the Germans"—which meant it was the Germans

who were making all these strange things happen. They were why these things were happening. Now we knew about WHO, WHAT, WHERE, WHEN, and WHY. We still didn't know exactly who the Germans were, but WHY could help us answer some important questions.

In December, we spent the usual fortnight at home for the holidays. The house felt cozy and warm, and we had a lovely Chanukah and even celebrated Christmas.

On the first night of Chanukah, our non-Jewish neighbours—Auntie Hewitt and our tenants, the tall blonde family who lived in the flat on the second storey—joined us for a little party. Leslie and I helped Mummy bake a sponge cake, which made the whole house smell wonderful, and we also had matzoh ball soup and potato latkes. Leslie and I showed the tenants' little boy, who was two, how to spin a dreidel, and each of us got five pennies for Chanukah *gelt*. For the first time, I lit the menorah, though Mummy carried it to the sink because she was afraid it would tip over and burn down the house. For the rest of Chanukah, we lit one more candle each day, and every evening, Daddy gave Leslie and me five pennies each.

On Christmas, the tenants invited us up to their flat. They had a small tree decorated with candy canes, Christmas balls, and chains made of paper, and an angel on the top. There were presents under the tree, wrapped in red or green paper. Soon, we were opening them and the boy got a funny book about Father Christmas, some alphabet blocks, some wooden trains, and a yellow lorry. Leslie and I would get to play with them, so they made us as happy as they made him. There was a present for Leslie, a set of small racing cars, and for me there was a lovely flowered tea set. I wanted to stay for the midday meal because for dessert there was going to be plum pudding with hard sauce and biscuits shaped like Christmas trees, bells, or stars. We couldn't stay though because the food wasn't kosher, but it still felt good to be there.

A few days after Christmas, my mother took Leslie and me on the bus to an enormous store with lifts to buy us some new shoes. After shopping, we had fun walking about and seeing the Christmas trees and the bright lights. By midafternoon, it was quite chilly and was starting to get dark, and we were eager to get home. My mother decided to go by Tube because it was the fastest way home. We trudged over to the station and when we reached the entrance, we saw something that was terribly

peculiar. People were queuing up and they were carrying blankets, pillows, small cases, and even mattresses! Why would they be doing something strange like that? Was the train taking them somewhere where they were all going to sleep? My mother didn't even try to explain. She just frowned, held her nose, and shook her head no.

When we arrived home, Mummy rushed into the kitchen, then into the larder, and soon she had carrots and potatoes and green beans on the table. She was going to make her tasty vegetable soup. These days, Mummy kept a pad of paper and a pencil in the kitchen, and when I wanted to know a word, I drew a picture and she wrote the word. If I wanted to ask a question, I wrote it and she provided the answer. It was important to know about those people in the Tube station, so I grabbed a pencil and scribbled, "Why train?" I ran over to Mummy and gave her the paper, but she shook her head NO. She was too busy cutting up vegetables to answer. Once again, I would have to wait.

I didn't know that those people were actually planning to sleep in the Tube (also called the Underground, part of our subway system) station! It was one of many public air-raid shelters all over the city, some in basements of churches or other buildings. Brick structures had also been built to hold up to fifty people, but they could collapse if a bomb hit nearby. Although some of the Tube stations were not safe either, they were the most popular shelters. The government tried to discourage people from sleeping there; troops needed to be able to move through, but many largely ignored the government's advice. Later, during the Blitz, many Londoners would sleep there because their homes had been destroyed and they had no other place to go; eventually, more than 177,000 of them would sleep in the Tube stations every night. People queued up early, then camped out on the concrete platforms or on one of the three-tiered bunks provided by the government. After midnight, when the trains stopped running, others spread out on the tracks. It was musty and cold and there was no privacy, but Londoners made the best of it. They played cards and joked and managed to enjoy themselves.

Most of the bombing was expected to be in London, but people were turning to blackouts and shelters in cities all over Britain. Outside the cities, large numbers of people actually moved into caves. After a while, commuter trains would be making special stops at two huge caves southeast of London, in Kent.

Back at school, because of the short days and the cold weather, we spent most of the time inside, working hard in the classroom and having fun in the dorm. Once in a while, Sylvia and Shirley kept secrets from Catherine, Ruth, and me, but most of the time, we all got on. Every night we parked ourselves and our stuffed animals in one another's beds and shared our treats from home, although lately, we were bringing back less. Now, when the lights went out, it was very dark because all the windows were covered with black curtains. Every night, Miss Stern stormed in and closed them with great care, and as soon as she left, we climbed out of bed and drew them back. It was a good thing she caught us, because what we were doing was against the law and the school could have been fined. Even when the curtains were open, we didn't get any light from outside. It was totally dark out there because the light that had always burned brightly on the street was off.

Poor Ruth sometimes stared sadly at the photograph of her mum and dad in the silver frame. The odd looking man with the white beard was no longer around. How curious that he had left all those children at our school and disappeared! Catherine helped Ruth, combing her hair, inviting her into bed, sharing goodies from home, and teaching her signs. I still wasn't sure I liked Ruth, but having her around wasn't as bad as before.

Cold weather and snow kept us from the world outside the stone wall. Now that we weren't taking walks and seeing all those changes out there, Mrs. Benham didn't talk about them. During the week, except for the black curtains and the darkness outside, it was almost as if those changes had gone away.

Unfortunately, those changes hadn't gone away at all. In fact, London was changing more than ever. That became clear during my trips to and from home with my father. As usual, he showed up every Friday after the midday meal. By now, he looked not only nervous and sad but also quite tired. The bus still had those metal screens on the windows, and I was still afraid we would miss our stop. By now, street signs had been torn down—to confuse the Germans. But it confused us, too! More sandbags were piled against buildings, and the windows of stores, offices, and homes were crisscrossed with tape. Now everyone carried a box with a mask inside. More women seemed to be on the streets than men because men were at military posts around Britain or over in France. Many

women who had previously stayed at home were now farm hands, bus conductors, railway porters, machinists, or crane operators, and in some aircraft factories, most of the workers were female. The clothes were different, too. Dresses were shorter and shoulders looked wider. Those shorter skirts were in style because they were easier to move about in and they used less fabric, which was needed for clothing the troops. Lots of people, both men and women, were wearing uniforms. Both sexes were in the armed forces, many women serving as nurses or in other roles that did not require fighting. Huge guns aimed at the sky were sprouting up everywhere—on rooftops, in parks, and even on lorries. They were ready to shoot down enemy planes, and the ones on lorries could race to wherever they were needed. People's eyes were on the sky, even though nothing was falling from there.

On weekends when it wasn't too frosty outside, Leslie and I were allowed to go out and play in the garden. My mother always wrapped us in layers of warm clothing, making sure that every button was fastened and that our wool scarves were carefully tied. When she stepped back inside, we took the scarves off and waved them around. Sometimes, we stayed out there while the snow was falling and opened our mouths wide and caught the snow with our tongues. It was fun to make snowballs and aim them at the empty ceramic stand in the middle of the grass. After lots of practice, Leslie was able to hit it from far away. One day, Daddy helped us make a snowman, with a carrot for a nose, black jellydrops for eyes, and red ones for the mouth. He even brought out an old, grey, pinstriped jacket, a black bowler hat, and a striped tie so our snowman would be smartly dressed. Whenever the neighbours peered into the garden, they laughed.

That winter, Leslie and I seldom went to the park or the shops because it was icy and Mummy was afraid we would fall. When she went out for groceries, Daddy or Auntie Hewitt stayed with us. Leslie and I pretended that the table in the parlour was a tent, and sometimes the tenants' little boy brought down his toys and we played there. Some nights, Leslie and I were allowed to sleep in the tent, and we brought a torch and made shadow puppets. The mattress still smelled musty, but we were used to it.

So far, except for the table in the parlour and the black curtains that were on all the windows, the changes that had been taking place were

outside. However, later during that winter of 1939–1940, a big change occurred inside our house, and it was the worst change of all. Suddenly, Mummy stopped baking, so those wonderful smells from making challah or scones or sponge cake or macaroons no longer filled the house. When we sat down at the table in the dinette, we missed the warm slices of challah with melted butter, the soft scones with gooseberry jam, the buttery sponge cake, and the sweet macaroons. Actually, now we had less food of any kind, and we were mostly eating tinned food that had been in the larder for a while. One day, I went in to fetch some milk for Mummy. The larder had always held butter, meat, and fish, but none was there now. On the shelves were only a few tins of vegetables, and in the enamel bowls on the floor were an uncooked chicken and one bottle of milk. We also were no longer visiting the sweets shop, which meant I had no sweets to take back to school.

The food shortage occurred because German submarine attacks had made it difficult to move goods in and out of Britain. January 1940 was when food rationing began, and soon, every family had a booklet with coupons that were used in the shops. Up to that time, food had been plentiful, but now, everything was becoming scarce. Butter, bacon, ham, sugar, and meat were rationed. Poultry and rabbit weren't rationed, but they were not available in butcher shops and were expensive if they could be found at all. Sometimes, a group of people brought a pig and slaughtered it secretly because it was against the law to kill animals without a permit. Milk, tea, cheese, fruit, fresh and tinned vegetables, and tinned fish would be in short supply or impossible to get during most of the war. Fresh fish was scarce because most of Britain's fishing fleet was busy helping the Royal Navy.

Later, in the spring of 1942, Britain would receive shiploads of American food such as dried eggs and milk, vegetables, cheese, and tinned meats. However, from the start of rationing in January 1940 until then, British people had a diet that was close to starvation. My family was fortunate to know the man in the sweets shop, who sometimes sneaked us some goodies. It wasn't very much though, and of course, it wasn't the food we really needed. Even though few people had been injured or killed yet, the war was beginning to take its toll.

What we experienced from the autumn of 1939 through the winter and into the spring of 1940 came to be known as the Phony War, or

Sitzkrieg. Everyone was expecting a full-scale war to begin, but it didn't. On October 9, Hitler issued orders to his generals to carry out an attack on the West as soon as possible, but they wanted to think about what they had learned in Poland and reorganize. The British and French planned to move into Belgium to hold back the Germans before they entered France, but because Belgium was neutral, it would not allow Allied troops into the country. Bad weather made it hard to carry on bombing, and British daytime bomber attacks on German naval bases met with heavy losses. All of these developments delayed the full-scale war that Britain was expecting, but it would not be long before that war would begin.

An Unfriendly Place

One cool, sunny morning in February 1940, I was awakened by a jab instead of the usual tap. Miss Stern was dashing about, and she seemed to be in a big hurry. She ran over to each bed, bent down, and pulled out the case that was under it. In a flash, mine was there on the floor wide open. Catherine and I glanced at each other, shrugged our shoulders, and frowned. Soon, everyone else was doing that, too. Miss Stern rushed from box to box, pulling out our clothing and throwing it into our cases. If she found biscuits or sweets, she didn't seem to notice and threw them in, too. When all the cases were packed, she flicked the lights and pointed to the wall, and we queued up and marched into the bathroom. We quickly gathered our washcloths, soap, toothbrushes, and toothpaste, wrapped them in our towels, and carried them back to our beds. When Miss Stern pointed to our cases, we threw the wrapped up towels in and then put on our winter uniforms. We trudged down to the dining room to a hasty breakfast, then quickly had our service in the assembly room. It felt like that morning so long ago when we had gone to stay in that little village. Could we be going there again?

We hurried back upstairs, where snowsuits, mittens, scarves, and hats were waiting on our beds. The older girls helped us into them, and we hurried down to the front door where Mrs. Benham was standing with the boys. The day was clear and, although some patches of snow remained, it was milder than it had been for some time. It felt as if spring would be here soon. We tramped out through the huge wooden

doors and down the path to the front gates, where lots of cars were lined up. Like before, the first one was Mr. Benham's, and he opened the rear door and lifted all nine of us into the back seat. He checked that our hands were safe, carefully closed the door, then climbed in and sat behind the wheel, with Mrs. Benham next to him. She turned around and shook her finger at the boys, who were fighting over who would sit next to the window behind her. This time, with Ruth in the car, it was even more crowded than before. I was next to the window behind Mr. Benham, with Ruth, Catherine, Shirley, and Sylvia between me and the boys, so at least I didn't get kicked. For most of us, this was an adventure, but poor Ruth looked ready to cry. As soon as we were moving, she rested her head on Catherine's shoulder and fell asleep. I wasn't tired at all, so I stayed awake and looked out the window. We didn't seem to be going to that village again, but where were we going?

The winter landscape was barren—no flowers in the gardens or leaves on the trees—so it looked different, but the houses were familiar. As we drove, the houses became more and more spread out, and because the window was open a bit, I could smell the air. It smelled like that wonderful fresh air at the seaside. Could we be going to Brighton or to Hove? I hadn't seen Grandpa Sam and Auntie Julie for a long time. Perhaps I would be seeing them soon.

The car slowed down in front of a long, three-storey red brick building, sitting high on a hill back from the road. It was surrounded by a gently rolling grassy area that was a lovely bright green, and it didn't have a wall. Behind the building was a wonderful surprise. Calm and blue and stretching on forever was something I had missed so much— the sea! Visiting a seaside boarding house in winter was an odd thing to do, but it was jolly good to be on holiday again. We turned onto a curved driveway, which led up to some stairs and two wooden doors, and Mr. Benham stopped the car. He stepped out, then opened the door and helped us all out, and we marched over and tramped up the stairs.

We stepped inside to a wide corridor with a room on one side and a table with a vase of flowers on the other. Shortly, we began marching along a narrow corridor where we found another surprise—lots of rooms on both sides and children queued up outside of them. This wasn't a boarding house; it was a school. All the children were dressed in uniforms, the girls in dark green jumpers with white blouses and the boys

in dark green trousers with matching neckties and white shirts. Some of the children stared at us as if we were odd, and a few older girls pointed and turned to each other, laughing.

We climbed some stairs to the second storey and shuffled into a medium-sized room with lots of grownup-size beds. They were close together, with no boxes in between, and it was crowded in there. Mrs. Benham led our group to a corner away from the door and pointed to each of us and then to a bed. The order was the same as in London, which meant that Catherine was on one side of me and Ruth was on the other. All the windows had black curtains, which were open, and I rushed over to look outside. There, with the sun making it sparkle, was the sea, which was lovely indeed. I was quite happy sitting there and staring out the window, but then the smell of breaded fried fish drifted up to our room, and we were ushered downstairs for lunch.

We tramped downstairs and into a large, square dining room that had rows of long tables with benches. Lots of children were seated near the door, all dressed in dark green and white, so we knew they were all from this seaside school. At each table, boys sat at one end and girls sat at the other. Our school was seated at the back of the room, but to get back there, we had to pass children who pointed to us, laughing, and covering their mouths as if they were telling secrets. When we finally sat down, Mrs. Benham brought over a tray of food. We had the breaded fried fish, which was dreadful, while the children from the other school had roast beef with Yorkshire pudding, which wasn't at all fair. What made it worse was that some of them pointed at our food and sneered.

When we had finished eating, we queued up and marched outside to a playground behind the school. The students from this school were playing together, rather than in separate groups of boys or girls, but they stayed away from us. Some children on the climbing bars were glowering, so we stayed away and played a game of tag. It was a beautiful day, and it would be lovely to take a walk on the pebbly beach. Catherine and I pointed toward the water and winked at each other. We knew exactly what we wanted to do. The problem was that the yard had no hedges to hide behind, so slipping away would be difficult. Then we spotted something on the grass that could be useful to our goal—a small ball. We would play catch, away from the playground, throwing the ball back and forth a few times so no one would think we

were doing anything odd. Catherine would throw it too far and I would chase it, and she would run after me. Then we would disappear and walk along the beach for a while. Of course, as soon as I missed the ball and Catherine started chasing me, Mrs. Benham came running after us. How did she always know what we were up to? Oh well. We would take that walk on the beach some other time.

Mrs. Benham had the class queue up and march inside, down a corridor, and into a classroom. It looked like our classroom in London, but we had to share it with the nine-year-olds from our school. The room had a long bookcase with three shelves that separated their class from ours. We didn't do any serious work. We just sat at tables or on the floor and played with toy cars and blocks or looked at picture books. It made us all very happy.

After tea, we marched to that room upstairs. Our cases were piled against a wall, and each girl grabbed her own case and dragged it over to her bed. When Ruth opened hers, she urgently began turning over the clothing and looked ready to cry. She was clearly searching for that photograph of her mum and dad. Catherine reached under a frock and found it, which made Ruth smile. I was feeling sad for her, so I invited her over to sit on my bed and look at some picture books. After a while it grew dark outside and became quite cold. We didn't know the time, but before long, the older girls were there helping us get ready to retire. I asked one of them if we were in Brighton and she said yes. Mrs. Benham popped in to close the black curtains, then left us alone.

So far, I had mixed feelings about this new boarding school The children were mean, the food was horrid, and it was cold in the dorm, but being here might not be all bad. We would not have to work so hard, and even though it was winter, it was terribly nice to be at the seaside. Best of all, Miss Stern wasn't here, so we wouldn't have to be on watch all the time for that shadow under the door. The large beds were roomy, so all five of us could sit on one bed without being cramped. That night when we brought out the goodies, five girls and five stuffed animals were on my bed. We didn't have many biscuits or sweets left and whatever we had was stale, but we gobbled down some shortcake biscuits that weren't too bad. We were cold and tired and wanted to go to sleep. Catherine, Ruth, and I slept in my bed, and when we pulled the covers over us, we were a bit cramped, but warm.

Suddenly, I felt a heavy tap on my shoulder. Was it morning so soon? The black curtains were closed, so perhaps they were blocking the bright sunshine and we just couldn't see it. Mrs. Benham was there, doing something that was peculiar and puzzling. She was flashing her torch around the dark room and pulling us all out of bed, urging us to slip into our snowsuits, hats, socks, and boots. Within minutes, we were carrying our blankets and pillows and following the light from Mrs. Benham's torch out into the dark corridor where Mr. Benham had the boys in a queue. We all quickly followed the light down a dark staircase. Then it got even worse, because Mrs. Benham turned off the light and led us outside. It wasn't morning at all. In fact, it was pitch black out there, and it was freezing cold. We trekked across the grassy area, trying to avoid patches of snow, but in all that darkness, it was difficult to see.

When we reached the playground, Mr. Benham was waiting for us. He flashed his torch down on the grass, and there we saw something odd—a green door that was flat on the ground. I had never seen anything like it before. Why would a door be on the ground? Where could it possibly lead? Were we going to hide from someone? Mr. Benham grabbed hold of a handle and pulled the door open, directing us to climb down a ladder into an enormous underground room. It was absolutely dreadful down there—dark, cold, damp, and musty. The floor was made of dirt, like in that playhouse behind our garden at home. The room had only one lantern, hanging from the ceiling, so it was quite dark, which made it hard to see what was going on. More and more children, both boys and girls, were climbing down that ladder, and the large space was now getting crowded.

Mrs. Benham led our class over to a corner where there were some quilts on the ground. She told us to put our pillows there and to lie down, and when we did, she placed our blankets over us. We lay there with our snowsuits, hats, socks, and boots on, which made it hard to turn over, and we were shivering. I had left my mittens behind, so my hands were especially cold, and tucking them into my sleeves didn't help much. Catherine was lying next to the boys, and they kept rolling over and kicking her and she kept kicking them back. Did Mrs. Benham really expect us to be able to sleep here? Suddenly the lantern began to flicker, and it was harder than ever to see. The teachers and some of the children were looking up and holding their ears. Did that mean that aeroplanes

were passing overhead? Perhaps they were going to drop something. That must be why Mrs. Benham had dragged us out of that warm comfortable bed and down to this horrid place. We were all terrified, and it took a long, long time to fall asleep again.

I felt a tap on my shoulder, and it was light inside the underground room. That door in the ground was open, and children were climbing up the ladder. Mrs. Benham helped us fold our blankets. She took them and our pillows and handed them up to Mr. Benham, who was kneeling outside, and he gave them to some older girls. We climbed up the ladder, and he grabbed our hands and pulled us out onto the grass. It was sunny and I welcomed that wonderful smell of fresh seaside air after being in that musty hole, but the air was still frosty.

After that, some nights we fell asleep in our warm, cozy bed upstairs and woke up there in the morning feeling happy. Other times, we settled down in our beds but were awakened in the darkness with a jab. Then we had to follow Mrs. Benham down the stairs and across the grass to spend the rest of the night in that dark, cold, damp, musty room. The worst nights were the ones when, as soon as the sun went down, we tramped across the grass, climbed down the ladder, and stayed in that horrid room all night.

In the classroom, Mrs. Benham tried to do some teaching, and we went over the questions every day, but sharing the room made work difficult. Both classes tended to peer over the bookcase and not pay attention to the lesson. Sometimes when the other class was out and Mrs. Benham was writing on the blackboard, the boys sneaked over and snatched the other children's pencils. When those children came back, they made a big fuss, which got us all out of doing our work. It was nice to be having so much fun, but I did want to get more practice asking and answering questions.

During the time at that seaside boarding school, we had little to do with the children from there, and nobody tried to bring us together. We had classes in different parts of the building, stayed in separate dorms, played on opposite sides of the playground, and most of the time, had different food. That school even had a separate room to sleep in under the ground. Once in a while, some of the children in green and white smiled, but others frowned, and most of them ignored us. We did not feel particularly welcome.

That evacuation in February 1940 was to the School for the Deaf, Eastern Road, in Brighton. It was a Christian school with seventy-five pupils (our school had thirty-five). They did not welcome us there for many reasons. For one, in those days, people did not easily accept anyone who was of a different faith. Also, having us there was extra work because we followed kosher laws, which made it necessary to prepare special food. With our school there, the classrooms and the dorms were crowded, and the school had had to build a separate air-raid shelter for us. Because our stay was temporary, no one had felt it was worth the trouble to forge a relationship between the two schools.

We seemed to be staying at this new school forever. It wasn't like our visit to that little village, when we had gone back to London right away. We weren't going home on weekends either, the way we usually did, and nobody was receiving parcels from home. Now, we had only a few biscuits and sweets left, and soon, we would have nothing to share.

However, on one warm, sunny afternoon, a few children did go home. It was in April, when the crocuses and daffodils had come and gone. We were too young for religious training, so I didn't know the name for Passover yet, but I knew it was that time of year. That morning, we had been playing tag near the rear door, and the kitchen help had carried in some boxes of matzoh. We didn't have a seder at school, but we did eat matzoh instead of bread. Parents could have their children at home if they were willing to fetch them, and that afternoon, some boys and girls were waiting in the driveway with bags or small cases. It made me feel hopeful. Perhaps a bus would pull up and Daddy would jump off, and he would run over and hug me. Then we would climb onto the bus and wave good-bye to everyone and be on our way home. It didn't happen, because my father was busy making blackout curtains. That was a pity because I had always loved Passover. My Auntie Hewitt and our tenants from upstairs usually joined us for our seder, even though they weren't Jewish. It was boring when everyone was supposed to pray, but it was great fun when we had to find the missing matzoh. If only I could be at home with the family. I was beginning to worry about them. With all those changes taking place in London, was everyone all right? Were those guns still sprouting up everywhere? Were people's eyes still on the sky? Maybe by now something had actually fallen.

By then, unknown to us, the Phony War was over and the war everyone was expecting had begun. On April 9, 1940, Hitler's troops invaded Denmark and Norway. Then, on May 10, they began their invasion of France, the Netherlands, and Luxembourg.

The German troops roared across France, and within two weeks, British and French troops were trapped with their backs to the sea near the French town of Dunkirk. The British government put out an emergency call, and volunteers appeared in fishing boats, steamers, firefighting boats, ferries, yachts, and other small vessels. More than 200,000 British and almost 140,000 French troops were transported across the Channel to safety in England. Our Prime Minister, Winston Churchill, called it a miracle.

Still, it was a very dangerous time for Britain. The French did not want to fight another costly war like World War I, so on June 17, 1940, they asked for an armistice, and one was signed on June 22. The armistice meant that Germany would not attack France, but that Nazi rulers would be in power there and that the southern half of France would be allowed a very limited form of self-government. Some French citizens joined the Free French banner of Charles de Gaulle in London while others set up resistance movements inside France. By then, the Nazis controlled all of northern Europe. Wherever they ruled, most people struggled to live as best they could. Jews, however, were becoming more and more afraid, and there was good reason to be worried about Uncle Jacob and his family, who lived in Paris. At this point, the British stood alone against Nazi-occupied Europe, and the future looked grim.

One thing that helped to keep us happy in Brighton was walking along the pebbly beach. Catherine and I didn't get to go there by ourselves, but when it was warm enough, the class took walks there, and Mrs. Benham allowed us to take off our socks and shoes and run into the water. During the spring, however, changes occurred along that beach. Suddenly, an ugly fence made of heavy wire appeared, with sharp pieces of wire sticking out, and it stretched along as far as you could see. Harry ran over and touched it, and his finger began to bleed. Because of that fence, we could no longer go near the water. Then one day, there was a long, deep, muddy hole that ran through the grassy area in front of the school. We had to walk along a wooden plank to get

across, like at the bottom of Wormholt Road. Soon, huge ugly metal towers that looked like giant fans began sprouting up along the beach. Aeroplanes were flying over more than they ever had before. At night when we peaked through the curtains, we saw rays of light moving about in the sky. They were pretty, but what were they for? Why were all these changes taking place?

One morning in class, Mrs. Benham drew pictures on the blackboard and told us what these new things were: barbed wire fence, trench, and radar station. Still, she didn't tell us why they were there. When I raised my hand to ask, she said, "later," and moved on to arithmetic. The beach had been so beautiful and it had always felt so good to run into the cool water. Why would anyone put up a fence there? The grassy area in front of the school was so green and pretty. Why would anyone dig a long hole across? And those tall towers were so ugly. What could they be for? Well, if Mrs. Benham wouldn't tell us, perhaps the older girls would.

Later, I ran up to one of the girls and asked about the strange things that were showing up around the school. Now I was able to use the WHY question. Now, finally, I was going to make sense of it all. Getting some answers was going to make me feel a lot better. I thought for a moment, then signed, "WHY FENCE, TRENCH, TOWERS HERE?" When the girl answered "BECAUSE GERMANS," I signed back, "PLEASE TELL MORE." Her answer did not make me feel better. It was "GERMANS HERE SOON. NEED PROTECTION." We still didn't know who the Germans were, but we knew that they were bad. And because they were bad, we surely didn't want them here!

That word *protection* aptly described the changes that were taking place. Barbed wire and trenches had been set up to hold back the Germans if they landed there. The towers that resembled giant fans were radar stations. Radar was a recent invention, an electronic device that could "see" across vast distances. Radar equipment would detect objects like aeroplanes while they were quite far away, and it could measure how far away they were. Thus, before the German planes reached their targets, British aeroplanes could be sent into the air to intercept them, and ground troops could use their antiaircraft guns. Radar would play a huge part in helping us to defend ourselves against the Nazis. Those searchlights at night also would help to locate enemy planes.

One morning in the classroom, I tried to ask Mrs. Benham if the Germans actually were due to arrive, but all she did was frown. A cloth bag was next to her desk, and we could see a newspaper inside. We weren't supposed to read it, but sometimes when Mrs. Benham stepped out, we would run over, pull it out, sneak a glance, and put it back right away. Now I hoped she would leave the room so we could get to see it. Of course, that morning, Mrs. Benham didn't leave, not even for a minute!

On other days, Mrs. Benham did step out, and we actually were able to see the newspaper. Everything in it was frightening. That word *WAR* was always there. Sometimes, there were photographs of that man with the dark moustache and those wild eyes and, sometimes, images showing lines of soldiers marching, or mothers and children looking sad and confused, or buildings that were on fire. The paper never seemed to contain anything nice. However, one day when spring had turned to summer, there was a photograph on the front page that was different. It was just a group of men with soldiers' hats, looking out on some water. Maybe they loved the seaside, like me. How nice to see something happy for a change.

Actually, that photograph was not as innocent as it seemed. In fact, one of those men was Hermann Göring, head of the German Air Force, standing with some of his staff. They were on the French coast, looking across the English Channel. They were only about twenty-one miles away from Britain, and they intended to invade soon.

Hitler issued his orders for that invasion of Britain, Operation Sea Lion, on July 16, 1940. The Germans were going to cross the English Channel at the narrowest point some time in September, when the tides would help them the most. Troops would sail across a corridor between two thick fields of mines patrolled by submarines on either side. By August, German soldiers would be practicing how to land in barges launched from France, and the bodies of about forty of them would wash up on English shores. The British expected the Germans to land at any moment, and when someone thought they were near, church bells were rung as warnings.

For Hitler's troops to be able to get across the English Channel and make a landing, it was essential that the Germans have command of the air. To get this control, the German Air Force had to destroy the Royal

Air Force (RAF). Thus, the Battle of Britain, the first major air war in history, began. It lasted from July 10, 1940, to May 10, 1941.

Phase I of the Battle of Britain was from July 10 to mid-September, 1940. At first, the German pilots attacked Channel shipping and ports to draw the RAF pilots into battle. Then, on August 13, the Germans launched a huge attack on England's south coast, with daylight bombing raids on areas where lots of factories were housed. Fierce battles took place in the sky as the RAF fighters tried to turn back the waves of German bombers and fighters, and many were fought by pilots in small planes called Hurricanes and Spitfires. To the surprise of the Germans, the British were brave and fought well and Hitler's forces lost many men. Because Hitler did not want to try to land with the Royal Air Force intact, he admitted defeat on September 17, but maintained a plan to invade later.

In early August, something happened that made it clear how dangerous conditions were in Brighton. One warm sunny afternoon, we marched out to the playground. The older children were already there and they were upset. They kept pointing out over the water and signing "AEROPLANE FIGHT." I glanced over in that direction, but saw nothing. I ran over to one of the older girls and asked if she had seen anything. She said that she had seen two aeroplanes out over the water and that they had been fighting. They were making a loud booming sound that she had been able to hear. One of the planes had left a trail of smoke, then had burst into flames, and soon, it had fallen from the sky. It had hit the water and disappeared, and a huge fountain gushed up. Her account frightened me. One had fallen out of the sky over the water, but what if the next one fell on us?

We would not actually leave Brighton until August 21. Considering the conditions, I'm surprised that we stayed so long, but it was not the fault of the staff. They had been looking for a house all over the country, and it was not easy to find one to meet our needs.

It still terrifies me to realize how close Britain came to being invaded by the Nazis. And I still have a hard time believing that my friends and I were only about seventy miles west of where they intended to land. I cringe when I picture German soldiers marching up to that school in Brighton. Surely they would have been brutal to all the children there; to them, we were "inferior" because we were deaf. Perhaps they would

have been even more cruel to those of us who were not only deaf but also Jewish. What a blessing that the invasion planned for September 1940 was called off.

The Most Beautiful House

When a poke on the shoulder woke me up to bright sunshine, and when I saw Mrs. Benham dashing from bed to bed, it was clear that it was time for another move. I knew from our calendar work that it was August 21, 1940. Mrs. Benham proceeded to pull our cases out from under the beds, as if she were in a big hurry. This time, however, we didn't have to grab our belongings and throw them in because they had been kept in the cases the whole time in Brighton. Catherine and I glanced at each other, shrugged our shoulders, and winked because we were both happy to be leaving. It had been lovely to be at the seaside and not to have to do much work, but the food was horrid, the children were mean, and sleeping in that underground room was awful. Also, because of the ugly fence, the big long hole, those giant towers, the searchlights, the aeroplanes flying over, and that fight in the sky over the water, the place felt dangerous. Anyway, by now, we were used to moving to new places.

After a hasty breakfast of porridge with milk and plain bread, we had a short morning service in the usual place, the front corridor. Then we rushed back up to the dorm with Mrs. Benham, grabbed our cases, and dragged them down the stairs. When we stepped outside, the air was sunny and warm, the dew sparkled on the grass, and that fresh smell of the seaside air was all around. The cars were lined up on the curved driveway and, as always, Mr. Benham's was first. He picked up our cases and placed them in the boot, then helped us into the back seat, and he and Mrs. Benham climbed into the front. We fought over where everyone would sit because we all wanted to be near the windows. I ended up in the middle with the boys kicking me, but after a stern look from Mrs. Benham, they stopped. Soon, we were on our way, and this time, Ruth rested her head on my shoulder.

At first, we followed the road we had arrived on back in February. This time of year, the landscape looked the way it had when the family was on summer holiday, with leaves on the trees and colourful flowers

everywhere. One thing was strange, though. Some of the road signs were missing. Any signs that remained had been painted over to hide the names. We passed a small railroad station, and the sign with the name of the stop had been taken down.

We turned onto a different road that felt less like the seaside. The road twisted and turned, and there were lots of trees. We passed through pretty little villages like the one we had stayed in before, with little shops and rows of white buildings displaying window boxes full of flowers. Could we be going back there now? If so, I should like to visit that place with the hanging sign with the mug, where people were having a party! After a while, we turned onto a narrow winding road with little cottages that had roofs made of straw and garden plots full of vegetables. All around were fields of tall grass where horses and cows were grazing and, in the distance, gentle hills. By this time, the boys were punching each other and shoving me, and we were all eager to get out of the car. We also were curious about where we were going. Would we be staying again at someone else's school? If so, we hoped that, this time, we would feel more welcome.

Finally, the car slowed down, and ahead of us was the most beautiful house. It was three storeys high, about the same size as our school in London, and it looked like a castle. It was made of stone, with small-paned windows that opened outward, tall brick chimneys, and ivy growing up the walls. A long curved stone path with bright golden yellow flowers on both sides led to a wooden door with a little window made of coloured glass. On one side of the house was a hedge, and on the other was a garden full of vegetables and fruit trees. Mr. Benham stopped the car, then helped us all out, and we waited for him to open the boot and hand us our cases. It did not smell like the seaside, but it did smell fresh and sweet.

Mrs. Benham led us along the path, up two stone steps, and into a large room. Inside, too, the house was beautiful. It had a winding staircase that had a carved, dark wood banister, and next to the staircase was a table with a vase of flowers. The walls were made of dark shiny wood, as were the floors, and a plush rug with a dragon design lay on one of them. I didn't see any long corridors lined with doors, nor any other children around. Perhaps this place really was a castle, and it was for us alone.

Soon, pupils from the other cars were filing in, and we climbed up the winding staircase. Mrs. Benham told the boys to wait and she led Catherine, Sylvia, Shirley, Ruth, and me into a pale green, square room that was much smaller than our dorm in London and a bit larger than my bedroom at home. There were five beds and they were grownup size and each of them was for one person. They were very posh. Every one of them had a rose-coloured blanket and white linens, and the white pillowcases had scallops around the edge and white stitchery. Between the beds were little tables with drawers. I peaked out into the corridor and saw that the rest of the girls were going upstairs. That was good because now the older ones wouldn't be able to boss us around. Ruth was afraid of them, and even though they taught us lots of signs, we preferred to be in separate rooms. Even this beautiful place had those ugly black curtains, but they were open and there was a lovely view of a field with horses and cows. On one wall was a tall cupboard dresser, and Mrs. Benham assigned everyone a drawer. Mine was one up from the bottom, which made it easy to reach.

After we had a chance to unpack, Mrs. Benham had us queue up and file downstairs to a dining room that had tables that seated only six. When we had finished eating, we proceeded on a tour of the building and the grounds. The boys our age had a room on the opposite side of the second storey, and the older boys and girls were on the third. Downstairs, next to our dining room, was the room for the staff, which had high ceilings and walls made of wood and large windows with panes that looked out on a garden with rosebushes. Next to that room was a huge kitchen, and behind that was a larder with floor-to-ceiling shelves and some enamel bowls on the floor. Not much food was there—only a few tins on the shelves and lots of eggs in one enamel bowl and two bottles of milk in another. One lovely large room had a fireplace, a flowered couch and matching armchairs, little tables with lamps and vases of flowers, and a rug with a swirly pattern. Another room was large and almost empty, with bats, balls, and soft mats on the floor, clearly for indoor sport.

Outside, we strolled through the garden full of fruit trees and vegetables and a greenhouse where peaches were grown. When we passed some hedges leading to the rose garden outside the dining room, Mrs. Benham shook her head no, which meant we weren't allowed there.

Behind the house were some small white cottages, and children were filing into them. Mrs. Benham pointed to one and we tramped over and stepped inside. The cottage had a blackboard, a bookcase, nine small desks, and a fireplace. This must be where we would be taking our classes.

Mrs. Benham told us about our new home and wrote some sentences about it on the blackboard. She gave us black-and-white notebooks and told us to copy the sentences. This was Havering House, also called Milton Manor, and it was near the village of Pewsey, in Wiltshire, about a two-hour drive west of London. Until now, it had been a mansion owned by a wealthy family, which is why it was so posh. What a pity I have no photographs of our stay there! Film, like so many consumer goods, was simply not available. Sylvia raised her hand and asked if we would be sharing the house with another school and the answer was no, which made us all cheer. Shirley asked how long we would be staying here, and Mrs. Benham said she didn't know.

We spent most of the afternoon outside playing hide-and-seek, follow the leader, and tag with the boys. At teatime, we had some fruit and cheese, then filed up the winding staircase to our cozy room. Mrs. Benham popped in for a moment to close the black curtains and turn out the lights, and after she left I turned on the torch. Everyone ran over to my bed and we shared what was left of our goodies—a box of butter biscuits and some jellydrops. After a while, Sylvia and Shirley moved over to Sylvia's bed, but Catherine and Ruth stayed and we got under the covers. I was liking Ruth, and having her there was nice. We were all exhausted and fell asleep right away.

In the morning, Mrs. Benham awakened us with a gentle tap. What a relief that we hadn't had to rush anywhere during the night. We put on our pale blue summer uniforms and filed downstairs for breakfast. We had our morning service in the room with the flowered couch, then queued up and marched out to our cottage.

Before long, we were all seated with our notebooks and pencils out, ready for class. Our first subject was arithmetic, and we were supposed to copy some addition problems from the board. However, there was a newspaper on Mrs. Benham's desk, and two of the boys jumped up and ran over and grabbed it and held it up in front of the class. They were quite excited, and kept pointing at the front page and signing "AEROPLANE FIGHT." Displayed on the front page was a photograph of two

small aeroplanes, just like the ones over the water in Brighton, and one of them was on fire. Mrs. Benham told the boys to stop signing and calm down, but she wasn't cross.

In fact, Mrs. Benham surprised us. She dashed over to the cupboard, pulled out some newspapers, and placed them on her desk. Would we actually be able to look at them while she was here? Would we be able to point to photographs and ask about them? I thought about all the questions I wanted to ask. I had so many. Who was that man with the dark moustache and those wild eyes? Why was that building with the dome on fire? Why were there so many changes on the streets and in the park? Why were those awful things on the beach? Perhaps, finally, I was going to know why all these strange things were happening. Perhaps, finally, I would be able to make sense of it all.

Mrs. Benham spread out some newspapers on her desk, including the one with the photograph of two small aeroplanes. She told us to gather around. Sam pointed at the aeroplanes and asked "Who?" Mrs. Benham wrote on the blackboard that England and Germany were fighting a war in the sky.

In one newspaper was a large photograph of that man with the dark moustache and those wild eyes, and we pointed and asked who he was. Mrs. Benham ran to the blackboard and wrote that he was Adolf Hitler, leader of the Nazis—bad people who had power in Germany. She pulled out a map and pointed to one place that said ENGLAND, which was here, and another that said GERMANY, which was far away.

In another newspaper was a building with a dome, and it was on fire. Shirley pointed and asked what it was and Mrs. Benham wrote that it was a synagogue in Germany that the Nazis had set on fire. Why had they done something terrible like that? Mrs. Benham shrugged her shoulders and said it was because they hated the Jews. Why? Nobody knew.

Finally, we were actually talking about why these strange things were happening. We had wanted to do this for such a long, long time. Perhaps Mrs. Benham didn't think we were old enough before. Now that we were eight years old, finally, we were ready. This class was very exciting indeed.

In one newspaper was a photograph of a beach with a barbed wire fence. It was just like that fence on the beach near school. We all pointed to that, and Mrs. Benham showed us BRIGHTON on the map.

She pointed to THE ENGLISH CHANNEL. That was the name of the sea. The Germans were trying to land in England and the fence would hold them back. That was what the older girl meant when she said "Germans here soon. Must protect," and it was why we had left Brighton so fast. Well, thank goodness we had.

All the newspapers contained photographs of things we had actually seen. Mrs. Benham showed us LONDON on the map. The papers showed photographs of two women sitting on a bus with those metal screens over the windows, of sandbags piled against buildings, of windows crisscrossed with tape, of a family in a little house with a dirt floor. One picture showed an aeroplane with some long, round things falling out of it, and on the ground, one was exploding. Mrs. Benham said they were bombs. That must be why people were always looking up at the sky! I tapped Mrs. Benham and asked if that photograph was taken in London. No, it was in Germany, so we all began to smile. It was part of a Royal Air Force raid on Berlin that took place on August 2. Mrs. Benham said not to worry about bombs falling on London. That was not going to happen. Anyway, people knew how to protect themselves and they would be safe, and we were going to win this war.

I wasn't so sure of that. Perhaps Mrs. Benham wasn't telling the truth. Didn't she know that we could read? There, in huge letters on the front page, was IS LONDON NEXT? My stomach was hurting, and I was beginning to shake. Would bombs actually be falling on the city? For a while I hadn't thought much about Mummy and Daddy and Leslie. Now I was worried about them. London must be terribly dangerous. Perhaps bombs were falling there now, right on our house in Wormholt Road. Were Mummy, Daddy, and Leslie safe? Was I ever going to see them again?

Our work in class and other activities kept us busy, and we settled into a routine. After breakfast and our meeting when we sang "God Save the King" and recited The Sh'ma, we filed over to our cottage. We worked on speech, speechreading, reading, writing, arithmetic, and penmanship. In speechreading, different sentences still looked the same and we still guessed a lot, but I was getting better at it. I watched the teachers when they were chatting and got to know school gossip such as which people they liked and which ones they didn't. We also were learning something new—Hebrew. It was especially hard work because

we had to read and write a whole new kind of letters. They went from right to left, which was very odd indeed! Every afternoon, we filed into the room that had the soft floor mats, where we did calisthenics or ran around the edge of the room, and then it was time to play outside, which took place behind the house, unless it was too wet. The yard had no playground so we played catch, follow the leader, hide-and-seek, and tag. Sometimes, when the older boys worked in the vegetable garden planting carrots or picking tomatoes off the vines, Catherine's brother would sneak us tomatoes to hide in the pockets of her cardigan, and we would run behind a hedge and munch on them. When we couldn't be outside, we played jump rope or hopscotch or pat-a-cake in the large room with the floor mats.

Three days a week, something happened that was very special to me. The boys marched out, and Mrs. Ballinson came into the cottage to teach the girls sewing. She was older than Mrs. Benham and was tall and had short brown hair and wore little round spectacles. We had no sewing machines here, so we did our stitchery by hand on little scraps, and we learned to do cross-stitches, backstitches, and blanketstitches. It felt so good to be working again with a needle and thread and a piece of cloth. The last time I had done any sewing was during a visit to Daddy's shop last autumn, and that was so long ago. Daddy would be so proud of my work now. I could see him running his eyes over it with great care, smiling at me, and saying "beautiful." Miss Ballinson said that our sewing machines were being sent from London and that they would be here soon. I couldn't wait to be running the cloth along under the needle again, the way I had with Daddy in his shop. The bad part about sewing was that it made me miss him so much.

In the evening, we stayed up in our room and looked at picture books or chatted. Once, Miss Ballinson brought up socks with holes, and we sat around a table and she showed us how to darn them over a wooden frame. Sometimes, she brought up socks and a wooden frame for each of us, and we sat on our beds and darned socks for the troops. Every evening when the lights were out, the five of us still gathered on one of our beds and shared our biscuits and sweets, though by now, we had almost nothing left.

Here in the countryside, everything became part of a lesson, so we learned lots of new words. We walked around the grounds and looked

at the flowers and learned their names—crocuses, daffodils, tulips, roses. We strolled through the vegetable garden and wrote the name of everything there—onions, carrots, spinach, potatoes, tomatoes, parsley, and kale. When they appeared at the table, we had to ask for them by name, with perfect manners, of course. Animals were an important part of life in the countryside—puppies or kittens that were just being born, the hens that laid eggs in the henhouse, the robins we fed bread to near the kitchen door. Sometimes when it was warm, Mr. Benham appeared with a fishing rod and we tramped down to the river. We didn't catch many fish, but it was lovely to sit on the bank, dip our feet in the cool water, and throw pebbles in and watch the ripples. Mrs. Benham wrote little stories about what we did, and we had to answer questions using WHO, WHAT, WHERE, WHEN, and WHY.

I never missed a chance to get into mischief. When it was warm enough, we had to go without shoes. There were almost none available in stores, so our old ones had to last as long as possible. I wanted to wear mine out so I would have to get some new ones. Mummy would object to my going barefoot because it could give me a chill. She would insist that I wear shoes all the time. I secretly wrote her a letter about it, even though letters going home were supposed to be checked by the staff. I asked one of the kitchen helpers who rode his bicycle to town to post it for me. He told Mrs. Benham, and for punishment, I had to pull out weeds in the teachers' garden for a whole week! Another time, when the class was tramping around in a field, we saw some plants growing that had long, flat, fuzzy stalks. A horse might find them tasty, I thought, so I fed some to a brown horse who was grazing nearby. Suddenly he reared up and bolted straight across the field! Those tall plants were stinging nettles, and that poor horse must have been in dreadful pain. Another day, the class was marching in a queue along the winding road into town. It was a good opportunity to show off, so as we marched around a bend, I dashed out into the middle of the road. A lorry was speeding around the bend, but I didn't see it, and before long I had flipped up onto the hood! Mrs. Benham almost fainted. It was a miracle that I was still alive. After that, we always had to walk in twos.

Even here in the countryside we saw reminders of the war. All the windows had those black curtains, and Mrs. Benham closed them carefully every night. Lots of aeroplanes flew over, and whenever one passed,

the teachers looked up and frowned. One night, we woke up suddenly because the house was shaking. Mrs. Benham rushed into our dark room with her torch on and pulled us out of bed, and we had to grab our blankets and pillows and follow her down a dark staircase. It made every one of us start to worry. Could we be going to some dark, cold, damp, musty underground room, like the one in Brighton? Actually, we ended up in that pretty room with the flowered couch, and Mrs. Benham said we would have to sleep there. Catherine and I ran over and climbed into an armchair while others placed their blankets and pillows on the floor. It was better than that horrid underground room, but we couldn't really lie down in that chair. When the house started shaking again, everyone was terrified, and that night we didn't sleep at all.

The aeroplanes that flew over at night just after we arrived at Havering House were probably traveling to and from the Midlands. From August 19 to September 6, as British planes withdrew to the interior, the Luftwaffe had to fly there to destroy centres where fighters were being built and to bomb RAF bases. Sometimes we had to rush downstairs because the moon was full, which made us especially easy to see. The teachers always worried that the Germans would drop the unused bombs on us on their way home!

After a while, we were worrying more and more about what was happening in London. Since we had arrived here on August 21, there had been almost no letters or parcels for anyone. Every day when the post arrived, we all hoped there would be something from home, but there almost never was. Catherine was the only one in our class who received anything—a small parcel from her mother that contained some Turkish Delight. Was she able to mail things because she lived in Southend-on-Sea, rather than in London? Were those in London unable to get or mail anything? What a very frightening thought!

Now that we weren't going home on weekends or holidays, we received more religious training in school. In addition to morning services, we were writing some words in Hebrew and reading stories from the Bible, and we celebrated the Jewish holidays. For Rosh Hashanah, we said a few prayers and Mr. Hart blew a curved horn called a shofar. I couldn't hear anything, but the boys and girls with some hearing frowned and held their ears. At Yom Kippur we prayed, and the older children fasted from sundown one day to sundown the next. The children

only a bit older than we were fasted for half a day. Mrs. Benham said we would fast next year, but we weren't in any hurry.

Sukkoth, which came in October, was the autumn holiday we all loved, and it was especially nice to celebrate it in the countryside. We watched the older boys use pieces of wood to build a small sukkah in the grassy area behind the house, and we helped them gather the branches for the roof. Soon it was filled with autumn leaves and hanging fruits, and it looked beautiful in the bright sunshine. Inside was a long table with a blue velvet cloth and bowls of apples, red and green grapes, pears, dates, and figs. Also on the table were plates filled with fresh loaves of challah, which made me think of Mummy. In class, we had learned that Sukkoth is a harvest festival that begins five days after Yom Kippur and lasts seven days. For the festival, we build small huts to remind us of the temporary dwellings of the Israelites during their journey in the desert after Exodus. When it was our class's turn to spend a few minutes inside the sukkah and have a taste of bread and fruit, I snatched some extra grapes and passed them to Catherine to hide in the pocket of her frock. Later, we enjoyed them behind the hedge where we usually had our tomatoes.

One cold, foggy morning when we stepped into our cottage, Mrs. Benham said to copy the sentences on the blackboard. She pointed to the door and stepped outside. On the floor next to her desk sat her bag with a newspaper inside. She might not want to share it with us today, and we simply had to see it. Perhaps there would be some good news. We hoped to see that there was no war in London. That news would make us all feel a lot better. I ran over, pulled out the newspaper, and spread it out on the teacher's desk. Everyone jumped up and gathered around. On the second page were some photographs, and they did not make us feel better at all. Many were like the ones we had seen before, with buildings in ruins and mothers and children looking sad and confused. One photograph was of a huge aeroplane, with one of those bombs falling from it. Across the top of the page was a terrifying phrase— MORE BOMBING IN LONDON. Everyone pointed and started to frown. My stomach was hurting, and I was beginning to shake. When Mrs. Benham stepped back inside, she was surprised, but she looked sad rather than cross. She hadn't been sharing the news with us lately. Clearly, she didn't want us to know what was happening. This news

was very bad indeed, and it made us worry again. I had to see my family, especially Leslie. If only I could be inside our cozy house, smelling Mummy's challah baking. If only I could be in the garden playing with Leslie or helping Daddy water the flowers. Perhaps one of those terrible things had fallen from the sky and it had landed on our house. Perhaps one had landed on my father's shop. Were Leslie, Mummy, and Daddy all right? Was I ever going to see them again?

By this time, Phase II of the Battle of Britain, the massive attacks called the Blitz, had begun on London and other cities. It lasted from September 7, 1940, to May 10, 1941. Germany sent wave upon wave of bombers, and by mid-October, when the RAF was better at shooting them down, they were coming in almost entirely at night. Some nights, the raids went on from sunset to sunrise without stopping, and by November, no part of the city was spared. Sometimes, the Germans used land mines, packed with explosives, that drifted to the ground on parachutes and exploded with great force. Some bombs didn't go off right away, but exploded later, when people were back to their normal activities. German fighters even swept down to machine-gun people who were trapped out in the open. With the city blacked out, the German pilots needed to see their targets, and they provided their own light by dropping incendiary bombs, which set off blazes that lit up the city for blocks around. Thousands lost their lives, were injured, or became homeless, and much of London was destroyed.

In mid-November, the Luftwaffe began a new kind of air attack, focusing on cities with lots of factories and key ports—cities such as Coventry, Liverpool, Manchester, Birmingham, Plymouth, Bristol, and Hull. Throughout these new attacks, the Germans continued to bomb London, and the assault would go on even beyond May 10, 1941, when the Battle of Britain ended. We had good reason to be worried about our families.

Getting On with It

Autumn turned into winter, becoming much colder. Every day when the post arrived, each of us prayed for a letter or parcel from home, but almost nothing ever came. Catherine's mother had sent that box of toffees, but none of the other girls in our room had received anything. All we had to share at night were the toffees and a few butter biscuits that were stale.

We were more and more worried about what was happening at home. Every night when it was time to retire, someone was in tears. It was hard to fall asleep, and I lay awake thinking about Mummy, Daddy, and Leslie. Had there been bombing in Shepherds Bush? Had a bomb hit our house on Wormholt Road? Was the family safe?

In the cottage, Mrs. Benham kept us busy. We read stories such as *The Town Mouse and the Country Mouse, Rumpelstiltskin, The Frog Prince,* and *Pandora's Box,* and we answered WHO, WHAT, WHERE, WHEN, and WHY questions about them. We worked on grammar, practicing plurals, putting in commas and periods, making two sentences into a compound sentence, and writing paragraphs about things we did. We began to realize that some words were synonyms—spectacles and glasses, weep and cry, frightened and afraid. We wrote about events taking place in school, and we looked at pictures and wrote about them. If our grammar was wrong, Mrs. Benham corrected it and expected us to rewrite everything properly. Our work had to be precise. In one lesson in which I was describing a recent walk, I wrote "Mr. Benham fell down," and it was corrected as "Mr. Benham slipped and fell." When I said "Perhaps I have made a mistake," it was changed to "Perhaps I am mistaken." We had to copy everything from the blackboard or chart into our notebooks and do it neatly. If it wasn't perfect, we did it again.

In spite of the hard work, we had fun in class. Sometimes when Mrs. Benham corrected our grammar, she was quite funny. When I described an uncle as having "a brown eye and a rather dark hair," she drew a cartoon of a person with one eye and one hair that was sticking straight up, and wrote "Poor uncle!" When she turned to write on the blackboard, we signed to one another (still forbidden). Of course, when she was about to turn around, we stopped.

One of the many activities we enjoyed outside the classroom was going to Pewsey. One brisk, sunny afternoon when Mr. Benham drove us there, we stopped to watch the blacksmith make horseshoes. It smelled awful in the shop, and we didn't like watching the horseshoe being nailed to the hooves because we thought it must have hurt. We meandered over to the shop where you could buy sweets, and the shop owner, Mr. Waghorn, smiled at us as usual. (Too bad there were only some jellydrops and a few Cadbury bars and we had to give him ration coupons.) Afterward, we tramped over to the cinema where we saw a

film starring Clark Gable. I don't recall the name of the film, but he was quite handsome. Another day, when it was cold and wet, Mr. Benham drove us to the cinema to see Disney's *Snow White and the Seven Dwarfs*. The wicked stepmother was terrifying, but it was lovely at the end when the prince arrived. Little Ann Benham went with us, and on the way to the cinema and back to the house, she sat on my lap in the car. Back in the cottage, Mrs. Benham taught us how to sing the dwarfs' song. After that, she expected us to march to our cottage singing "Hi ho, hi ho, it's off to school we go." She said it would improve our speech, and perhaps it did.

The first snow arrived and covered the countryside. It was quite beautiful, especially when the sun came out later and the snow and the sky were a soft lovely blue. Sometimes it was colder than it had ever been in London. We wore hats, mittens, scarves, and Wellingtons, and we had cardigans under our winter coats, but we were cold anyway. During play time, we often tramped through the snow down to the frozen river and went ice-skating there. My ankles kept collapsing and I fell down more than I skated, but Shirley and Sylvia were able to skate backwards and make figure eights. They showed off a lot, and whenever they started, Catherine, Ruth, and I turned around and looked the other way. We loved it when the boys knocked into those two and made them fall, which always made us laugh. It was great fun tobogganing on little hills out in the field, and sometimes the teachers had us pull one another on sleds and made us speak in the process. For example, Mrs. Benham had one of us tell the others to go or stop and which way to go, and we had to use our voices or we couldn't play.

One day in December when the sun was shining on a blanket of snow, we were tramping around behind the house, following some footprints made by the birds and making our own footprints in the snow. Mr. Hart appeared at the rear door, waving at me and gesturing for me to come. I glanced at Mrs. Benham to see if it was all right, and she nodded her head yes. I tramped over to the door and stopped to shake the snow off my Wellingtons. Then, as I followed Mr. Hart into his office, my stomach began to hurt and my heart was beating fast. There might be a parcel or a letter from home, but there also could be some news that was bad. Perhaps a bomb had fallen on our house or had landed on my father's shop.

When we reached the office, Mr. Hart shuffled over to his desk, and on it was a pile of different-sized parcels. Could one of them actually be for me? Mr. Hart smiled and after sorting through the pile, pulled out a medium-sized parcel that was square and had a string around it. Would this one have my name on it? Could it actually be from the family? I peered at the parcel, trying to see the writing, but there wasn't any, and I wanted to cry. Right away, Mr. Hart turned it over and began to smile. My name was there and the handwriting was Mummy's! It really was from home! It might mean that everyone was all right. My hands were shaking, which made it hard to get the string off, but after fumbling a bit, I managed to pull it off, tear the paper, and open the parcel. There was a box of chocolate wafers with vanilla fillings—my favourite biscuits! There was also a bag of Pascall marshmallows with "Ann" written on it, for little Ann Benham. I couldn't wait to show the biscuits to the girls. Tonight, we would have quite a feast!

The parcel also contained a letter. Although I was eager to read it, the thought was making my stomach ache. It was so important to know what was happening at home, and yet I was so afraid. As I unfolded the letter, my hands were shaking again. What was it going to say? Was the news going to be good or bad? I started to read the letter, and, actually, it was quite a pleasant surprise. Mummy sounded cheerful and said nothing about the war. Perhaps she thought that here in the countryside we didn't know about it. Everyone at home was fine and they were "getting on with it." Daddy was working hard in the shop, and Auntie Hewitt always asked about me. Everyone missed me terribly, and Leslie talked about me all the time. My mother had taken him by train up to Manchester and left him with our relatives there, but he had cried so much that, after a fortnight, she had to go up there and fetch him. She didn't say why he had gone, but, of course, I knew. There must have been bombing right there in Shepherds Bush. Still, the letter and parcel made me very happy indeed.

I glanced over at Mr. Hart's desk. On it was a newspaper, and I could see that terrible things were still happening. One photograph showed a mother holding a baby inside a church where a wall was missing and there was no roof. In another photograph, children were in a Tube station, and they were sleeping in beds stacked on top of each other.

> My darling brother Leslie,
> I am very well
> and hope you are too. How is Miss
> Allen? I hope she is a very kind to
> you. Can you send me some more
> comics? I will send you some comics
> if I have plenty of comics.
> Mummy send me some tomatoes.
> We had a film on Saturday. It
> was called "I rust Peggy", "The Under
> the Microscope," and the "Happy Isle".
> We enjoyed ourselves. I hope you
> will like this letter. Please write
> to me at once with Mummy's next
> letter.

A letter I sent to my brother Leslie.

Something about it was familiar—the name of the station—South Clapham, the station near our school in Nightingale Lane! Did that mean that our beautiful school had been bombed? Worst of all was the writing at the top of the page: BOMBING GOES ON AND ON. I was thrilled about the letter and parcel, but those words made me feel awful. As long as there was bombing, my family was in danger.

Soon the other girls began hearing from home. The next day, Sylvia was called to Mr. Hart's office. She returned to the cottage with a box of lemon creme biscuits. A few days later, Catherine was called to the office. Her mother sent not only some homemade macaroons for Catherine but also a separate parcel containing mints for Ruth. Whenever anyone in the group received a letter with good news, we were happy, and when someone received a parcel, we were thrilled.

Now that we were hearing from our families, we started writing letters home as part of our English lessons. It not only provided a means of staying in contact but also gave us a way to practice English grammar. Our letters almost always began the same, with "My dear parents" (or anyone else), followed by "I am well and hope you are the same." We learned how to thank someone for a letter or parcel, to ask for news, and

to tell about life at school. We closed the letter with the proper "Your loving daughter" (or son or sister or granddaughter or friend). To help us think of things to tell our families, Mrs. Benham asked us questions about events at school. What was the weather like today? What did we see in the garden? What are Sylvia and Shirley able to do on the ice? After we answered the questions using sentences and Ms. Benham corrected them, we included them in our letters. In my letters, I also wrote a lot about the girls, especially Catherine and Ruth. At first, the sentences were short, but after a while, they became quite long.

I was beginning to realize how far I had come in getting people to understand me. When I was little, the only way to get anything had been to kick or scream or bite. After a while, I learned to find something I wanted and point or pull someone over to it. Later, I learned what to do if I wanted something that wasn't there—gesture or try to say it or find a picture or try to draw one or write down the word if I knew how to spell it. Of course, here at school, making someone understand me was easier than at home because the teachers were skilled, the older girls showed us how to fingerspell and sign, and we could fingerspell and sign to one another. Even in a place like the dining room, where we were supposed to ask for something in proper English, if we didn't get it right, we could point to it or ask someone for help. When we were writing to someone, however, it was different. Making someone who wasn't there understand us could be very difficult indeed. That person couldn't see my face or body, so the only way to make him or her understand me was to write in proper sentences. Because writing was so important, I became better and better at it.

In my letters, I was never shy about asking for things—money, a paintbook, a paint box, a notebook, envelopes, stamps, comics, white polish for my shoes. In one letter home I said, "I am very excited because you will send me a parcel with some coloured wools another time. Yes, I want shoulder straps for my navy blue skirt. Please will you send me some navy blue wool and a pattern for a jumper for myself?" Sometimes I gave my parents a choice, "Which do you prefer to send me—biscuits or a Swiss roll?" If I expected a problem finding something, I told them where to find it. When asking for a 1940 calendar, I reminded them that it was in the dinette. In one letter, I said, "Please will you send me my nursery rhyme book? My book is upstairs in my bedroom."

In one letter, I asked for brand names, asking my parents to be sure they sent Palmolive soap and Phillips toothpaste. Once in a while I was quite bold, as when I wrote, "Why have you not sent me a parcel for a long time? What is the matter with you? I am very disappointed with you." I sent letters not only to my parents but also to Leslie, Grandpa Sam, Auntie Hewitt, and other relatives and friends.

Of course, writing home was for more than bringing people up to date and getting them to send things. Letters showed how much I missed everyone and how worried I was. In one to Leslie, I asked, "Do you think London is too dangerous for you?" In one to Grandpa Sam in Hove, I said, "I am sorry because you have a lot of air raids." I wrote to my parents, "I hope there are no German bombs in Shepherds Bush." Another time it was "I hope London has no air raids for a long time." In a letter to Auntie Hewitt, I asked, "Are you nervous about the air raids?" In spite of our comfortable life in the countryside, the bombing of London was very much on my mind.

I tried especially hard to stay close to Leslie through my letters. Sometimes, I played the caring older sister, asking if he was clever in school or reminding him to be obedient. In one letter to him I said, "I am always looking at the photos." I asked Mummy for a tie so I could mail it to Leslie. In a different letter, I requested that she mail a card to me and keep it a secret, so I could send it to him.

In the cottage, we continued to have religious instruction, and the next holiday was Chanukah. We learned about how the temple was restored after the Syrians had tried to destroy our religion. We read a story about the dreidel, which was used in ancient times when the Jewish people were not allowed to get together to pray. The Jews pretended they were playing with the top, and the four Hebrew letters on the dreidel stand for words that mean "a great miracle happened there"— the miracle being getting the temple back from the Syrians. During the eight days of the holiday, we gathered every evening in the dining room after tea, and Mr. Hart lit the menorah and we all said a prayer we had practiced in Hebrew class. There was no Chanukah *gelt,* but one evening we had a Chanukah party, with potato latkes, macaroons, and apple juice. The boys in our class sat on the floor and played with dreidels while the girls sat on folding chairs and chatted. It was the first time we weren't home for the holiday season, and nobody's family

showed up, so we were all a bit sad. I missed Christmas, too, with all the decorations and lights outside and visiting our tenants upstairs.

Late in the winter, we began to see signs of spring, an especially lovely time in the countryside. We took long walks in the fields, and by mid-February, everything was beginning to come alive. One field was carpeted with snowdrops, another was full of lovely golden yellow aconites, and the hedges were adorned with hazel catkins. Toward the end of February, we wrote about daffodils beginning to appear, clumps of snowdrops in the grass, and small, tight buds on the trees. I also wrote that we had seen a newborn lamb. We must have read about Mary and her little lamb because I said that its fleece was "white as snow."

Soon it was warm again, and one lovely spring day when we marched into the cottage, Mrs. Benham had a newspaper on her desk. She was reading it and she was clearly interested in what it said. Did it contain good news or bad? Perhaps it would bring more bad news. Perhaps the newspaper said that a bomb had fallen on Shepherds Bush. My stomach was hurting and I was beginning to tremble. The teacher looked up and gestured for us to gather around her desk, and we all rushed over.

We looked down at the newspaper, and Mrs. Benham pointed to a sentence in big letters on the front page. We were able to read pretty well, so we stood there and read it together. I couldn't believe what it said. It was what we had been wanting for so long, and I shall never forget those words: BATTLE OF BRITAIN OVER. HITLER TURNS ATTENTION TO RUSSIA. That must mean that no more bombs would be falling on London! Mrs. Benham pulled out her book with the map saying ENGLAND and GERMANY, and she pointed to RUSSIA and showed us that it was far away. Everyone started to smile, and we all jumped up and cheered. Catherine asked if we could go home and visit our families. Mrs. Benham said we wouldn't be allowed to go home just yet. Then she gave us some wonderful news: That Sunday, our families would be visiting us at school.

All week, we couldn't think of anything but visiting day. It was hard to pay attention in class, and often, Mrs. Benham looked cross, pointed at someone, and rolled her eyes. That week must have been the longest week ever. After classes on Friday, Mrs. Benham helped us tidy up our bedroom, and I even bent down and peeked under the bed to see if any dust was there. Since Mummy thought it caused breathing problems, if

there was any there, I wanted to get rid of it. It was important for everything to be perfect.

Finally, Sunday arrived, sunny and warm, and we were filled with excitement. The older girls came down and helped us take our baths. I put on a yellow frock with smocking that Daddy had made in his shop, though by now it was a bit tight. I wore yellow socks with white lace and my white shoes with the ankle straps, even though the shoes cramped my toes. I brushed my curls just the way Mummy used to do it. It was so important to look beautiful for the family.

We marched down to the dining room for the midday meal, but I didn't feel like eating. I was too excited about seeing Mummy, Daddy, and Leslie. I couldn't wait to show them our beautiful school here in the countryside. I would take them on a tour of the building and the grounds and, now that my speech was good, they would understand me. It was hard to believe that the family would actually be here soon; it had been such a long time since we had been together. Mummy had promised in her letter that they would visit today. Then again, perhaps I shouldn't get too excited. What if they don't show up?

After the midday meal, we went outside to play on the grass in front of the house. Other families were starting to arrive, but there was no trace of Mummy, Daddy, and Leslie. When a huge black car pulled up and Catherine's mother jumped out, we rushed over and cuddled with her. Sylvia's parents arrived, and a bit later, Shirley's. Perhaps my family wasn't going to be here after all.

All the parents smiled at Ruth and cuddled with her, but after a while, she shuffled across the grass and sat down under a tree. She must have been feeling terribly sad because her eyes were filled with tears. At least our families were in England. At least we had heard from them. Most of them were actually here, and mine might be here soon. Ruth hadn't heard from her family at all. They were far away in Germany, and she might never see them again. I walked over to Ruth, sat down on the grass, and put my arm around her.

After what seemed like forever, I saw a bus in the distance, and it was speeding up the road toward us. Perhaps the family would be on that bus. As it came closer, the bus slowed down, and then, finally, it stopped. I jumped up, ran over, stood on my toes, and tried to peer through the windows. I saw only strangers, and they were beginning to stand up and

form a queue. Soon, one by one, they appeared at the door and stepped down onto the road. There was no trace of Mummy, Daddy, or Leslie, and I was ready to burst into tears.

Then a boy who had silky brown hair and was in tan knickers and a brown checkered pullover appeared at the door. It was Leslie! He was followed by a woman in a pale green frock with a matching lace collar, lisle stockings, and black-and-white shoes with little heels. Mummy! Next came a man in a grey wool suit, a white shirt, and a wide tie with stripes. Daddy! It was such a relief to see everyone. Mummy and Daddy were thin and they looked tired, and Leslie had grown taller. My heart was beating fast as I ran toward them. The family had arrived after all, and I was so happy. I grabbed everyone and cuddled and didn't want to let go. We had been very fortunate indeed. The Battle of Britain was over, and we were all alive and well and together again.

Still, this was a sad day for Ruth. I ran back, grabbed her hand, yanked her up, and pulled her over to meet everyone, and we all cuddled. I turned to Ruth, shrugged my shoulders, smiled, and signed "Maybe your family soon." When she smiled back and nodded her head yes, I was happier than ever.

Looking Back

Looking back, I realize how fortunate I was during the Battle of Britain and, indeed, throughout the war. After the war, I learned more about what it had been like during the bombing in London, especially during the Blitz, when the worst attacks took place. Except when my mother took Leslie up to Manchester, the family and Auntie Hewitt remained in Wormholt Road. In spite of eventual bombing in Shepherds Bush, the family slept in the Morrison shelter in the parlour. Not even once did they consider sleeping in the Underground, where there was no privacy, it was dirty, and people had to use pails for toilets. Whenever she spoke about it, my mother scowled and held her nose. For her, the sanitary conditions there would surely have been worse than a direct hit by a bomb.

Daddy described how difficult life was during the war and how life had changed. In the morning, he might walk outside and see smoldering ash, mounds of broken glass, and deep bomb craters. When he left

for work, he never knew whether his shop would still be there. On the way home, he could be blocked from a street while the police were trying to take apart an unexploded bomb. People got used to doing with less. Britain had to be supplied by sea, and the Germans were doing their best to stop ships from reaching port. Most of what did get through was needed for the war. Almost no consumer goods were available; everything from toys to furniture had disappeared from the stores early in the war. People threw nothing away; salvage squads collected scrap iron, rubber, and other materials that could help us win the war. Even aluminum pots and pans were collected to be melted down and made into planes. Rationing was in effect not only for food but also for clothing and petrol.

Britain's survival required that everyone pitch in, and every able-bodied citizen did, with some working up to ninety hours a week. My father was pressed into service as a fire-watcher, helping to spot fires before they got out of control. Others grew food in victory gardens or collected money for widows and orphans. Many civilians who were exempt from the draft because they were not in good health or were too old or too young for military service served in the British Home Guard. They were trained to protect the home soil in the event of an invasion. People whose children were away from home missed them terribly and worried about them. It was a very difficult time, but the British accepted the blackouts, the shortage of fuel, the food rationing, the clothing coupons, and other restrictions because they were determined to win the war. They used ingenuity, for example, a deaf woman had tied a string to her foot and hung the string out the window; when the air-raid sirens went off, the local warden pulled on the string to wake her up.

When the Battle of Britain was over, London was not going to be as safe as we expected. Although the worst bombing took place during the Battle of Britain, from July 10, 1940, to May 10, 1941, German pilots would still be flying over and dropping bombs on London later in the war. Also, from June 13 to June 20, 1944, London was attacked by Hitler's V-1 rockets—small, pilotless, jet-propelled planes that carried a ton of explosives at more than 300 miles an hour. Then, in early August 1944, V-2 rockets, which carried a ton of explosive at supersonic speed and were almost impossible to intercept and destroy before hitting a target, reached London. Actually, these attacks on London worked

against Germany. The V-1 and V-2 rockets, though dangerous, allowed British ports to continue functioning and, thus, enabled desperately needed military supplies to reach Allied troops on their march to Berlin. These new air attacks did not last long because the main launching sites were captured by the Allied armies late in August 1944.

The Battle of Britain was Germany's first defeat in World War II. By launching the Blitz on London and other cities in 1940–41, Hitler caused enormous damage and suffering. However, by turning his attention to the cities, he failed to destroy the Royal Air Force, and therefore ended his chance of invading England. If the Luftwaffe had continued its assault on the RAF, Britain's air defenses would have been destroyed and Hitler might have succeeded with his invasion. If he had conquered England, he would have controlled almost all of Europe, and he and his allies would have ruled most of the world. Thank goodness his victory was not meant to be.

During that long period when the Battle of Britain was over but the war was still going on, the family would visit me at school perhaps twice a year. Once in a while, I would even go home. On one holiday in London during the summer of 1944, the V-1 and V-2 rockets were being launched against the city. Mr. Hart must have thought it was unsafe there because my parents had to lie and say that we were going to Cambridge. I never saw any rockets, but I was stunned by now much London had changed. The damage had been enormous, and everywhere were bombed-out buildings, broken glass, and the smell of burning wood.

When Daddy was bringing me home that summer of 1944 and we got off the bus at the bottom of Wormholt Road, he looked uneasy. It was clear that something was wrong. When we reached our house and stepped inside, though, it was the same as before. The Morrison table was still in the parlour, and the dinette looked as cozy as ever. I couldn't wait to run out into the garden. I wanted so much to see the area near the kitchen where the mint and spinach were growing and the ceramic stand set in the middle of the grass. I especially wanted to see all the beautiful flowers. I dashed through the kitchen, past the larder, and out through the rear door. When I saw the garden, I was shocked. Mint and spinach still grew near the kitchen door, and the ceramic stand was filled with geraniums, but all the other plants and flowers were gone!

Even worse, our neighbours' house and two or three others were no longer there! At the end of our garden was nothing but a huge, ugly hole in the ground—a crater. Leslie made the sign for aeroplane and made a gesture that showed something falling out of it. A bomb had fallen there! I never learned whether the neighbours survived. We were fortunate that it hadn't landed on our house. I sat down on the grass, and even though I was twelve years old, I burst into tears. I felt not only terribly sad but also very angry at those horrid Germans. How could they do that to us?

Something even worse happened because of the war—we lost some members of the family. My mother's brother, Uncle Alf, was killed in a car accident during a blackout. Just as my father had feared back in the autumn of 1938, my Uncle Jacob lost his life during the German occupation of France. Daddy also lost two younger sisters there. Jacob's son, Willy, was found in a concentration camp by a relative who was a chaplain in the army.

Actually, it is quite remarkable that so many of us fared as well as we did. I shudder to think about the summer of 1940, when nearly all of northern Europe was under Nazi control and the Germans were planning to launch their invasion from the French coast only twenty-one miles from Britain. In spite of all the dangers, Mummy, Daddy, Leslie, Auntie Hewitt, Grandpa, and Auntie Julie, and many relatives, neighbours, and friends survived the Battle of Britain and the rest of the war.

Although those of us at the school had still faced risks, those evacuations of the Residential School for Jewish Deaf Children enabled us to avoid the massive bombing in London. Our school building at 101 Nightingale Lane was used as an aliens' reception centre for women and was badly blasted on two occasions. Throughout the war, pupils and staff managed to remain safe—initially, at the building in London, during our short stay in Newbury, back in London, at the Christian school in Brighton, and finally, at Havering House. Remarkably, our education and our social life at school were disrupted very little because we had remained together through all the evacuations. None of us had to adjust to new surroundings on his or her own, like British youngsters sent to the countryside and millions of children all over Europe who were separated from their families. None of us was left behind in the

city with school closed and nothing to do but roam around, like so many children. During a time when the British were near starvation, we were growing food in our own garden and were well-nourished. Most important of all, we were not in a country controlled by the Nazis. If we had been, we would surely have lost our lives because we were Jewish and deaf.

We never dreamed we would be kept away from Nightingale Lane until a year after the war ended, but students and staff did not return until May 13, 1946. Even then, although repairs had been carried out, the building would need more work to make it safe and attractive again.

Those Jewish deaf children from East Berlin who arrived in England in July 1939 suffered terrible losses and showed great courage. One girl's family emigrated to America without telling her why or even saying good-bye. They left her behind because deaf people weren't allowed into the United States, and she didn't see her family for four years. In 1942, in her early teens, this brave girl traveled alone on a war ship filled with troops, and the crossing took a month. She wasn't allowed into the country until her parents claimed she had been trained as a farmer. As for Ruth, her parents, her grandmother, and her brother had to travel to faraway Shanghai for refuge because it was the only place that would accept them. Her grandmother and her brother returned to Germany in 1942, thinking it was safe, and they perished in a concentration camp. Ruth went on holiday at the seaside with the Benhams because she had nowhere else to go. In a recent letter from Ann Benham, I learned that she and Ruth had been like sisters, and that Mr. and Mrs. Benham had been thinking of adopting the deaf girl. Although Ruth heard from her parents twice a year through the Red Cross, she wasn't reunited with them until November 1949, aboard the *Queen Elizabeth* in New York. She recognized her father, but her mother's appearance had changed so much that she was unrecognizable. It must have been sad for Ruth to hear about the rest of her family, but at least she was with her parents again. Ann Benham met them in New York in 1960, but since then, she and Ruth have lost contact.

Ruth and the other girl, both reunited with their parents, were more fortunate than most of the children who arrived from East Berlin. They never saw their families again. In spite of that tragedy, all the children

who came to England were blessed. Under the loving care of the RSJDC staff, they were safe during the war and acquired useful skills. Later, they settled in England, the United States, and Israel and have since led happy, productive lives. In spite of their terrible losses, life for the children who joined us at RSJDC has been good.

Looking back, I am grateful to so many people. First of all are my parents, who cared so much and were willing to send me away to be with others who were better able to guide me. Next is Leslie, my beloved brother and dear friend, to whom I still feel so close. I am indebted to my Auntie Hewitt, the friendly neighbour who recommended the Residential School for Jewish Deaf Children. My heart is filled with thanks for the staff members of the school, who believed in the ability of deaf children to learn, who had such enormous patience, and who were so highly skilled in their work. They freed so many from isolation, ignorance, and dependency by providing the gift of language, by inspiring us to learn, by establishing a solid religious foundation, and by teaching us practical skills. Attending RSJDC prepared me to feel comfortable in both the deaf and hearing worlds—a great help throughout life. I am grateful to my fellow pupils, who taught me a natural, easy way to communicate and provided emotional support and a sense of community. Catherine, my best friend at school, is still as important as ever. We correspond by mail or by e-mail. She has visited me in New York, and we get together in England from time to time. I must thank the Royal Air Force pilots for fighting so bravely, the British people for refusing to submit to the Nazis, and the Allied forces for helping us win the war. They all fought so hard and sacrificed so much to break the Nazi control of Europe. Without them, my loved ones, so many others, and I would not have survived.

Life has been good to me; both personally and professionally, I have been fulfilled. I have been blessed with a long and happy marriage to my husband Fred, a deaf American. We have four wonderful hearing sons of whom we are very proud. We have many grandchildren, who are a great pleasure, and recently, we have even become great-grandparents. We are observant Orthodox Jews, are active in deaf organizations, and take great pride in the growth of a respected worldwide deaf community. The dressmaking skills I acquired from my father and at RSJDC have served me well, enabling me to become a young seamstress in the high

couture industry in London and, later, to run my own dressmaking business in New York. I have also worked many years as a paraprofessional and as a teacher of children and of adults, both hearing and deaf, which has been quite satisfying. I am fortunate indeed to have survived the Battle of Britain and the rest of that terrible war.

I Dared!

Frances M. Parsons

In 1970, Dr. Mervin Garretson, who was then the Executive Director of the Council of Organizations Serving the Deaf, visited Argentina to see how deaf children were being educated. While he was there, a group of deaf adults asked him to send a spokesperson on behalf of deaf children. Being very shy and a reluctant public speaker, I was leery when he recommended me. I asked him to clarify the purpose of making this trip, but he answered evasively, assuring me that all I would do was sit with the parents of the deaf children and share my family experiences with them. I was not at all sure how I could help families in Argentina, but I decided to go.

I arrived in Buenos Aires in early June of 1971 and was greeted warmly by a small welcoming committee—a hearing teacher, a hearing father, a deaf mother, and the president of the Argentina Association of the Deaf. While driving toward the city, the teacher, Iris, and I had a long conversation, until I told her we had to stop because the sun was going down and I could not lipread her. She was silent until we reached our destination. I was confused when Iris appeared agitated and the members of my welcoming committee began to argue with each other. It turned out she was stunned to learn that I was deaf! All the VIPs, government people, professors, and teachers were expecting a hearing professor from

America! It was my turn to be shocked when I learned I was to present lectures about the teaching methods used in the United States. I threw up my hands and was all for returning to the States.

Iris changed her mind when the group pointed out to her how well I could speak, in spite of my deafness and my ability to sign, and I could be a role model. So they all begged me to reconsider. I refused to listen. I was furious and cursed Dr. Garretson for letting me walk into this trap. Finally we agreed that I would visit a model oral school. The principal was astounded when we arrived unannounced. She asked us to return on the following day, but I had made a firm decision to leave Argentina.

Reluctantly the principal welcomed us to the school. I was flabbergasted to see teachers loitering in the halls, leaving children unattended. The principal led me to a classroom where the students were having intensive speech training. As she opened the door, I took a quick glance around the room—there were no blackboards, no pictures, no papers or books, no crayons or pencils. Six five-year-old girls sat on hard benches around a semicircular table. They all looked bored as they waited their turns for speech training.

In this classroom, at that moment, my life changed forever. I watched incredulously as the teacher reached out and clutched a little girl's hair and pulled her head backward. The teacher then whipped out a pair of metal tongs, gripped the girl's tongue, and twisted hard enough to make the girl jerk. This small child looked at me as she licked her bleeding tongue. Her eyes were brimming with tears that pleaded with me to help her.

Horrified, I asked the teacher why she had done this. Her explanation was it would correct the pupil's pronunciation. I realized then that these children had no one to speak for them, and so I decided on the spot that I would become their advocate. I stayed in Argentina for three months. With Iris as my interpreter, I gave interviews to television, magazine, and newspaper reporters; presented lectures to professors, teachers, parents, and government people; taught and worked with the teachers of the deaf, showing them how to combine basic sign language with speech; visited schools inside and outside Buenos Aires; and took advantage of every opportunity to publicize Total Communication (the method of using sign language, speech, speechreading, and any other

communication mode that will help deaf students learn) and the combined method (the simultaneous use of signs and speech).

Thus began my global campaign to encourage other countries to incorporate sign language into deaf education. During the academic year, I taught at Gallaudet College, so I was able to travel during the summers. My second trip was to the Bahamas. At first the British principal assigned me to work with the British teacher for the slow and emotionally disturbed deaf children because the hard of hearing children were forbidden to learn any form of sign language. The slow learners responded enthusiastically to learning fingerspelling and signing. Our work was so successful that the Bahamian government brought me back to Nassau four more times and they formally accepted Total Communication (T.C.).

In 1974 I was invited to implement T.C. in the Philippines by lecturing, meeting, and working with parents of oral-trained deaf children, teachers, audiologists, college professors, and government people. After a week of successful seminars at De La Salle University, I went to the Peace Corps Headquarters in Manila to propose the first deaf Peace Corps program for deaf volunteer teachers. During the trip back to Washington, D.C., I stopped over in Southeast Asia and the Middle East, where I introduced the combined method and alleviated widely held fears that signing would prevent deaf children from speaking.

In the 1970s, most deaf children around the world attended oral schools—schools where sign language was forbidden and never taught. When I visited a school in Chile, the principal bluntly ordered me not to sign while I was in the classrooms. Slowly, though, some countries, like Iran, Thailand, the Philippines, and several African colonies, began to question the reliability of oral-only training. Since the Commonwealth countries were dominated by England, Manchester University trained all teachers of the deaf in the rigid oral philosophy. When I arrived in Trinidad, the principal was at first doubtful about Total Communication, but he permitted me to give it a try. He was amazed that his pupils' rate of learning accelerated through the combined method. The following year, he attended the Commonwealth Convention in Manchester, where he highly recommended T.C. to teachers from India and other countries.

By 1975 I was receiving a flood of invitations, so I asked Gallaudet College for a leave of absence for the year 1976. The Gallaudet College

Alumni Association (GCAA) and some Gallaudet faculty and staff members generously contributed to my travel fund through the help of Donna Chitwood, the editor of GCAA's publication, and each country provided a place for me to stay while I lectured about the need for implementing signing in classrooms and worked with the teachers and principals. Before I left, I discussed the Total Communication philosophy with Roy Holcomb, who was known as the Father of Total Communication, and he gave me his full support and plenty of advice.

I began my journey in January 1976. I brought along *A Basic Course in Manual Communication* (Silver Spring, Md.: National Association of the Deaf, 1973), which is commonly referred to as the "ABC book." It was so effective and so popular that all the non-English-speaking schools I visited had this book translated. They wanted to incorporate at least 400 to 500 American signs in their own signing vocabularies for the sake of breaking down the communication barriers between countries. My main message was the same in every country: The happiness of the children should come first, their education second, and their speech third.

❧

I went to Dulles airport outside of Washington, D.C., on a snowy January day. My itinerary alone promised adventure—Iran, India, Ceylon, Thailand, Malaysia, Singapore, Hong Kong, Taiwan, the Philippines, Australia, Ethiopia, Kenya, Mozambique, Swaziland, South Africa, Madagascar, Tanzania, and Nigeria. To supplement my lectures in all these places, I carried a frightfully heavy briefcase and shoulder bag, which were stuffed full of material. I had four reels of 16 mm. film, pamphlets and papers about the Model Secondary School for the Deaf (MSSD), Gallaudet, Total Communication, and Dr. David Denton who was then the superintendent of the Maryland School for the Deaf. I also carried Dr. Richard Cornett's drill book and instructions on Cued Speech, *A Basic Course in Sign Language*, and a transcript of a marvelous lecture that Dr. Merrill had given in Japan titled "New Measures of Credibility." I felt that each one of these items was necessary for my journey but the thought of lugging them all reduced me to a quaking form. Luckily, I had my faithful suitcase porter so I was able to pile everything on to it and roll it all the way to my plane.

The plane took off during a snowstorm and arrived in a sunny and warm London a few hours later. My heart skipped a beat to see the Thames and other familiar landmarks. Incredible!

❦

Two weeks prior to my departure, two strange incidents occurred. For one year prior to my trip, I did yoga exercises to learn how to sit with my legs crossed so that I could blend in with people in other countries who traditionally sit cross-legged. I also wanted to build up my endurance for discomfort and hardship. One day, while in the midst of a deep meditation, I felt my heart stop beating and saw a blinding flash behind my closed eyes. I struggled to open my eyes and when I did, I looked around, feeling like a different person. That feeling persisted throughout the whole year until the day I left Africa. I felt something was following me, protecting and guiding me.

The second strange event happened when I, on a friend's recommendation, sent my date, time, and location of my birth, and nothing else to an astrology center in Ceylon. Up until then, I hadn't believed in astrology. But three days before I was to leave America, I received the report and was astounded to read the following:

> You are now under Rahu, which indicates Muslims. Therefore you are traveling to a country predominated by Muslims. Success in that direction is shown. You will become highly religious during this period.
>
> This is the most favourable period for you. You will have happy promotions and favourable services. Wherever you go you will be honoured and respected and such recognitions will be in foreign countries rather than in your motherland.
>
> Many travels are shown. You will be associated with good people such as professors, bankers, legislators and churchly people. Most of your efforts will be brought to a successful end.
>
> Being a poisonous planet, acid poisoning is likely, Beware of reptiles and electricity, as dangers from same are shown.

After a one-hour–and-a-half wait at Heathrow, I effortlessly wheeled my heavy load to the plane while other Iran-bound passengers looked on enviously as they struggled with their overloaded bags. The moment I sat down in my seat on the plane, I fell asleep and did not feel the take-off nor behold my beloved London from the skies.

Iran

Tehran, January 12

In Tehran, Iran, I stayed with Julia Samii, an American married to an Iranian and a good friend with whom I had stayed for more than one month during my 1974 trip. One night, after writing in my journal while sitting cross-legged on a bronze Persian stool, I switched off the light in their television room and walked down the stairs in the dark. Only faint moonbeams shone from the foyer to light my way. Thinking the large landing at the end of the steps was the floor, I stumbled and felt a shooting pain in my foot. Gritting my teeth, I hobbled to a kitchen chair to sit and check my foot. The chair had a broken leg and collapsed; I found myself sprawled on the floor counting the stars. The speed with which Julia arrived from the upstairs bedroom amazed me. I insisted that my injuries were nothing serious. I had shown her my horoscope before that evening (which she hadn't believed), but now she exclaimed, "Your horoscope says beware of electricity!" I shrugged my shoulders and said, "It just happened." It took all of my stamina to hobble across the yard to the guest house.

The next morning, Julia had her chauffeur drive me to a hospital to have my foot x-rayed. The doctor wrote in Farsi and the nurse spoke Farsi. I felt ignorant and wished Julia were there to interpret. The doctor handed me crutches but I refused them because I had my pride and was determined to get around on my own. After the examination, I sat stoically in the waiting room with an elastic bandage around my elevated foot and waited for Julia's chauffeur to return to pick me up. Julia and her co-coordinators had to reschedule the programs I was to speak at and when I did lecture, they made sure I had my foot propped up on a stool at every event.

Julia worked with Miss Samineh Baghcheban, the director of the National Organization for the Welfare of the Deaf and the director of two Baghcheban Schools for the Deaf in Iran and she brought me to meet her during my stay in Tehran. Samineh explained that she had become involved with deaf people because of her father, the late Jabbar Esgarzadeh. He had been born in Erivan, Russia, in 1884. As an adult, he became a newspaper reporter and published several magazines. During the Russian Revolutionary War, he returned to Tabriz in northwest Iran,

where he had family, and became a teacher. He earned a reputation as a good teacher who developed new and more efficient methods of teaching his young pupils. One day, he noticed that three deaf brothers had followed his hearing pupils into the classroom and were cowering in a far corner. At that time in Iran, deaf children didn't go to school and most people thought they couldn't be educated. The parents of these boys, however, had hoped that by sending them along with their hearing brothers, they might learn a bit. Their confused eyes touched his heart, so he pantomimed all his stories, inspiring the deaf boys to smile. Afterward, the memory of the looks in their eyes continued to haunt him, so he began using his spare time to find ways to communicate with them.

Jabbar went on to found Iran's first kindergarten for deaf children and changed his name to Baghcheban, which in Persian means *gardener*, because, as he said, "If there must be a name for one who teaches little children, let me be called Baghcheban." These children were his little flowers and he was determined to help them grow. To aid that growth, he developed a phonetic hand alphabet, which evolved into Iranian Cued Speech.

He was always zealous and enthusiastic about teaching but his thick beard and rough-looking face often frightened the tiny deaf children. When his daughter Samineh was a small child, he would have her approach the terrified pupils and press her small hands to their faces. They would open their eyes at her soft touch and then she encouraged them to lipread Jabbar.

By the time Jabbar passed away at the age of eighty-two, seven years before my arrival in Iran, his little shabby classroom had expanded to a modern three-story building that accommodated 210 pupils and 41 teachers, administrators, and administrative aides. In 1975, the school, in cooperation with the local teachers college, began offering a nonofficial teacher-training course in educating deaf children. It was Samineh's dream to see branch schools open in other parts of Iran.

Samineh had gotten her master's degree in deaf education and had gone to the teacher-training program at the Clarke School for the Deaf, the leading oralist school in the United States. She firmly believed in oralism aided by Cued Speech and was more than ready to accept two signed languages for all ages. But she also had a keen interest in the latest teaching method: Total Communication.

I learned that after my 1974 visit, much controversy ensued about the kind of sign language to adopt in Iran, but now Total Communication was here to stay. Iran was the first country to prefer calling signs "English signs" instead of "American signs." Deaf Iranians argued, "We, as international people, speak and write English, not speak or write American." English signs were implemented as the springboard to Farsi signs: both followed a nation's spoken and written language rather than a school's or a community's language. Julia Samii assured me, though, that my work had not been wasted: She said that my presence, with my ability to speak and use sign language, was living evidence that sign language did not take away speech, but rather makes people more expressive. She and Samineh asked me to teach English signs as well as the Total Communication methodology to the Baghcheban School teachers from 8:30 to 11:30 a.m., and the deaf adults from 6 to 7 p.m. throughout my entire stay in Iran. I agreed to do it.

After our meeting with Samineh, Julia and I went to the Parents' Center, which consisted of several preschool classes, an audiology department, a doctor's office, an ear-testing room, an earmold laboratory (where a deaf assistant made earmolds), a waiting room, and a meeting room for parents. Black-cloaked women with their deaf children sometimes traveled two hours or more by bus to this clinic twice a week for parent training with their children under the teachers' supervision. I was told that inbreeding among families in tribes and small had caused deafness to become rampant. There was no law prohibiting marriages between cousins.

In addition to the original school of Samineh's father, we visited the second Baghcheban School for the Deaf, which had been built on land that Farah Pahlavi, the Empress of Iran, had donated. At the school we met Alice Burch, an American, who taught English to deaf Iranians using English signs. English as a second language was being introduced for the first time to the upper-grade students. To the teachers' surprise, the older students began using these signs to communicate with the younger ones in the school.

And to my surprise, Alice's students, who had begun English lessons only three months earlier and attended class for little more than an hour twice a week, were not only quite fluent in English signs, but also able to speak English almost perfectly. How had this been accomplished I

wondered? Alice explained that Farsi had two alphabets: a phonetic alphabet and a script alphabet similar to that of Arabic. Samineh's father had based his manual alphabet on Farsi's phonetic alphabet. So Alice would write an English word on the blackboard, then, using the Farsi phonetic alphabet, she'd write how the English word should be pronounced on the left next to it. An Iranian teacher would write the Farsi translation in script on the other side. I lost no time taking close-up pictures of these three different forms.

Throughout my stay in Iran, I visited, presented lectures, or dined at the National Organization for the Welfare of the Deaf, two other schools for deaf people, a Parents' Center, a vocational and rehabilitation center, and a government compound. Alice frequently accompanied me as my interpreter. Often there were TV cameramen who filmed me while I was being interviewed. At one point, Alice exclaimed with a grin, "They have been introducing you to everybody, even Her Excellency, and they never mentioned my name!" I did my best to field some of the trickier questions diplomatically, such as when one person asked if Iranian deaf children should be sent to an American school for a better education. I answered that the Baghcheban School was very good for the Farsi-speaking children because it was now well on its way toward accepting Total Communication and its teachers were all required to have master's degrees.

When I showed the slides of Kendall School and MSSD to parents, I would point to one showing Mervin Garretson signing with a student in front of a computer and emphasize that he was the Deaf principal of MSSD. I also explained how sign language could enable many deaf people to be promoted to higher positions in their jobs. When I was with Samineh, she would present me as evidence of that, since I was a college professor.

In addition to all my other activities, I had the honor to be invited to the Shah's royal palace. Farah Pahlavi, the Shah's wife and the queen of Iran, was a big supporter of deaf education and rehabilitation and wanted to improve deaf people's lives and opportunities in her country.

When we were first invited to meet Her Excellency, Alice and I worried that we did not have the proper attire. Even in our fanciest clothes,

we looked like ragamuffins compared to the fashionable and sophisticated women accompanying us. Those women eyed one another, each hoping to outdo everyone else with her fashionable attire and hairstyle. I was extremely self-conscious about my moccasins, which were the only pair of shoes I could wear until my sprained foot healed. During the hour we waited for Her Excellency to make her grand entrance, we sipped tea, nibbled pastry, and met numerous VIPs. When she finally entered, flashbulbs popped and heads nodded, and there was much fuss about serving her food and drink. Ghamar, a friend of Julie's who was also there, was determined that I be introduced to the queen. Ghamar pushed through the packed crowd with Alice and me close at her heels. When we finally reached Her Excellency and introduced ourselves, Queen Farah did not seem to notice our humble attire but appeared fascinated with Alice's flying hands.

After our visit to the royal palace, Prime Minister Hoveyda's wife invited Julia and me to a private dinner at her home and a viewing of the then-current American movie *The Sting*.[1] When we arrived for the dinner, the sight of their beautiful mansion left me speechless—walls and stairs were covered with curves and ovals embossed with heavy calligraphy. Curvy lines snaked around the swimming pool, gardens, fences, balustrades, stairs, rooms, windows, and furniture. Heavy crystal chandeliers hung from the ceilings, crystal drinking glasses embedded with gold calligraphy sat on tables, and nineteenth-century Iranian paintings displaying a hint of the influence of early Italian Renaissance paintings (particularly Giotto and Duccio landscapes) decorated the walls. Gold-inlaid plates with heavy gold knives and forks lined the dining table. Our party of eight walked to a long table that was loaded with exotic food—enough to feed 100 people. Guards stood behind us, watching closely so that the golden wares would not be stolen. All I could take from the table was an embossed matchbox that has been stored safely at the Gallaudet Archives.

After the feast, we walked up three flights of curved stairs to a private circular movie room. I sank into a soft plush chair with a huge footstool. Coffee tables laden with fresh fruit, honey with almonds, wine, tea, and more were scattered about. Servants with white gloves glided in and out to tend to our every whim and wish. Women paraded around the room in long evening wear while I tried to look invisible in

my casual attire. But everyone seemed more interested in my speaking ability than my clothes because they had all wrongly believed that deaf people were mute.

꧁

Throughout my stay with the Samii family, Michael, their youngest son, and I developed a close relationship. Whenever Julia and her husband went out, Michael preferred that I stay with him rather than a regular babysitter. He shared the same name, and was the same age as my own grandson, Michael. We played games together, talked, and cuddled. He continually asked me why I was always writing in my journal, and I explained that I wanted to share my experiences with Gallaudet faculty members because they had funded my global journey to campaign about Total Communication.

On the last day before I left for India, he asked me to buy him stamps featuring Jesus Christ, the Virgin Mary, St. Peter, or angels at a stamp shop in each country I visited and give them to him in person when he visited America. He drooled, "I want a milkshake! Soda pop! And pineapple cheesecake! Grape juice! Hawaiian Punch! An American hamburger!" I promised him that he would have all of that during his visit. Then the taxi arrived and I got up to leave. The way Michael looked at me made my heart melt. He said, "I will miss you. I really will miss you!"[2]

India

New Delhi, January 27

I arrived in New Delhi long before dawn in a light drizzle. I breezed through the health and passport sections of customs, but once an inspector saw those reels of film I had packed for my lecture, pandemonium ensued. And after I managed to clear customs, I discovered no one was at the airport to meet me. When they learned this, taxi drivers and porters suddenly crowded around me, but I stubbornly stood my ground until I could find the right person to make a phone call for me. Lack of sleep and all that sudden attention had reduced me to a state of gibbering exhaustion—especially since I had that heavy luggage. Finally, a policeman noticed that these men were hassling me and came to my rescue.

He warned me not to leave the airport until after sunup. I learned later that only two days earlier, a British nurse had taken a taxi after dark and had been murdered. Her dismembered body was discovered stored in the trunk of a car. Exhausted, I lay on the hard dirty bench in the airport to doze with my belongings next to me. When I woke up, I panicked after realizing that my luggage was missing. How could I present lectures and demonstrate films and slides to audiences for many months to come without my materials?

I stared dumbly at the open door of a hangar between the airport and a storage building. For some unknown reason, it looked familiar to me. A hunch prompted me to walk toward the door, cross the alley, meander through rows of shelves to find my luggage tucked away in the back of a shelf. I knew I had never been there, yet I had seen that place!

❧

After fruitless calls to Mr. Gupta, the headmaster of the Government Lady Noyce School for the Deaf, and Dr. Dilip Nandy, general secretary of the Association Indian Federal of the Deaf (AIFD), I hailed a taxi. Just as we pulled out, another Indian man suddenly hopped in next to the driver. The way they exchanged looks made me nervous, and I was about to scream "Stop!" when an airport guard signaled for our taxi to pull up. He ordered the passenger out, checked the driver's ID and the tag on the back of the taxi, and wrote down his name. He looked toward me and saluted with a nod of approval.

When I arrived at the office of the AIFD, a group of deaf assistants gave me a warm and sunny reception. They immediately served me slightly spiced hot tea. Dr. Nandy arrived and handed me a staggering list of programs that were to occur from January 27 through March 17 in New Delhi, Calcutta, Banares, Bombay, Bangalore, Mysore, Hyderabad, and Madras.

For the whole month I was in New Delhi, I visited ministries of education, schools, hospitals, palaces, hovels for the poorest of the poor, and all kinds of residential homes and apartments. I lectured and met with people from all walks of life. Writers and editors bombarded me with questions about my life, my work, my education, and above all, how I, as a deaf person, could talk. Camera flashbulbs popped. Teachers, headmasters, parents, wealthy donors, and government officers demanded, or

asked for, my presence. A number of them doubted my deafness, so I had to write to Hortense Auerbach, my chair at Gallaudet, and ask her to rush me a copy of my audiology chart as evidence. I talked and talked until I began to lose my voice. My hostesses were alarmed and prescribed all kinds of remedies lest the audiences think I couldn't speak.

India's shops, offices, schools, and public buildings displayed pictures of the national leader: Indira Gandhi. There were posters everywhere with her picture and the motto: "She stood between order and chaos. She saved the Republic." Like the Empress of Iran, Prime Minister Indira Gandhi exhibited a keen interest in the welfare of deaf people.

That evening of January 29, Mr. Gupta surprised me with a request: He asked if I could teach sign language to his school's forty teachers in ten days. I agreed lickety-split, but after I gave it more thought, I pointed out some possible problems. A group of forty people was too big for a manageable class, the time was too short, and the teachers had no textbooks to practice with at home. I had only one copy of NAD's ABC book. It's better than nothing, he said, and his teachers were enthusiastic. I accepted. I had to pinch myself. It was beyond my wildest dreams! We were taking the first solid step forward to accepted signing in India.

January 31

I took a motor scooter taxi to the Government Lady Noyce School where the first sign language class was to be conducted, probably the first ever in the whole of India. Some teachers came on time, some arrived late, but all responded enthusiastically regardless of my misgivings about the lack of textbooks. Mr. Gupta invited me to the schoolyard where all the teachers and children gathered for a mass prayer. A male teacher gestured for the children to stamp their feet loudly first apart then together in a military style. Then all bowed their heads in prayer.

I have seen "the deepest of the private lives of the foreigners." India's customs and cultures were often confusing to me. I occasionally forgot that sometimes their gestures might mean something entirely different to what I was used to. In India, I once hailed a taxi and asked the driver if I could get in. He nodded his head, and when I was just about to climb in, he roared angrily. It dawned upon me that his nodding head meant "No."

On February 2 I wrote

It would cost me a mere 60 pais for a bus ride of over sixteen kilometers from South Delhi to the northern extension; but after I waited twenty minutes in the cold morning, a bus came with so many passengers that I could not get on. It was a good thing that my host Lawyer Ahuja had written down the Hindi for Raj Ghat so that I could show it to a two-wheeler taxi driver. It cost me 6 rupees 40 pais or about 70 cents (8 rupees and 70 pais equals 1 dollar), but riding with the ringside view was very interesting. We rode by mud abodes, brick hovels, and straw-matted lean-tos or tents with many Indians still sleeping.

❧

One day, while walking to sign language class, I decided to try to find a back road to the Government Lady Noyce School. I took a wrong turn into a narrow alley lined with small hovels. Realizing my mistake but having too much pride to back out, I went through the labyrinth and became the focus of every person who lived there on next to nothing. The people were not hostile but appeared genuinely surprised to see me in that location. Many readily offered assistance in pointing out the right direction, yet three times I entered the wrong courtyard or arrived at a dead end where half-naked, shivering children followed me. I had to be careful not to step on fresh human feces in the alleys. Skeletal, lice-infested dogs wobbled weakly by and tore at my heart.

Finally I arrived at the school and was surprised to see that the class size had doubled. Some deaf children walked in timidly and sat behind or alongside their teachers. Out of the corners of my eyes, I noticed how quickly these children, all smiles and sparkling eyes, picked up sign language. Despite the fact that they had no books, they remembered what I had taught them last Saturday.

In early February, I met Prime Minister Indira Gandhi. Her small, delicate stature surprised me after seeing all of the pictures showing her as a tall monumental figure. She looked thin and tired, though her countenance indicated a strong will and determination. She held my hand and said, "Thank you for helping deaf children." After my photograph with the Prime Minister appeared in the national newspapers, people began to recognize me everywhere I went.

At my meeting with Indira Gandhi.

I was staying at the YWCA (at fifty cents per night) in the factory region. One day, I noticed the nearby Vishwaytan Yoghsnram, Yoga Research Hospital. I realized I wanted to do some yoga exercises, so I visited the hospital and met with a Dr. Shards. To my amazement, when I arrived at his office he was not in a yoga position on the floor, but seated behind an executive desk and was very well dressed. He was equally startled by my appearance and my deafness. He asked about my health problems by writing on a piece of paper. I replied that I had no problems and wanted a convenient place to exercise. Because of my good health, he rejected me as a patient. So I quickly added, "My ears have problems and I cannot hear." He then admitted me as a patient and asked me to be at the hospital at 6:15 a.m. the next day.

I argued with myself all night—should I or should I not go? Finally my curiosity got the best of me. Woozy from getting up in the cold, misty morning, I walked briskly through the deserted alleys, past warehouses and factories, until I came to the hospital grounds and met a group of warmly clad men and women meditating or practicing yoga. I was led to Dr. Sharda who was dressed in white balloon-like trousers

and a long white tunic. He also wore a heavy gray cloak and a colorful woolen cap. He looked at me, and seemed disappointed I was there. Apparently he had hoped I would chicken out. He reluctantly signaled to his assistant, circling his finger around his ear like "crazy" to indicate my deafness.

Dr. Hioshi, the assistant, gesticulated for me to pick up an odd-looking tin pot. He instructed me to wash the little pot and fill it with hot water from a small tank. He then told me to drink four pots of hot water! As I drank, he kept pushing me down into a squatting position. After the third pot of water, I called it quits since I was close to retching, which was just what he wanted me to do for this purification exercise. He led me to a circular pit over which other clients were vomiting water. I obeyed but hated that ritual of retching. After a job well done, he led me back, gesturing for me to fill one more pot. He then took me to a large wicker basket, pulled out something white, and put it in my pot. I then noticed an Indian next to me swallowing a long white strip of gauze.

Horror seized me. That, I could never do. He pushed me down into a squatting position, but I deftly switched to kneeling instead. He motioned for me to put the spout of the pot into one nostril. When I turned my head sideways, water ran out through the other nostril, much to my surprise. After using up half the water, I did the same thing to the other nostril.

Dr. Hitoshi then led me indoors to a cold room with windows that had no glass or shutters. Yoga exercises in India were a far cry from those in the States . . . and I didn't like them. Instead of gently encouraging me to cross my legs as my yoga instructor back home would do, he forcibly yanked my legs across and nearly pulled my hips out of their sockets. I decided to ask Dr. Sharda if I could perform my own yoga exercises in the afternoon.

Dr. Sharda refused and told me to make my choice: keep up his form of yoga or forget it. I went for the next three mornings, but I avoided the stomach and nostril cleaning rituals by sneaking into the yoga room. The third morning, I was walking confidently to the hospital in the swirling mist under the feebly glowing street lamps. Then suddenly, the lights blinked out and I felt terribly alone.

I was wrong—I wasn't alone! An arm went around my throat in a hard grip, and I felt something sharp against my cheek. To this hour,

I am thankful to Mops, my longtime friend, for inviting me to go with her to a gym in Hyattsville, Md., where the police demonstrated self-defense techniques. Our instructor had emphasized that, if attacked, we should "keep cool." But at first I panicked. Then, recalling the policeman's demonstration and warning to keep cool, I felt for his elbows, which was difficult because he was squeezing my throat. I turned my head sideways and downward slowly to sink my teeth into his arm. He yanked it back while I pushed his elbows up with a hard jerk. I gleefully and bloodthirstily kicked him in his groin. I picked up my now-broken pair of old glasses and raced back to the YWCA. Wasn't my horoscope's warning to beware of electricity true?

All day long and late into the night, I ached from head to toe. I felt as stiff as a ramrod. The next day, I was to meet with the president of India, Fakruddin Ali Ahmed, whose palace made the U.S. Capitol and the White House combined look like they belonged on the island of Lilliput. The interior decoration left me speechless. Even the private gardens impressed me and I have never been fascinated with flowers and plants. Still aching from the attack, I barely managed to wobble into my meeting. The president greeted all of us, saying, "Namaste," but when he saw me, he immediately extended his hand for a warm handshake. He thanked me for coming to his country to help with the Deaf community. We enjoyed an amiable chat and I found myself liking him.

Calcutta

My second visit was with Principal Dhun Adenwalla who had a thirteen-year-old deaf daughter named Dinaz.[3] When I first met Principal Adenwalla, I was waiting for her on the porch of the YWCA. She approached, looked at me questioningly, and asked, "Ms. Parsons, do you use your hands when you talk? I teach only the oral method at my school."

For the sake of her deaf daughter, she founded the private school with thirty pupils ranging in age from three-and-a-half to eighteen years with five teachers. All the students wore hearing aids. Dinaz had already learned a lot: biology, science, physical education, algebra, geometry, history, grammar, and English. Generally in the Middle East, Far East, and Southeast Asia, parents either mollycoddle their deaf children or hide them in shame. Dhun saw differently and taught Dinaz to

be independent in every way. That impressed me to no end. I suggested Dinaz attend Gallaudet College and offered to help her.

Dhun had the children take breaks from oral teaching and do mime. I asked her why. She explained it was strenuous to lipread, and mime let the pupils exercise and act. I replied, "Well then, why not encourage them to use sign language? It's the best remedy." After I left, she thought it over and flew with Dinaz to Bombay to take signing courses.

In Calcutta, I made the usual rounds of lecturing and showing slides and films at schools and auditoriums, confronting the skeptics. Male teachers outnumbered female teachers. When I spoke at the Bengali School for the Deaf, the teachers did not accept my talk and were silent. The headmaster there had been to the Clarke School for the Deaf in 1955, but he felt that those children received a pitiful education because they had no ear phones or hearing aids. Then I visited the Bengal Club for the Deaf where I was honored to be served an Indian supper while all the members stood around the table and watched me eat alone.

Calcutta was dirty and crowded. A deaf couple took me sightseeing to temples where I had to take off my shoes and walk on filthy floors. When we left, beggars crowded around me and a leper held out his fingerless hand. In the streets, men pulled heavy wagons while others pushed from behind. Many people trotted by, pulling rickshaws. A beggar had just died on the sidewalk with his hand up for a coin, and two other beggars ripped his tattered robe off. Traffic snarled. Long stops occurred for cross road clearance. Rain poured—not like cats and dogs, but like allosaurs and dinosaurs.

I gave Dinaz and her teachers a lot of time to think about Total Communication. I was permitted to demonstrate signing and speaking English to the little children. They imitated signing "Goldilocks and the Three Bears" until on the last day, one boy suddenly caught the cue. With his eyes brightening and his face shining, he jumped up, ran to the blackboard, pointed at each word and signed the whole sentence. He was screaming, "I know! I know! I like it! I want it!" That was the turning point. Sign language was accepted at his school.

Banares

No deaf Indian was at the airport to greet me. So, gritting my teeth against my fear, I took a rickshaw to DAK Bungalow, the cheapest

hostel. It was very hot and dry, and on the way, we passed numerous lumbering water buffalo and oxen pulling overloaded wagons, other rickshaws, some buses, very few cars, and even some camels.

My bare-looking bungalow was not appealing. I had no towel, no pillowcase, no sheets, and no toilet paper. I hit the ceiling and demanded all of these things. I was immediately provided with everything but a sheet. I whipped out a gauzy pareau that I had bought in Tahiti and covered the filthy mattress with it.

I wanted to go to the Ganges River and see the religious rites that took place there, but first I had to meet with the father of two deaf boys. I took a long, bumpy, and jarring ride through the hodgepodge streets full of open residences, shops and restaurants, sleeping cattle, sacred cows, and frolicking goats. Many people looked startled to see me riding through that section of the city. The rickshaw boy kept asking people on the street for directions every few blocks in order to locate the house. When we arrived, the father was stunned to see I had come alone. He said his sons searched for me at the airport, different hotels, and eventually DAK where they learned, to their horror, I had already left.

His sons returned, much relieved that I was still in one piece. They invited me to their deaf club, which was a tiny, a mere cubicle. I was the first deaf foreigner they had ever met. All the deaf men stood in the alley, crowded around me while the club president sat on the cubicle's floor. Not one woman was present. Why? The women could go out only in the daytime.

The club members asked me to demonstrate American signs. I asked each of them what they did for a living, and they responded: watch maker, painter, artist, bus mechanic, electrician, printer, jeweler, and sari makers.

Another day, a deaf friend and I meandered through mazes of narrow, crooked alleys, dark halls and rooms, little shops, and temples. Beggars followed us like leeches. A leper held out handless arms. A little boy exposed his hunched back with crooked spine. Peddlers hawked their wares at me, holding out fingers for six rupees, then five, then four. When we got on a bus and it began to pull out, one beggar cajoled me into giving him three rupees.

During my stay one rickshaw driver in particular became attached to me and saw to it that I always rode on his rickshaw and was well cared

for. "I like you," he said. On the last day, he made sure I reached the airport on time, and I gave him a generous tip, enough for him to live on for a month.

Bombay

Then I was off to Bombay for a month-long whirlwind of visits, lectures, and so forth, which Behroz Vasha, my gracious hostess, had arranged.[4] She was a die-hard oralist, a speech therapist, and a director of a model oral school who I had met two years earlier. She whisked me from the airport to her apartment, which was cooled by fans. She showed me an agonizingly long list of programs and schedules that nearly floored me. Despite that, I was delighted. Two years ago, I had failed to convince her of Total Communication's value but she had been impressed by my speaking ability. I had some difficulty reading her lips because of her accent. She drilled me in the use of the speech sound and also corrected my pronunciation. I wailed, "But I have just been corrected on these very words." She replied, "You are in India and I know the right pronunciation." I'd had my speech corrected in the United States, the Bahamas, Trinidad, and then India—not to mention Australia. I said I'd return home with a heavy British accent, and she replied, "Why not? You're a citizen of the world!"

One afternoon when Behroz went to the market, I wanted to take a bath, but there was no water heater. As a guest, it was a taboo for me to get my own pail, pour water in it, set it on the stove until it was steaming hot, and then lug it to a bathroom where I would squat and douse water over my body. It was a servant's chore to prepare a hot bath. Since the Indian servant could only speak Hindi, I gestured that I wanted a bath by clenching my fists and rubbing them up and down my sides. He bowed out to the kitchen, and I made myself comfortable to read and wait for the water to steam.

Presently my hostess returned, her sari flowing gracefully after her, and asked, "Do you want broth?" I shook my head with a smile. (I didn't like soup and the day was sweltering.) She left. The servant entered a minute later with a perplexed look on his face. He gestured, his fists moving up and down for bath. I nodded and started to get up. He waved his hands that he was not ready and bowed out of the room.

In a matter of time, she sailed in, her sari flying behind her. "Do you want broth?" "No," I replied lamely. This same scenario happened two more times until she, livid with fury at her servant's lack of understanding, dragged him into the room by his ear. He cowered, near tears. She said, "He insisted that you wanted broth."

"Oh! Oh! I want a bath." She stood frozen with shock on her face. This convinced her to learn fingerspelling because it was easier to communicate using this method and avoid misunderstandings because of our varying accents. She then recognized the benefit of Total Communication.

I returned to Bombay after Behroz had arranged many presentations so that I could convince people to add Total Communication with speech therapy. But talking all the time disastrously caused me to develop acute laryngitis several times. She called her doctor, and he prescribed a remedy that helped me recover temporarily. She also asked her Parsee friends for throat remedies. Behroz was worried because she needed me as proof that sign language didn't prevent deaf people from using their voices. While I was in bed recuperating, Behroz explained that she and other friends in the city were descendants of Parsees-Zoroastrians who fled from Persia to Bombay in the seventh century. The Parsees were only a fraction, about one-third of one percent of India's 500 million people. The Hindus made up about 85 percent.

In Persia, centuries ago, the Parsees had respect for the sacred soil and believed that no decaying flesh should spoil it. Their dead had been eaten by vultures for centuries. In Bombay, the Parsees built the Tower of Silence on which their dead were placed. Behroz pointed it out to me while we were walking in the hanging gardens, and I could see vultures circling above ready to swoop down. Bodies of men, women, and children were laid out, often with the bones broken up, on slats so the cleaned bones would fall through to pits where they turned to dust. Water from springs washed the dust back into the earth. The thought of the vultures gave me an uneasy feeling and, with some hesitation, I asked one of the Parsees how she felt about it. The reply was, "Oh, that's nothing. It's so quick."

I appeared on both the TV news and in the *Times of India* (a nationwide newspaper), which caught the attention of the governor of Ali. He

was inspired to call the Society for Administration of Rehabilitation and Relief to collaborate on starting a training course for teachers of the deaf. He had a committee member from the Society interview me. I was also asked to return in August to assist with the teaching of 400 American signs to the teachers and deaf adults.

I lost my voice a dozen times from talking at schools, auditoriums, clinics, hospitals, United States Information Services, and other places. I lectured to standing-room-only audiences and visited many schools for deaf people. Word about my talks had circulated among the Indians, so toward the end of my visit, the audience had doubled. On the last day, Behroz was offered funding for a model school!

One day, a prominent Indian gentleman phoned Behroz, asking if he could have the honor to treat me to dinner. I wanted to rest but she persisted, saying he was the most affluent man in India and could give a huge endowment for her school. Reluctantly I went out.

He tried to make me feel at home by opening the door for me to pass instead of using the Indian custom of women following the men. He pulled out my chair for me at the restaurant. He ordered wine, which was an unheard thing of in India, raised a glass of wine to toast, and asked, "Will you sleep with me?" I was petrified. I thought he must have overdone the American custom. I said nothing and kept a poker face.

After he escorted me back to Behroz's home, I screamed at her, "He is NOT a gentleman like you said. He was brazen. He had the nerve to ask me to SLEEP with him!" She wouldn't believe me and phoned him. Then she looked at me with a mixed expression on her face and said, "He mispronounced. He was trying to say, 'Will you SIP with me?'"

❧

Dorothy Souza, who was my friend, interpreter, and escort, was very dedicated to teaching deaf children. She took me sightseeing during our spare time. Instead of going to historical landmarks, she took me to Bombay's dark side. She said, "I know you would go anywhere and not be afraid." When we walked over the train bridge, she pointed out Dhobi Ghat, an outdoor laundry with separate water tanks, each tended by one man. Often the same tank had been tended by the same family through generations. Each man took a huge pile of laundry to

his tank. Squatting, he soaked and then washed them by pounding them on the ground with a rhythmic swing over his head. He rinsed each article in a community tank and hung it to dry over a big dead tree trunk, or spread it on the grass along the road. Imagine dust dancing on them as cars roared or trucks rumbled by!

After making me swear not to tell Behroz or anyone else, Dorothy also took me to the "Street of Slave Girls" where very young girls—nine to twelve years old—were sold into slavery by their parents as "entertainment" for men. As in China, it was customary for poorer parents to murder baby girls if they thought the girls might be an economic drain on the family. As a result, there were many unmarried men who couldn't find "suitable" mates and instead sought out prostitutes. When newly arrived at a flesh factory, the girls were imprisoned behind bars where male customers paid the "lords" of the bordellos for their services.

Once these girls became accustomed to this life, they would sit on the outside steps in heavy makeup, colorful attire, and flashy baubles. Or they picked up men as they rode in decorated buggies pulled by prancing white horses. Then they paired off to brothels beyond the iron bars. I managed to snap two pictures of the girls without being caught and reprimanded by the "lords."

Dorothy brought me to this street to show me a twelve-year-old deaf girl who was enslaved.[5] However, the girl was allowed to attend a Christian church. Unfortunately, one of the lords spotted me with my camera and ordered us out of the area.

Hyderabad

Hyderabad was dominated by Muslim culture—Muslim languages, mosques, temples, hooded black shawls on women, Muslims customs, Muslim food, Muslim this and that. I had stepped into a different world—the Persian world. This picturesque city had beautiful public buildings built in Arabic, Persian, and Moorish styles. It made me feel as if I was in fairy land.

My presentations and lectures were different in Hyderabad because of the large percentage of deaf adults and teachers in the audiences. I gestured, pantomimed, and fingerspelled using the manual alphabet and earned deafening applause.

Wanting to treat me to a curd-shake, my deaf hosts took me to a bazaar that was cluttered with sidewalk shops full of glass bangles, filigreed silver and gold, perfumed oils, jasmine soap, and exotic incense. When we came to the man who prepared the shakes, my stomach quailed at the sight of him. He was sitting on the floor with his feet among the shake ingredients: butter, milk, water, curds, and sugar, which were covered with crawling flies. Not wanting to offend my hosts, I managed to down the drink, which I thought of as a "fly shake."

There were many people with deformities in Hyderabad. One day, a boy of about ten came to me with a begging hand extended. I nearly fainted when I looked into his face. His eyelids drooped to his cheeks, his lips hung over his chin, and skin rippled all over his face. He had to pull his eyelids up to see. My hostess gave him a coin without looking at his face. There were also large numbers of people walking on all fours like monkeys. It was said that they were born with "locked hips." My hostess explained that these deformities were either the result of intermarriage among family members or venereal disease in the last stages. Sex and venereal clinics were everywhere, but many Indians refused to go until it was too late.

Mysore City

When I arrived at Bangalore airport, I decided to take a cab to my next destination. Once again, a seedy-looking man got into the taxi's front passenger seat after me. I was too sick to protest, but a policeman saw my taxi and stopped it. He ordered the man to get out. We then drove to a convent where Miss Manohara, principal of the Mysore School for the Deaf, welcomed me. She was going to accompany me to her school in Mysore City.

She persuaded me to go into Mysore City by bus. Unhappily, I stood on the smelly, overcrowded bus. When we arrived in Mysore City, Miss Manohara hailed a buggy drawn by a small donkey, and we began a whirlwind of sightseeing, which included a Gothic cathedral, cream yellow municipal buildings, hospitals, offices, and institutes built in the style of grand palaces. We also saw the Mysore Palace with its many domes, colonnades, arches, turrets, and a central tower.

At every temple and statue of a goddess we encountered, Miss Manohara had to stop and pray. She'd turn around three times, bow,

make circles with her hands, and then touch her forehead to the ground. At one point, I decided I didn't want to follow her any farther, so I sat on a garden bench and watched monkeys swing from tree to tree while she continued this ritual over and over again.

I suddenly had a strange thought. Why was this bench in the middle of overgrown grass? I asked her, "Are there snakes around here?" She shook her head. A few moments later I realized I thought this meant "No" when in fact it meant "Yes," and I practically flew out to the open path.

By nightfall, we finally reached her school. To my dismay, she continued to worship her goddesses, praying, circling, and touching aromatic petals of flowers. A lantern shone eerily, throwing off our long, grotesque shadows. We went into the school and into her office where, one by one, deaf boys came stealthily in, and I introduced myself to them. The boys were experts at gestures and had never been taught to speak. They even used American fingerspelling. They all looked bright-eyed, alert, and happy—a contrast to most of the deaf oral children I'd seen in India who seemed lackluster and depressed. One ten-year-old boy suffered the same malady that I had seen in Hyderabad—it was commonly called "Monkey's Walk." He explained that he was born with his hip joints not functioning and walked on all fours, using shoes for his hands and going barefoot. Despite his condition, he smiled and smiled, and joined the other boys crowding around me and asking me many questions.

At last, at last, at last, it was bedtime. My host apologized for the state of her humble, bare-looking house. But I told her, "This is better than many places I've been to." (I never say that I've been to worse places.) She warned me to check the floor toilet by squatting over it with a flashlight. "Why?" I asked. "Just in case there is a cobra inside!" she warned. When I went to use it, it took all of my willpower to balance over it, squatting on wobbly legs.

Then I insisted I sleep on the floor since she was a few years my senior and her house had only one tiny bed. She nodded "No" (and added "Cobra goes up the crack of the floor"). So she put two small low tables together with a chair at both ends, and I slept atop that; it was the most miserable night because the chairs kept sliding out, which caused the tables to separate. Numerous times throughout the night, I'd have to pull everything together again.

During my three-day visit to this city, I was so ill with an intestinal ailment that I barely made it through my visits and lectures. But I managed to rest between the presentations and soldiered on. Strangely, I never visited inside Miss Manohara's school.

Madras

Miss Boyd, the Irish principal of the Madras School for the Deaf, generously fed me with familiar food: boiled potatoes, cucumbers, raw carrots, tomatoes, lettuce, whole wheat bread, and peanut butter. It was heavenly not to suffer any more spicy, unsavory, or pungent dishes (up until then I had gamely been trying to eat the native food of each region but found that most of those dishes didn't agree with me). And I could read her lips easily. Although she was receptive to allowing sign language in classrooms, she warned me that there would be a strong resistance from the teachers at Little Woodford, a small and very strictly oral school.

Miss Boyd was right about the resistance. During my visit to Little Woodford, I was forbidden to take photographs. The eyes of the preschool children looked tired and dull. I had seen the same exhausted looks when I visited the Clarke School for the Deaf back in the States. But at Little Woodford, the principal was astounded that I spoke well. She dragged me from classroom to another, saying, "She speaks very well. You can do that, too."

I resisted telling the principal that I ALSO use sign language, but I saved that argument until she invited me to present my talk to her pupils' parents the next evening. I agreed but, to her chagrin, I deliberately signed simultaneously with my speech at the presentation. The principal hopped up, picked up a drum, and banged on it. She strutted back and forth between the audience and me. I complained to Miss Boyd about her discourteous behavior. Miss Boyd just grinned from ear to ear and said, "You had her rattled! You got those parents asking me to set up tonight's meeting so they can hear you talk and ask you questions!"

I was then better prepared to confront the hostile reactions from the teachers at the next presentation after I showed the film depicting Gallaudet students signing in the classroom. The teachers hotly argued that sign language would confuse deaf children and diminish their abilities to lipread and speak. They also believed that sign language was not

a valid method of communication with hearing people, would not improve the family relationship, and would retard the children's learning.

One pointed out, "The deaf would be too busy signing to each other, and we wouldn't know what they were talking about." I smiled, "That is EXACTLY how we, the deaf, have been left out throughout our lives with your talking to each other, and we don't know what you are talking about." I sensed that the audience was shocked at my response.

Another school in Madras, however, warmly welcomed me. Sister Rita, the headmistress of the Little Flower Convent school, arranged my presentation for the next day. Forty attractive young teachers attended and were receptive to using Total Communication. As I walked down the stairs of the three-story school, a nine-year-old deaf boy stopped me and gestured, asking if it was true I used sign language. I nodded. He put his arms around my waist and signed, "I love you."

In the late afternoon, I decided to walk on the nearby beach. Miss Boyd wouldn't let me go alone and sent two girls to accompany me. Imagine the girls, eleven and twelve years old, chaperoning me! They bombarded me with questions about American deaf children, which I enjoyed tremendously. This was also my first opportunity to see the Indian fishermen using curved, raft-like *kattamavar* boats that could fold after the use, while their wives sold fish from wicker baskets. Most of the fishermen shamelessly wore nothing but their birthday suits as they pulled their boats to the sea.

Miss Boyd had arranged for me to speak at six training centers for deaf adults, a parents' association (many parents were receptive to signing and wanted to send their children to Gallaudet), and the Deaf club, with some sightseeing squeezed in over five days.

On the last day, Miss Boyd and I reminisced over the successes and failures of the programs and discussed the different schools all over India. She mentioned that she felt Mysore City School for the Deaf was one of the worst and most depressing. Could that be the reason Miss Manohara maneuvered me away from a classroom visit? Had she been too ashamed to allow me to see the inside of the school? Yet I pointed out that those children were granted the heavenly gift to sign and fingerspell, and the ones I had met outside the school had looked happy, regardless of whether their school lacked the proper facilities.

We bade each other a fond farewell and I went to the airport in a taxi, which got a flat tire en route. I barely made it in time to catch my plane. I rushed to the counter and was told, "Airport tax. Fifteen rupees, please." I fished the money out and an airport worker stamped my boarding pass. An inspector at the passport and visa desk looked at my visa and then at me as though I were an alien caught in the act of conducting a terrible felony. He passed it to another inspector who also looked at me suspiciously. I cringed to learn that my visa had expired and I had overstayed twenty days in India. It was a nightmare. My passport was confiscated, and the officer ordered me to be sent to jail! I quickly showed them the newspaper clipping with the photograph of me meeting Indira Gandhi and I was then spared from being hauled off to jail.

I frantically made a phone call to Miss Boyd while my plane to Ceylon took off without me. An immigrant officer was merciless, blasting orders through his thick moustache and gesturing for me to return to the city's main immigrant office. My airport tax was refunded, my boarding pass was returned, and my plane ticket was stapled back to its original place. I filled out four long pages of reasons, declarations, passport numbers, on and on. Finally, I met with the top director of immigration who sneered at me. I showed him the address of the Madras School for the Deaf, so I was permitted to return there to wait for the next plane to Colombo, Ceylon. I sent a cable explaining the delay to Mr. Cooray, headmaster of the first school for the deaf in Ceylon I was to visit. Miss Boyd and I spent the rest of the day discussing teaching methods, maladies, taxi drivers, horoscopes, and everything else under the sun. I told her of my earlier intestinal problems and she warned me to never drink from a glass that had been shared among numerous people because so many people in India suffered from intestinal illnesses.

While waiting at the airport for the next plane, I observed a large tour group of Americans and was not proud of them for their "cock-of-the-walk" behavior, their immoral dress, and the way some of them treated the shopkeepers. It was a small comfort to hear the natives say that the Japanese tourists were the worst (although when I visited Japan, their hospitality, manners, and behavior were excellent), French tourists were the second worst, and the Americans, third.

Ceylon

Colombo, March 18

Once again, I arrived at the airport with no one to meet me but heavy, sultry, equatorial humidity. This time, my prolonged stay in Bombay was the reason. The mail service was frightfully slow in reaching my international hosts, and Principal Cooray apparently never received my telegram and didn't know when I would be arriving. With the help of an airline agent, I called Principal Cooray, who suggested I take a taxi to Mount Lavinia—a thirty-six-mile ride. It was past midnight and no taxis were available, so the agent found an ordinary man to take me in his old car. The agent assured me it was safe, but my knees knocked in fear during the entire ride.

The long shadowy road was lined with trees of bananas, papayas, mangoes, and breadfruit and exuded loneliness and isolation. My stomach was tight. The driver simply kept his eyes glued to the road until we arrived—to my tremendous relief.

Principal Cooray explained that earlier he had brought a van with some schoolchildren to welcome me at the airport. Mrs. Dassanayaka, one of the deaf children's mothers, had prepared a sumptuous dinner for me. When I didn't show up at the airport, they thought I had cancelled the visit.

I stayed at Mrs. Dassanayaka's sprawling plantation house, which was shared in happy harmony by two families—one Catholic and the other Buddhist. Villashini, her deaf daughter, hoped to take the Gallaudet entrance exams at the American embassy and bombarded me with questions.

As in India, it was customary to drink coffee or tea upon rising; except the locals in Ceylon also served me papaya. An hour later, we had breakfast: milk rice, *pittu*, and coconut bread. For our afternoon dinner, we had dhal, snake-gourd, lady fingers, and *mukunu wenna malluri*, although I have no idea what they were. At least they were not spicy. In all my travels, Trinidad had the most abundant varieties of vegetables and fruits, but Ceylon was a close second. This country also reminded me of Tahiti—many people wore sarongs and pareaus as well as saris.

The government school's children, having never seen a white deaf adult, stared and stared at me and refused to return my smiles. They sized me up and gestured behind my back. Undaunted, I emphasized that we were alike in our deafness, if not in our appearance, nationality, or language. The boys began to respond to me first, and by the time I stood on the stage with Mr. Cooray, the children accepted me with waving arms. I then showed the audience the film *Total Communication*. The children were astounded to see deaf white children signing in classrooms. They had been under the impression they were the ONLY deaf children in the world.

As I sat in the auditorium, a plump woman moved to the seat next to me and said, "I am a principal of Little Woodford School and have a deaf daughter. Can you come to visit us?" (Many oral schools are named after Woodford Oral School in England.) She introduced herself as Mrs. Wijetilaka and her daughter as Thushara. In her school, she heavily emphasized speech training as well as reading and writing. Since my heavy itinerary was booked up for the four days I would be in Colombo, Mrs. Wijetilaka persuaded me to stop at her school while en route back to India from Australia in August. Mr. Cooray agreed with her request.

By the third day, I came down with laryngitis so I took a break from my marathon lecturing and went downtown with Mrs. Dassanayaka. The sun climbed to its zenith, increasing the already intolerable heat. Since Mrs. Dassanayaka's car was in the repair shop, we took a bus downtown, which was like traveling in a sauna bath and steam room combined. After we got off the bus, I was tagging along behind Mrs. Dassanayaka when I suddenly felt faint and leaned against the wall. When I recovered and opened my eyes, I found a group of poor people had crowded around me like vultures, waiting for me to collapse so they could grab what I had.

My friend dashed back and took me to a shelter to rest. While there, I observed an extremely poor family of four who had their "homestead" on part of the sidewalk. From a dirty sack, the father took some opened tin cans, garbage wrapped in newspapers, and a small pail of water, which he gave to his wife and two tiny daughters. The mother wiped out the cans with her fingers and held them out for the girls to lick. The girls tore the newspaper bundles apart and ate the garbage with their tiny hands. The father then put the sack on his shoulder and hobbled away

in search of more food thrown in the streets, alleys, or behind restaurants. One girl accidentally spilled water on her filthy, ragged dress, and her mother whipped her with a stick. The older child then began to look for lice in her mother's hair. Further down the sidewalk, four teenage boys lay down for a siesta. They took off their *lungis* (wraparound waist sarongs) and covered their bodies to ward off flies.

Like South America, Ceylon was the land of *mañana,* or *tomorrow.* As a punctual person, I continually had to remind my hostesses and friends to get ready for our appointments. They turned a deaf ear to me. Punctuality meant nothing in Ceylon and I should have realized that it was futile. One day, I rushed through my shower and dressed quickly, only to wait forty-five minutes for the van to pick me up. I should have known better after my years of experience in Tahiti—islanders in the tropics are never prompt.

In a few months, I would return to Ceylon to visit the Little Woodford School run by Mrs. Wijetilaka. Her teaching method was oral but she, like Mrs. Adenwalla, encouraged breaks with games that allowed the children to gesture. Not only did they want me to come back, but I wanted to return to Ceylon.

Thailand

Bangkok, March 23

I was forewarned about Thailand's growing Communist party and its hostility toward Americans, who were being ordered out of the country within four months. Some communists had stomped upon and urinated on American flags. In fact, many Thais who weren't communists were also quietly moving out of their country though most remained in resigned hopelessness. They feared that the royal family would be overthrown within five years. I was also advised not to wear any jewelry because thieves would cut a person's finger to take a ring, tear an earlobe yanking an earring off, or tear skin while pulling off a neck chain.

I again arrived at the airport to find no one waiting for me. Mrs. Suvannus, the principal of the first school I was to visit, had given up waiting for me five minutes before we landed.

I ran into Margot, a French nurse who I had met in Colombo, at the Bangkok airport. She asked if she could join Mrs. Suvannus and me for

the ride to her hotel. But I couldn't guarantee that Mrs. Suvannus would meet me. Margot spotted a couple leaving in a taxi and decided to join them. She hastily apologized with "Be careful. A white woman is a white woman and anything can happen to her." We shook hands and she ran to get in the cab. After a considerable wait, I realized I HAD to take a taxi. I got in one and, once again, another man jumped into the front passenger seat as we pulled out of the airport. I felt queasy with fear. The passenger doffed his cap to me and gestured that he was just getting a ride home. We drove on and on along a long, isolated road in pitch darkness. When both men began to exchange glances and nods, I told myself, "Keep cool."

As the driver was slowing the car down by a ditch, I remembered my speech therapist kidding me about how I could rattle my voice, saying, "It is scary. It sounds like a death rattle." So I rattled my throat and acted like I was dying. The men exchanged frightened glances and the driver flattened the accelerator, driving like a devil to the city. He dumped me at a cheap hotel and didn't collect taxi fare.

The next morning, Principal Suvannus apologized for not waiting any longer and was astounded that I had left the airport by myself. I was just as astounded to see Mr. Niram, an oral-trained teacher, and the schoolchildren using English signs. I visited the school in 1974 and had been surprised to see schoolchildren using some English signs. I learned that two previous principals of the school had attended Gallaudet Normal School and had been taught by Dr. Elizabeth Peet who largely used Clerc's Standard Signs.[6] At first, Mr. Niram had strenuously opposed signing, but after my demonstration in 1974, he had a change of heart and taught himself some signs from the NAD ABC book. He then passed it down to his pupils and discontinued teaching Thai signs because they were not part of a structured language. Mrs. Suvannus wanted me to assist in revising a version of the ABC book with Mr. Niram. She also asked me to present at a weeklong conference in May with teachers from every part of Thailand. She offered to ask the ministry of education to pay for my extra plane fare from the Philippines to Malaysia, but unfortunately I was already committed to being in Hong Kong and Taipei during that time. As it was, my schedule was packed for the four days I was in Thailand. Fortunately for me, I gave only one presentation, which enabled me to rest my tired throat and communicate in sign.

I asked to stay on the school campus and share the girls' dormitory to save the school the expense of my hotel room and food. The school was closing for vacation, but I had the wonderful opportunity to communicate with girls who bombarded me with hundreds of questions. I was surprised to learn that some of them were motherless. The one that intrigued and fascinated me the most was a nine-year-old girl named Wilairat. She was tiny for her age and could pass for a five-year-old. Eagle's Club, a Thai charity, paid for her room and board. She had a peppery, piquant personality with a playful spirit. The older girls, however, ordered her around. Every time they gave her orders, I visualized them saying, "Cinderella, do this," "Cinderella, do that," "Cinderella, Cinderella," so I dubbed her Little Cinderella and held her in a special place in my heart. She, the lonely outcast, was overwhelmingly appreciative when I paid close attention to her conversation.

I was impressed by this school's liberal use of sign language, especially with Mr. Niram teaching the older girls' English signs. For the first time since Bombay, I enjoyed communicating without misunderstandings or groping around to decipher what was being said. The communication among these students was remarkably advanced and more varied than those in the oral schools. Their eyes reflected something I couldn't quite define—a combination of alertness, zest, and brightness.

For two sweltering days, Principal Suvannus had meals brought to Mr. Niram and me at the school meeting room. She also set up two whirring fans and brought lots of cold water and cool washcloths to dab our perspiring faces. Cinderella joyously flitted in and out of the room as a servant and helper throughout our work. In the dining hall, I shared with the deaf employees (cooks, waitresses, housekeepers), I listened to their high praises for their principal and her efforts to upgrade the school. They also spoke highly of Mr. Niram's dedicated teaching. Then they showered me with advice: Don't drink tap water; never ride alone in a taxi; don't ride in a three-wheeled taxi; don't wear jewelry; don't walk through alleys; and so forth.

I asked for their opinions about the differences between Thai and English signs when using spoken Thai as the official language. All

agreed that they preferred the sign language brought by the two former principals from Gallaudet College because English standard sign language was widely used in many countries such as the Philippines, Singapore, and Africa in addition to the United States. Some commented that using Thai signs blocked free communication with deaf people from their neighboring countries as well as within their own country.

On my last day in Bangkok, my friend Yuenyong, whom I had met in Honolulu several years earlier, and his wife Achara took me to the Deaf club earlier than planned. I was dying to run upstairs, take a cold bath, and fall into bed, but I stoically stayed up longer to be with them. At the club, I was surprised to see deaf Thai adults signing fluent English signs, so I had no problem conversing with them. Some of the club members owned small shops in downtown Bangkok and others were peddlers, but all claimed that after they learned English signs, their businesses grew because they could communicate with foreign deaf visitors.

Malaysia

Penang, March 27

Once again, nobody was at the airport to meet me when I arrived in Malaysia. I encountered some delay at the passport section when they questioned me about my planned month's stay. I explained that I had come to help the deaf children. They smiled and wrote down the expiration date, April 27, and explained that I must leave by that deadline. I asked an airline agent to look up the number of Mrs. Yahaya-Isa, who was the principal of the first school for the deaf—the Federation School—I was to visit in Malaysia. He put the call through for me but looked dismayed after a few rings—her five-year-old son had answered the phone and told the agent that his mother was out for the day. So I summoned a taxi driver. The driver knew the location of the school but told me the fare would be $30. I decided to wait until 5:30 when she'd be home, but the driver and the agent said that would be too long a wait. After some arguing, the taxi driver finally agreed to take me for $8.00. The drive was very long and we had to take a car ferry that brought us to the idyllic island of Penang, which reminded me of Trinidad, Hawaii, and Tahiti. Balmy sea breezes made it very comfortable.

Penang was immaculate—it was the second cleanest city I'd ever seen after Singapore. We arrived at the school, a lovely, streamlined compound. All afternoon I wrote reports on various schools in Madras, Ceylon, and Thailand. Suddenly Mrs. Saleena Yahaya-Isa stood before me almost speechless. For weeks, I had looked forward to meeting her because I'd heard such high praise of her work, and I liked her at first sight. We soon discovered, however, that she had never received my February letters from New Delhi. We stared at each other dumbfounded—all her plans for my visit were in May. Should I leave now and come back later? But that would leave me totally unprepared for Hong Kong and Taipei. What about Kuala Lumpur and Singapore? That won't do because they needed plenty of time to prepare for TV, radio, and newspaper interviews. Then I said, "Where there's a will, there's a way." She nodded and added, "But the trouble is, the Ministry has arranged to pay for your stay at a hotel in May." "Hotel?" I said, "I'd prefer staying with deaf girls in a dormitory." She was mollified and asked, "Would you like—not mind—to stay here?" I pointed out the value of living with a principal or teacher in order to speed up the learning of sign language. Her mind was made up. I would stay and she'd get the ball rolling. The following Monday began a two-week vacation for the students, and some of the teachers would be away, but I assured her it would be better than during regular school days. There were thirty-nine teachers in addition to several house parents who were eager to learn. Since I preferred to have no more than twenty in a class, the absent teachers wouldn't matter.

I learned that Mrs. Yahaya-Isa, who preferred to be called Saleena, had opposed the use of sign language for years until one of her students, Eleanor Culas, entered Gallaudet. Saleena protested when Eleanor, home on vacation, used signs, but Eleanor spoke out, saying "I am not ashamed to be deaf. I use sign language so as to let the world know I am deaf." Saleena was shocked by Eleanor's outburst—shocked into rethinking her perception of how deaf students should be educated. When Saleena attended a conference in England sometime later, she was the only one there to stand up and question the concept of pure oralism. She gradually began to meet others, such as Behroz Vasha of Bombay, who felt that a purely oral method was too narrow and limiting. She also heard and was impressed by Dr. Merrill's speech, "New

Measures of Credibility," which he gave at an international meeting in Japan in 1975.

In 1998, I found that, as in many countries, teaching English signs to deaf children had been discontinued in Penang. Saleena was concerned that foreign deaf people who wished to enroll at Gallaudet some years from then would face problems as a result.

When the children returned after their two-week vacation, Saleena introduced me to them in the auditorium, explained the purpose of my visit, and then asked, "Would you like to learn sign language?" "Yes! Yes! Yes!" shot up from them. "All right. She will teach us and we will teach you." Many students peeped through the windows to watch me instruct the teachers during after-school hours and readily picked up many signs. Ruth Pemberton, a visiting British teacher, was amazed at their accelerated learning. She had been attending my class during her ten-day stay and was now convinced of the value of Total Communication in deaf education. She also agreed that Cued Speech should be a part of the teaching method. We enjoyed very amiable relations in spite of our disagreement on which should come first for a very young deaf child, Cued Speech or Signed English. Being deaf, I strongly believed that a deaf child easily learned Signed English, which helped reinforce both written and spoken language. Ruth thought that a deaf child should have spoken language first. She admitted that teaching a child Cued Speech required extensive communication and individual attention. At that point, Saleena threw up her hands and exclaimed, "Not in this school! Simultaneous method of speech and signs will do!"

I never dreamed I'd be so busy. During the first week the children were back, Saleena gave me a desk in the administration office and granted me full authority to enter any classroom unannounced. It was a golden opportunity to observe the actual methods of instruction since the teachers were caught unprepared. At every other school I had visited, I was escorted by the principal or the teachers were notified in advance. What I saw in those unannounced visits dismayed me. The teachers focused excessively on teaching concrete concepts and taught very few abstract concepts. I discussed this with Saleena, then told the teachers not to offer too much assistance to the deaf children, otherwise their independent learning would be stunted. On my next round of visits, I noticed the teachers of classes of very young children were

not happy with my presence. One teacher reasoned that because the children were deaf, they needed extra help. I smiled at her but firmly explained that deaf children could learn and think as well as hearing children. She resisted and I persisted. I was upset but kept it hidden although she was outwardly upset. She quit my sign language class and complained to Saleena, who stood by me and pointed out that the teacher should listen to the words and experience of a person deaf since infancy. The next day, that teacher was back in my class and turned out to be my best student!

I also observed another teacher struggling to hide her frustration while her pupils openly showed frustration. She exclaimed, "I love deaf children but I have trouble getting what I want to teach across to them. It is so tiring." I suggested that she start teaching her class Signed Malaysian. In only four days, a miraculous change took place in her classroom. Not only did the children quickly pick up the signs, but they understood her and were attentive. She exclaimed, "Now I see why Total Communication is the ultimate answer!" I agreed but made it clear that an important part of Total Communication involves having the children write independently rather than only copying words or reading books. That teacher had been one of my star students, and she wanted to take graduate courses at Gallaudet, but the price of tuition dismayed her. In Malaysia, teachers didn't receive much financial aid for their educations, and their own savings were a pittance.

Unfortunately, my busy schedule only allowed me to go sightseeing on Saturday mornings and Sunday afternoons. In addition to the Buddhist temples and panoramic views of Penang, however, I did have an opportunity to observe a traditional wedding.

As in India, the couple saw each other for the first time at the altar. "Is that why she looks so solemn and sad?" I asked. Saleena replied, "No. If she smiles and looks happy, she is thought to be shameless!" Like everybody else, I sat cross-legged on the floor for two hours (and how I thanked my yoga practice). We were each given a tiny foam-rubber basket with an egg in it as a symbol of fertility. More eggs hung along the walls, nestled in the corners and over the doors.

When the wedding feast began, I was grateful to find that Saleena had brought peanut butter sandwiches along for me to eat. She often did that when we were invited to parties because she knew that many

Westerners had a tendency to suffer from intestinal ailments after eating Malaysian cuisine.

I witnessed another fascinating religious ritual, one that is outlawed in its native country, practiced by Tamil Indians living in Malaysia. Devotees fasted and were celibate for a week and prior to enduring having pins, nails, and hooks pierced into their skins. They would drag small wagons or carts with ropes attached to the objects in their skin. Long thin pipes were pierced through one side of the cheek to the other with teeth holding the poles. I could see their skins open up as the pipes went through. There was practically no bleeding. After the considerable march and climb up the steep steps to the temple, all foreign objects were removed from their bodies and faces, and they immediately splashed milk on their skins, which practically closed up, leaving no scars. I asked if it was painful. They said no. The lack of pain was due to faith. As for me, there is no inkling of faith. A mere injection into my veins would reduce me to a bag of shakes.

I felt I needed more time to work with the teachers and had my visa extended until May 27. I continued to teach, attend meetings, lecture, counsel, and encourage teachers and parents. Before I left for Kuala Lumpur, I was interviewed by a reporter from the Northern Malaysian Radio Station and also many newspaper reporters.

Kuala Lumpur

In Kuala Lumpur, I worked mostly with a man named Tan Yap who had been struggling without much success to promote Total Communication since 1964. He had turned to the Peace Corps for help but had no luck, so he formed a committee of influential people and teachers to aid deaf people. The local Lions and Rotary clubs helped with the teachers' salaries. I began my round of interviews, school visits, and presentations but also made appointments to meet with Robert Graulich, the director of the Peace Corps in Malaysia, and the Malaysian deputy prime minister, Dr. Mahathir.

Mr. Graulich was not only attentive to my explanations about the needs and dilemmas of Malaysian deaf people but was also interested in sign language. I showed him a copy of Dr. Merrill's article and pointed out the sentence, "The education of thousands upon thousands of young persons has been prostituted in the name of speech and speechreading."

Talking to the Malaysian Deputy Prime Minister Dr. Mahathir about deaf education.

Mr. Graulich had tea served to us and, after lengthy questioning, offered us at least four deaf volunteers—more than I had asked (I had asked for two). Tan Yap and I looked at each other happily. Afterward, I warned him not to say anything about the volunteers until after my interview with Dr. Mahathir at the Ministry of Education and after the agreement was officially signed.

The meeting with Dr. Mahathir proved to be a great turning point. Amid the popping of flash bulbs and under glaring lights, I entered his office suite amid to shake his hand. I paid no heed to the newsmen and began rattling away like a Model A Ford. I had been warned that he was an extremely busy man and so I was prepared to crowd all my information into ten minutes. However, he seemed to be so interested that the interview lasted more than forty-five minutes, much to my surprise and delight. He beamed when I praised the one Total Communication school as the best and most modern in Asia that I had seen so far. But I quickly followed that by saying the other schools were a national disgrace. What could be done? he asked. I explained why Total Communication as a teaching method was superior to the oral method because it used all forms of communication: lipreading, signing, and

mouthing or speech. I also explained that hearing people shouldn't decide what was best for deaf people without getting them involved in the decision-making. He nodded in agreement and promised that a law would be passed requiring schools to use Total Communication. He had impressed me as a man of his word. Before we left the meeting, much encouraged, I said to him, "Your name will go down in history in education of the deaf." He grinned, "No, it will go UP in history!"

Mrs. Wong, who was a friend of Tan Yap and my hostess in Kuala Lumpur, helped me balance my rigid schedule with my much needed rest. She turned away many interviewers except for one female radio reporter whom she felt was worthwhile. I was sleeping deeply one afternoon when Mrs. Wong gently woke me up, saying someone wanted to see me. "Please, I can't," I begged. But she persisted, explaining, "But this visitor is an Irish father, and his little son is deaf. He drove 300 miles to see you." I catapulted out of the bed and had a long supportive talk with him. We were stunned to discover that his family lived only a short distance from the Federation School, but he couldn't read Malaysian newspapers. He learned of me when he saw me meeting with Dr. Mahathir on television! After our long talk, he left much encouraged and had decided to meet with Saleena.

Singapore

May 8

I was overwhelmed by the huge welcome that awaited me at the airport in Singapore! The airport employees recognized me from my photographs in newspapers and my television interviews and rushed me through the health, passport, and customs sections without delay. Many deaf people had come to greet me. Photographers took my picture as I was presented with a bouquet of orchids. At a reception and press conference held at the airport, deaf people, reporters, hearing people, and especially the most prominent supporters, such as Dr. Goh, a medical doctor who was involved in improving opportunities for deaf people, and Mr. Lee, the influential leader and officer of the Singapore Association of

I had a wonderful reception at the Singapore airport. Heng is on my right in the Gallaudet College t-shirt.

the Deaf, gained my attention in turn. After the meeting, I went outside and was overwhelmed to see well-wishers holding banners printed with my name and the motto "Total Communication around the World."

I stayed at the home of Chin-Heng Lim, who had graduated from Gallaudet in 1975 when the university's teaching policy was Total Communication. I was delighted to see him again and was impressed by his leadership and diligent work in expanding Singapore's association of the deaf and its deaf youth group there. He had already increased the association's membership from 86 to more than 150.

I began my visit to the Singapore School for the Deaf with the Vocational Institute for the Handicapped. I found the facilities pleasant; other aspects of the program, however, were not quite so accommodating. The students were divided into oral and sign sections. The oral section studied English, while the sign section learned Chinese, which created what I described as a "havoc of prejudice" between the two. In the oral classes, the students lacked motivation, comprehension, and knowledge. Once sign language was given to them, however, they changed dramatically. How starved they were for learning!

Meeting with teachers, parents, and representatives from the ministry of education as well as visits to other schools followed. At one meeting, the teachers suddenly began to ask Heng for a few signs, and we all ended up sitting in a huge circle taking up sign language impromptu. I couldn't believe it. Yet I also met with strong resistance from people like Mrs. Neo, principal of the oral section at the vocational school. She wrote on a blackboard, "Not to belittle speech, use Total Communication." Mr. Lee marked off part of the sentence and changed it to the supportive message "Speech and SIGN—Total Communication."

Controversy raged over Total Communication. Some teachers boycotted my first lecture about various sign languages, but they were ordered by Dr. Goh to attend my second talk. They were glum as I showed the differences between conceptual gestures, American Sign Language, and structural signed language. Mr. Lee spoke vehemently, emphasizing the importance of educating deaf people, developing their minds and written language skills, and above all, instilling in them confidence and independence through the help of sign language. Observing the faces of the teachers, I saw some approved, some beamed, some doubted, and a few soured.

With a lucky stroke, a message reached Heng and me. We had a meeting with the deputy minister on Wednesday morning. The advocates of Total Communication rejoiced. We learned afterward that Dr. Goh, a prominent supporter of Total Communication, had performed surgery on the minister's son that morning and had taken the opportunity to tell the minister about me. When we met with the minister, we discussed topics such as recognizing educational graduate work abroad and providing financial aid for people pursuing teacher's certificates. He, having read newspaper stories about me, strongly supported sign language.

For eight days, I visited, talked, lectured, demonstrated, and gave interviews. I went to oral schools, preschools, newspaper offices, associations, and administrations. I showed the films *Total Communication* by Dr. Vernon McKay and *I Hear Your Hands* by Rita Corey over and over. One meeting with a group of teachers lasted three hours. I took over the floor, step by step, line by line. I explained, demonstrated, repeated, and compared the differences among International Sign, school signs, American Sign Language, Combined Method, Structural Signed English, and SEE II. I showed grammar, tense, and syntax in signs.

One by one the teachers began to ask questions, at first with solemn looks, later small smiles, and eventually broad beaming faces. It was a wonderful breakthrough.

I was so busy in Singapore that I lost weight, had a bout of fever, and suffered a sore throat. Whenever I could, I'd grab a few precious breaks to sleep deeply. Heng's mother prescribed Chinese herbs and a bottle of Chinese medicinal oil. At a banquet held on my last weeknight, Mrs. Neo, the Manchester-trained teachers, and others approached me. Mrs. Neo announced that they felt it was important to start learning sign language as soon as possible. Although everyone rejoiced, I would not be convinced until they actually carried it out.

Over the weekend, Heng and I enjoyed our time off by oversleeping, catnapping, and daydreaming. We spent hours signing to our hearts' content. Our ideas and suggestions volleyed back and forth, and from these plans, programs materialized. We also went sightseeing for a bit. I had visited Singapore in 1969. Then it was a quiet city with rickshaws and bicycles; now it had mushroomed into a modern "New York" with skyscrapers and miles of towering apartment buildings. Yet in spite of being overcrowded, the city remained remarkably clean. Family planning was prevalent. Every couple was only allowed to have two children, unless they were two girls (then they were allowed to try once more for a son). If they had more, they had to pay a tax.

To discourage the use of cars, the government levied an annual $1,000 tax on cars used for business and a lesser tax on private cars. During the dry season, the residents cooperated in saving water or they paid an astronomically high price on water brought in from Malaysia. The government also had a powerful clamp on drugs and crime.

At the airport, Heng and I didn't say farewell because I would be back for a day the following month. Instead, he said, "Deafness is a small handicap when we use sign language."

Malaysia

Penang, May 19

I stopped over in Malaysia and spend a week with Saleena before continuing on to Hong Kong. Everyone rejoiced after I told them about

Dr. Mahathir's announcement that a law would be passed allowing Total Communication to be implemented at all schools.

Mrs. Shank, the wife of the Irish man who had driven 300 miles to Kuala Lumpur to see me, brought her deaf seventeen-month-old son to visit. He was such a lively, happy-go-lucky bombshell with very blonde curly hair and alert icy blue eyes. Saleena had heard my talk many times before, but she listened as though it was her first time. Naturally Mrs. Shank asked, "Will he ever learn to talk? Will sign language help him to talk?" I emphasized the importance of giving him knowledge and developing his mind rather than focusing only on his ability to speak. I asked which she would prefer: for her son to speak and sign together and have a good command of written language or for him to receive total speech training, which might give him the ability to speak but with a limited vocabulary. She admitted that her husband's long drive and my willingness to talk with him, despite my fatigue, had been a great help to them. She and her husband decided to take sign language classes.

I revisited a classroom at Saleena's school and was overjoyed to see how much better the children could communicate then when I first visited a few weeks before.[7] They eagerly raised their hands and answered questions in sign language, with or without voice. I asked the teachers, "Now what do you think of sign language in the classroom?" All but one gave positive replies: "For years we searched for an answer to the teaching problem, and sign language is the answer," "Sign language is here to stay," "All teachers must learn sign language," "I've stopped teaching word by word and use whole sentences the children understand," "It's so easy to get it across to them!" "The children have been happy," "They've learnt so much in a short time," "I argued with the professor at teacher's training college. I defended Total Communication in 1974 and got an F for it! [My teacher] should witness our classes!"

The one teacher who was still strongly in favor of the oral method explained that she felt that children were unable to speak and sign simultaneously, and she preferred speech over sign language. This time I was as outwardly upset as she was. I unleashed a tirade, pointing out that deaf children's mental development was wasted when teachers focused solely on speech. "Forget speech," I said. "Don't correct their

speech. Let speech wait. Use sign language all you can and talk simultaneously. Let them read your lips and watch your signing at the same time. I want them to learn, learn, and learn as much as possible so they will be likely to have something to talk about later!" Her face froze. Afterward, Saleena summoned the teacher to her office and tried at length to convince her to use sign language and to listen to a deaf adult like me. I asked Saleena, "Is she Manchester-trained?" "No," Saleena answered, "she was trained in Melbourne." So Australia was no better than England at educating deaf people. I was forewarned that I'd meet strong resistance when I lectured in Australia.

Hong Kong

May 24

How Hong Kong had mushroomed since my earlier visit seven years ago! This magnificent, teeming metropolis was still expanding vertically, since it could no longer expand horizontally. I was welcomed at the airport by Miss Josephine Chan, executive secretary of the Hong Kong Society of the Deaf; Sister Theresa, principal of a convent school; and Mrs. Simon Lee, mother of a deaf son. They whisked me off in a Mercedes-Benz limousine to the Lee's residence.

Miss Chan had warned me that the oralist teachers, except for those at the convent school who were more receptive, might meet me with hostility. She had become interested in deaf education when she had gotten to know an eight-year-old deaf boy named Lam Fat Cheung and helped him with his education and to find a job. She eventually saw him through Gallaudet College. She also introduced me to two other students, Kam-Ling Choi and Hung Choy, and asked me if I could help them to be accepted at Gallaudet. Most people in Hong Kong were not concerned about deafness, which led to many deaf people resorting to crime to support themselves, which was one reason she became involved in trying to help deaf people. She said, "Imagine the adult deaf who cannot write and cannot lipread if they are not taught sign language."

Miss Chan planned a four-day whirlwind of visits for me at Cassova and Victoria Schools (both specialized in Cued Speech), the Hong

Kong School (which had four speech rooms—all equipped with earphones and "albatross" mikes with long cords so the teachers could move around freely), the Hong Kong Society for the Deaf, and the Hong Kong Education Department. I also had four appointments with different newspapers reporters.

Mr. and Mrs. Lee had a deaf seven-year-old son named Lawrence, who was lucky to have such devoted parents. They gave him not only love but also a sense of independence and an education. As soon as they discovered his deafness following a high fever at the age of two-and-a-half, they not only had him wear binaural hearing aids, but also taught him to read and write by the age of three. He attended morning classes at a regular school and had two private tutors (one for Chinese and another for English); then Mrs. Lee, an ex-teacher, tutored him in the evening. For a profoundly deaf orally-trained child, he had a large vocabulary and good speech.

His bedroom walls were covered with drawings, pictures, and numbers written in Chinese. Chinese-printed books were stacked on a table and desk. In his private classroom downstairs, drawings, pictures, and numbers written in English hung all over the walls and door. English-printed books overflowed cupboards, a table, and a desk. Educational toys were stacked in an adjoining room. In Mrs. Lee's dressing room, a small table with two low chairs for mother and son stood at the center of the semi-circular mirrored wall, in which they would sit to practice speech.

&

I was amazed at the large number of teachers from Victoria and Cassova Schools who attended my lectures. Mrs. Leung, the principal of the Victoria School, admitted to me that she didn't believe a purely oral teaching method or Cued Speech were beneficial and that she would like to have Total Communication implemented at her school. Unfortunately, she, like other principals, had their hands tied. The British educators, with their insistence on oral education, required the schools to use strict oral training; otherwise they would terminate any financial aid to the schools.

One day I gave Miss Chan four reels of film and my presentation papers to translate into Chinese. I then snuck to a corner of the lecture hall to catch up with scribbling in my journal and writing thank you

letters. An amiable female reporter from the *South China Morning Post* interrupted my writing and spent an hour and a half bombarding me with questions about my experiences, education, deafness, and personal life. "Must I answer these?" I wailed to Miss Chan who agreed with the reporter that readers would be curious about me. It took the reporter a long time to wrangle a few bits of information about my personal life from me. I was there to talk about Total Communication and deaf education not about myself.

After the interview, another woman charged toward me, saying, "I'm Inspector of the Education Department." She ranted on and on that I was the exception to most deaf people, that I was the most intelligent and special, and as such was not a proper role model for deaf people.

I interrupted her and told her to look at the products of oralism and asked why she felt it was necessary to give deaf children a break. I said that she should try to accept sign language to reinforce lipreading and see what sort of results she got. She fired back, "I watched the film of the Gallaudet classroom and that teacher did not fingerspell. That is *not* Total Communication!" Firmly, but politely, I answered, "Because you are not familiar with sign language, you missed her fingerspelling. And didn't you notice a boy fingerspell 'picnic'?"

She groped for further criticism while I continued: "The difference between a conceptual and a signed language does make a big difference, and the latter helps reinforce speechreading." I demonstrated what I meant—signing while I spoke. We volleyed our words back and forth as we walked down the hall, down the elevator, and out into the street, but I was not satisfied when we had to part. Her mind continued to run on a one-sided track. And, as an inspector for the Education Department, she held the power above all.[8]

Another newspaper reporter arrived, and I sat down to speak with her. She was unfriendly, and I could not tell whether she agreed with me or the oralists. She argued that hearing aids would improve deaf people's speaking abilities and insisted that signing would make deaf people look like clowns. I responded, "Haven't you noticed how wildly and clownish the oral deaf gesticulate and grunt? How badly they scramble word order?" She scribbled my words on her notepad. After the lengthy interview, she smiled, although I couldn't tell if it was genuine,

and quipped, "Thank you for your wonderful response." Was she for or against me? I couldn't tell the difference.

Later, when I was in Sydney, I received a note from Miss Chan with the words "I am not happy" and a clipping from the *Star* newspaper.

Turning a Deaf Ear to Mrs. Parsons?

The deaf in Hong Kong have no structural sign language in Chinese and, as a result, are behind in their studies, according to Mrs. Frances Parsons from Gallaudet College in Washington, D.C., the only institute in the world for higher learning for the deaf.

Mrs. Parsons says deaf sign language here is only conceptual, which enables them to communicate among themselves. But our deaf kids leave Form Four several years below that level in writing which is so essential to them. They are as a result frustrated and lonely and denied their proper place in society. Nearly all end up working in factories for low wages, are denied opportunities for promotion or a career. Her argument against lip-reading is that normal people listen 25 percent and think 75 percent, but lip-reading reverses the process to 75 percent concentration on watching and 25 percent on thinking. Mrs. Parsons is surprised to find us in Hong Kong so backward in helping our deaf. Just as backward in fact as the worse country in the world. And she wonders how it could happen when we are so enterprising in other directions. Yet Manila, only 600 miles away, is well-advanced. It would be a small thing for us to accomplish the change she advocates. We ought to do it to give our deaf kids a real chance in life, instead of keeping at least some of them little better off than monkeys communicating with one another in the jungle. Denying our deaf the total communication concept, Mrs. Parsons thinks, is like taking the crutches from a cripple. Mrs. Parsons has been deaf herself since birth, but she is an intelligent, kind and well-educated woman. How can we tell her she is wrong? How can we deny our deaf kids the opportunities she has had and the success she has made of her life? How can we turn a deaf ear to the plea of this wonderful woman who seeks only the understanding and support of we hearing people?

The *Star* reporter's blunt comments dropped a bombshell on Hong Kong's deaf education system. I tore my hair and climbed the walls. I had to rework my rigid budget to pay airmail postage and wrote letters of apology and explanation to all the schools I had visited in Hong Kong. I recalled how these wonderful friendly principals and teachers had welcomed me and, with a sickening and sinking feeling, wondered what they now thought of me.

Taiwan

Taipei, May 30

Wayne Smith, a tall, efficient American, arranged my three-day schedule in Taiwan. However, he mixed the sign languages of several countries while trying to communicate with me and at first absentmindedly spoke to me in Chinese. I wasted considerable time trying to lipread him. Yet, despite how tired I was and how heavily it rained, I enjoyed my stay in Taiwan.

Prior to my first meeting, I grabbed a 20-minute nap while he was in bathroom. Then to make up some time, we walked across a winding path of rice paddies, through alleys, across railway tracks, and even through the living and dining rooms of two houses, much to the surprise of their residents, until we reached a small train station.

We visited the Language Center where Wayne taught, the Ministry of Education, and the Taipei School for the Deaf, which had 800 students. They had been using Chinese Sign Language without any speech training. Administrators were considering setting up experiments to determine the best teaching method: pure oral teaching for preschoolers, Total Communication for the Taipei School, or Cued Speech for the Tainan School. The Tainan School alone had over 760 students. I thought this was a terrible idea. "Over my dead body," I protested. But they assured me that they would segregate the students only for experimental purposes until they could determine the best methods. Wayne and I talked until our faces were blue, arguing that oralism and Cued Speech should not be used for such staggering numbers of students even as an experiment. The sign language in Taiwan was so well known that many Hong Kong deaf adults went to Taipei to learn it.

Three newspaper reporters interviewed me, the first for more than an hour, and the last two for nearly two hours combined. I warned Wayne that reporters tended to manipulate and mislead the interviews, so we were extremely careful to avoid misunderstandings. The first reporter commented that I was the image of Helen Keller, and Wayne replied, "She's not blind." The following morning, however, one newspaper hailed me as the second Helen Keller and Wayne tore his hair in frustration.

On our return trip, we took a bus, as I was suffering from jet lag and it was raining so hard that we couldn't walk across the rice paddies. We arrived at midnight and I dove onto the bed—to find no mattress but bed boards with straw matting. Mosquitoes buzzed unmercifully and I barely managed to get a few hours of sleep. Before dawn, I dragged myself out of bed, feeling like a zombie, and Wayne and I began our journey to the train in a monsoonal downpour.

After a tour of the Taipei School, we met with the teachers in a conference room. The Q&A session buzzed with electrifying excitement. No one opposed sign language as they had in the other countries. The teachers concentrated on arguing about which was best: the unified sign language in Taiwanese, Chinese, or English Signs; conceptual or structural sign language; pure manualism; or the simultaneous method. It was a breath of fresh air to discuss sign language so amiably!

The next day Wayne and I ran into a series of transportation problems—we almost missed several trains and buses—and tried to make up the time by taking short cuts whenever we could. We managed to arrive at the Taiwan School on time at 8 a.m. Miss Wang, the dean of academic affairs, whisked us to the auditorium. I spoke while the white-gloved interpreter's hands flew in the most structural sign language I'd seen outside of Bangkok. The sight of more than 760 students filling the huge auditorium and their thunderous clapping hands took my breath away. I realized that it would be impossible to introduce pure Cued Speech to that many students. I was flabbergasted to see three closed-circuit televisions with two microphones propped up for us; I spoke while Wayne interpreted in Chinese and the interpreter signed to the audience.

After I spoke, some deaf students sang the Taiwanese national anthem to the huge portrait of Sun Yat Sen by following a song chart with blue Chinese characters and red phonetics, which the conductor pointed to with a long stick. They sang in perfect harmony. This method was similar to that used in Iran where the deaf children could pronounce words correctly by combining phonetics and standard vocabulary.

Afterward, we toured the school. I found the biology laboratory amazing with its models depicting the facts of life for plants, flowers, and humans. Except for Saleena's open-mindedness in teaching sex education at her school in Malaysia, the mention of this delicate subject was taboo in most Asian schools.

When we started to leave, Mrs. Wang complained about the difficulties deaf children experienced with language and grammar. I asked why there were so many hearing children, even adults, who also had difficulties with language, grammar, tense, and spelling. They got away with it, I argued, and deaf people suffered while educators bickered about how to improve their language. She had never thought of that. I suggested the remedy was intensive reading and writing, lots of drillwork on writing, and lots of simultaneous method conversation. She smiled and said she required all the students to keep daily diaries.

The school presented us with first-class train tickets back to Taipei, as a token of appreciation for helping the deaf in Taiwan, and we were royally escorted to the train station. When I left for the airport, Grace Lin Shiau, a researcher in the government's educational planning unit, assured me that sign language would never be eliminated in Taiwan.

Philippines

Quezon City, June 6

As my plane approached the airport, I remembered under what circumstances I had left Manila two years before. Back then, I was physically and psychologically exhausted after having endured weeks of battles against a wall of opposition firmly cemented toward oralism. I had sworn never to return to the Philippines. However, the Basilios, a lovely Filipino couple, had visited me in Washington, D.C., late in the fall of the previous year and persuaded me to revisit their country. To this day, I am thankful for their invitation.

After my plane landed, Ruben Bonoan, the father of a deaf daughter and an old friend, greeted me at the airport. He signed fluently, which was much more than I expected, and I was overwhelmed near to tears. In 1974, Ruben wanted to help start a model school. During that visit to the Philippines, he had frequently accompanied me and Carl Argila, an American living in Quezon City who was involved with deaf education, during our travels. On the last day of my 1974 visit, Ruben and Carl accompanied me to the Manila Peace Corps headquarters to propose sending the first deaf Peace Corps volunteers to the Philippines to

teach at the school. Forty-five minutes after we'd arrived, I convinced them to recruit these deaf volunteers.

My first day back in the Philippines, I had to visit my "pet project": the Southeast Asian Institute of the Deaf (SAID), a model school for Total Communication. I was delighted to see my old friend Jane Mac-Fadden again. She had given up her position at the Maryland School for the Deaf in Frederick, Md., to become a Peace Corps volunteer and serve as an educational consultant at SAID. She had done a terrific job revamping the curriculum and revising the teaching methods to follow Total Communication. She and I got to work preparing for a seminar that was to be held the following weekend.

It was great to again see the volunteers I had helped to recruit two years before: Pauline Spanbauer, Daisy Slagle, and Guy Vollmar. They had done magnificent and dedicated work in educating the Filipino deaf children as well as parents and teacher aides. Ruben, now director of SAID, repeatedly stated how grateful he and SAID's teachers were for the help the industrious volunteers provided. I recalled a controversial meeting I'd had during my 1974 trip with the parents who only wanted to hire deaf teachers who could also speak to teach at the school. They would not accept my assurance that one male teacher in particular, Guy Vollmar, would make a wonderful role model for deaf boys. In Filipino culture, however, boys grow up among women—mothers, aunts, grandmothers, maids, and *yayas* (nursemaids)—so parents didn't feel their boys needed a father figure. They refused to listen and voted against hiring Guy. So Pauline and Daisy were the first two deaf Peace Corps volunteers at SAID.

Back in the United States, however, Guy was not going to be thwarted. He quit his job, sold his car, and bought a one-way plane ticket to the Philippines. He volunteered to sleep in one family's garage, eat the family's leftovers, and teach at SAID at no cost. The parents were divided about accepting his offer. One side said, "He cannot talk! He is mute! That is not good for our children." The other group argued, "But look at him. He sacrificed his job and everything to help with our children!" The parents finally agreed to give him a try at teaching. Since he had very little money, Pauline and Daisy took a third of their meager income ($80 a month) and gave it to Guy for one year. By the end of the year, he had won the admiration, trust, and support from the parents

and other teachers. They asked the Peace Corps to accept Guy as a Peace Corps volunteer. Guy quoted the father of one of his deaf pupils: "At home, I am his father. At school, you are his father." Once the parents had realized the value and importance of deaf teachers, many children were transferred to the SAID from several oral schools.

The volunteers had not received a proper orientation before arriving in the Philippines and had suffered from culture shock, which led to some misunderstandings and hard feelings between them and the Filipinos. The volunteers suggested more careful recruitment and thorough orientation for all future deaf volunteers and hoped that I would take part in preparing new volunteers. All I could offer them was my instruction for a few evenings on how to respect foreign cultures. They had gone through so many trials since arriving in the Philippines, but inwardly I smiled: They had grown. They finally had adapted to Filipino life.

The director of the Manila Peace Corps office asked me to meet with Minister Stull, the head of the American embassy to discuss the possibility of increasing the number of volunteer teachers for the expanding school. Daisy and Pauline were nearing the end of their two years of service with the Corps, so replacements needed to be found. Minister Stull agreed. I sent word to Gallaudet that any seniors who were considering volunteering for the Peace Corps should contact Marilyn Galloway at the Gallaudet Placement Center. Mrs. Galloway and Dr. Tom Mayes at Gallaudet's Continuing Education Center had been coordinating the volunteers through my recommendation. Gallaudet and the Peace Corps have worked together ever since.

During the weekend "Seminar on Deafness" that Jane and I had prepared, I spoke with Salou Sobrepena, the mother of a four-year-old deaf boy, who I had met during my 1974 trip. Two years before, she had been a thin, nervous, and unhappy woman who worried about her profoundly deaf son. But now Salou was an official interpreter, and her ability to sign fluently and reverse interpret astounded me. It was fortunate that two years before her mother-in-law Rose had seen the ad for my 1974 seminar in a newspaper and encouraged Salou to attend. That night, she—like many other parents of deaf children—went home with hope. She telephoned some friends, the American parents of a deaf six-year-old daughter, and urged them to go to the seminar the next day. Though

the father of the girl believed in Total Communication, I had to con-
vince her mother that sign language was not dangerous. Salou brought
the mother to SAID again to see a video about Total Communication,
and afterward invited all of us to her home for dinner.

At dinner, I advised Salou to start teaching Eric fingerspelling while
waiting for the deaf Peace Corps volunteers to arrive in a few months.
That very night, Salou taught him how to fingerspell at bedtime, and
three weeks later, he suddenly made her fingerspell all the time. Seeing
her again in 1976, I was impressed to watch this confident, hopeful
mother communicate with her intelligent, active, and independent son.
Salou credited Pauline with teaching her sign language. She said, "It is
no surprise to me why my husband and I are so convinced with TC. We
will keep on holding its banner high lest our son might say to us later,
'You never tried hard enough to understand.' Total communication has
brought forth our deaf son from a world of complete silence to a world
of knowledge unlimited." Throughout my stay, Salou kept telling me
how deeply grateful she was that I had come to the Philippines two
years ago. She often imagined what her and Eric's lives might be like if
I had never made the trip or not conducted the seminar. When I left
the Philippines, she gave me a photograph of herself with her two chil-
dren. On the back, she wrote, "To dear Frances—one who is 'all ears to
all our pleas.'"

During one of my many appointments, I met with Dr. Maltilda
Valdez, head of the special education department at the University of
the Philippines concerning a new graduate program in deaf education.
The deaf Peace Corps volunteers were going to be collaborating with
the department and had, she said, already helped her more than "all the
doctors, medicine, pills, and hospitals put together."

I had a round of dinner invitations and I brought the volunteers
with me. I regretted that we never had the opportunity for a private
get-together. But Guy pointed out, "At least you have contributed
something to us. Almost everyday throughout your visit, we have lots
of decent food at every dinner and lunch given in honor of you!" All I
could say was that I was very proud of their dedicated work with the
SAID.[9]

When I had first arrived in the Philippines, I had a batch of letters waiting for me. One was from Australia. The father of a deaf son wrote, "I write with tears running down my cheeks. Have the heart to lend me your ear. Give me hope that my son, my deaf son, will grow up to become a useful citizen so he can teach deaf children." How did he know my whereabouts, I wondered.

Singapore

June 9

I returned to Singapore and met with Heng, Mr. Peng, and Mrs. Neo at the Singapore School to plan a program to be held after I returned from Australia. They were all shocked at how much weight I had lost because of the stress of traveling and lecturing. After the meeting, they dropped me off at the airport, where I learned, to my dismay, that my plane was delayed by two hours. I made myself comfortable and began to write in my journal. After I had written a few lines, a queasy feeling nagged at me. I approached an agent and showed her my boarding pass. Looking bored, she waved me aside and told me to wait. I sat down again and wrote another few lines but continued to feel uneasy. I went up to the agent again. She glared at me and pointed to my seat with an imperative "sit down!" I complied and resumed writing, but at the end of the third paragraph, an ugly feeling enveloped me. There were lots of passengers around, but I noticed their boarding passes were different from mine. So I made the agent find me another passenger who had the same kind of boarding pass. She looked at the number of the Quanta's flight I had tried to make her notice. There were three Quanta airplanes leaving within two-and-a-half hours, but mine was leaving within the next few minutes. Her face went white.

She pointed to the other side of the terminal. Forgetting the heaviness of my luggage, I yanked it the wrong way and sprained my shoulder as I raced to the right terminal. I was met there by three men who had been looking for me and had been calling my name over the loudspeaker. That is a hazard of deafness. I yelled angrily at the stupidity of that agent while the other two tried to calm me down. The moment I

boarded, two impatient maintenance men breathed sighs of relief as they pulled the inclined stairs away from the plane. We took off for Darwin, Australia, but I still did not have a phone number or address of my host-to-be.

Australia

Darwin, June 12

It was now winter below the equator, so it was pitch dark at 5:00 a.m. when we landed. As I waited in a long queue to go through immigration and custom inspections, I noticed the many good-looking Australian men with their rugged complexions, light brown or blond hair, blue eyes, and sinewy muscles. All wore very brief shorts with knee-length socks. I was fascinated by the various shades of blue eyes: deep blue, pale blue, icy blue, clear blue, soft blue, dark blue.

I had no idea whether anyone knew I was coming or would be meeting me at the airport. With my injured shoulder, I could barely carry my heavy case of films and had no information about schools for the deaf in Darwin, but I was determined to find some deaf children and their parents. I thought of looking up a deaf school's address in the phone book. Then I noticed an inspector who was looking from counter to counter. He looked at my visa form, saw my name, and turned to a bearded man to say something. The man approached me and asked, "Mrs. Parsons?" Speechless, I felt rooted to the floor. The bearded man hastily introduced himself as Gary Yates, a teacher of the deaf. It was a miracle.

He explained that Joan Marryat, a friend of mine who lived in Canberra, had contacted him and arranged for me to be looked after throughout my entire trip. I felt so overwhelmed and grateful. He also had special permits for my films, which allowed me to get through custom without any tie-ups—a stark contrast to all the wrangling I had to do with customs in other countries during this junket.

We got into his jeep and endured miles of lonely, bumpy road. He apologized and explained that the cyclone had damaged the roads. I found that Darwin was still recuperating from the devastation of Cyclone Tracy. People were living in tents, caravans, and lean-to shelters while they slowly rebuilt their homes. Some buildings had been reduced

to rubble, while those next door were only mildly damaged. Initially, weather forecasters had thought that the cyclone would not be a major threat to Darwin because its projected path was well to the north. However, early on Christmas Eve, Tracy passed the western tip of Bathurst Island, north of Darwin, turned around, and began to accelerate toward the city. From midnight until 7:00 a.m. on Christmas Day, the cyclone passed directly over the town. Less than 100 homes were left inhabitable. At the time, Darwin's population was about 30,000.

He asked if I would mind sleeping in a caravan next to his house. Quickly, I answered, "Even a floor will do!" By the time we arrived at his house, I had been awake for 24 hours, so I immediately hit the sheets. When I got up at noon the following day, I mistakenly thought I was back in America. During my Australian visit, it was a thrill to eat typical American food: mashed potatoes, peas, carrots, bread, butter, milk, and steak.

I found it difficult to lipread the Australian accent. In talking to Gary, I learned that he was an advisory teacher of the deaf and also a visiting audiologist for some aboriginal tribes. He and the assistant director of the Australian Education Department were very concerned with the education of deaf aborigines. He bombarded me with questions after I told him that my mother was part Indian and had taught Navajos. I could see that there were many similarities between the two situations. When deaf Indian children were taken from their families and educated in residential schools, they were viewed as "different" when they returned to their reservations. But there were often so few deaf children on a reservation that the U.S. government couldn't justify sending in a teacher just to teach them. In Australia, Gary explained that many deaf aboriginal boys suffer because they are unable to participate in the rituals necessary for them to become men in the aboriginal culture. They become social outcasts, and many are physically abused. Should they be moved to Darwin, educated, and sent back to their tribes?

After years of teaching via strict oralism, some Australian educators were beginning to question whether that teaching method was the best. Not fully convinced of the value of Total Communication when I arrived, Gary seemed persuaded of it before I left Darwin. He offered me a book of aboriginal myths as a present, and in it he wrote, "Thank you for your efforts with deaf children in general but particularly here in Darwin. Your enthusiasm and energy give me renewed life."

Alice Springs, June 13

When I lectured to teachers and government workers in the small, isolated town of Alice Springs, I began with the story of my dinner with the affluent Indian man who I thought had asked me to sleep with him. That brought laughter and broke the ice. I then went on speaking about the problems of the oralist method versus Total Communication.

My host in Alice Springs was Tony Kelly, an advisory teacher of the Southern Territory who signed so fluently it seemed that sign was his first language. During my time with Tony, he learned the American manual alphabet since I found his accent hard to lipread.

Alice Springs is located in central Australia, which was the home of many Aboriginal tribes. Many people in Alice Springs, like many people I met in Australia, were concerned about the education of deaf Aborigines. Tony took me to visit an aboriginal reservation at Areyonga. He told me about a deaf girl he knew who had lived in an Alice Springs foster home for ten years and learned English. When she returned to the reservation, she was regarded and treated as a "dummy" because of her deafness.

Tony had me sign a form releasing the Australian government from any responsibility for me during my time in Areyonga. (I found out later that two sisters ["sisters" is an Australian word for female senior nurses] had recently been killed by some Aborigines during an uprising.) After I signed it, Tony drove like a devil to leave my form with the proper authorities, drove in a blur back to his house to pick up lunch, and drove even faster to the airport where we dashed to two wrong terminals before we located the right one, 15 minutes late. A pilot and three government inspectors, however, were waiting for us. We then took off in a tiny one-propeller plane which flew slowly, giving us ample time to enjoy the magnificent view of the desert painted in red, then brown, then yellow, then speckled with bushes, with one long, thin, strip of dirt road. During our flight to Areyonga, Tony pointed out a valley full of palm trees, calling it "world famous." I gave a limp smile and answered, "World famous? I never heard of it!" Tony also pointed to the Finke River, which cuts a deep meandering line through the rolling hills, flat land, red cliffs, and gorges. "It is the oldest river in the world," he explained.

Areyonga was not on our map—it is an unmapped settlement for the aborigines. As we flew over it, I saw that it was tucked in a narrow gorge. As we came in for a landing on a short runway, thick with soft red dust, the plane sharply dipped one wing. Once we got off the plane, not a person or a building was in sight. But then a pick-up truck suddenly appeared over a hump of rocky hill, followed by an army jeep, which bounced in its wake of red dust. We clambered into the vehicles and began our trip to the settlement.

I first glimpsed some of the aboriginal children of the Pijantsatjara tribe in the settlement's schoolyard. I expected to see their running noses and ears, dust- and dirt-caked bodies, and faces and hair covered with lice and ringworms, but I was surprised to see blond streaks on black or very dark brown hair with a reddish glint.

We first went to a government hospital where Tony investigated the records of the aboriginal children afflicted with otitis media, or inflammation of the ear. A husband-and-wife nursing team operated the hospital, and a doctor flew in to see patients once a month, unless an emergency arose. At the time of our visit, the settlement was home to 200 Aborigines and 29 white people, including children. The settlement's single school once had five teachers but now had only one because most of Areyonga's 86 children did not attend. The settlement also had an administrative office, a new grocery store, and a few brick houses for the government employees. The Aborigines lived in shacks or lean-to huts.

At the hospital Tony found the deaf girl who had learned English during her ten-year education in Alice Springs and introduced us. She sat cross-legged next to her mother in the clinic room and refused to communicate, hanging her head down. I asked if I could take a picture of her, but Tony warned me not to show my camera because the aborigines already seemed angry. However, I cajoled, smiled, and pantomimed for her mother to allow me to take a photograph of her daughter. Suddenly, the flash on my camera went off, jolting her out of the chair. I gestured an apology with a surprised look.

What I learned at the hospital reminded me of the situation on the Yuma Indian reservations before World War II: a language barrier, culture shock, failure of white people to devise strategies to accommodate the minority culture's traditions, the women's distrust of doctors, disregard for hygienic care, failure to ensure that babies were fed properly

and bathed regularly, and health problems caused by the physical, economic, and social environment. The Aborigines had to depend on the Australian government for food and shelter, which causes the deterioration of their social structure and the loss of their independence. Tony showed me the notes in one of many records of people with otitis media: Right ear—pus, flies, ragged hole; left ear—dull, red inflammation, fitted with hearing aid bone conductor. I learned that all deaf aboriginal children who were fitted for hearing aids simply yanked them off, threw them on the ground, and trampled them—they didn't want to be seen as different from the other children.

Tony explained his opinion: "If we have a prelingually profoundly deaf Aboriginal child, then we should offer him the best education available in Australia. We should send the child away for education until he or she is old enough to make a decision to come home or stay in the deaf community in which he had been educated: 'Deaf need deaf.'"

We had to wait nearly two hours for the return of our tiny plane. When it finally arrived at the runway, we quickly shook hands with the aboriginal driver and then we were off. Up in the air, we could see the beautiful setting sun slanting its long red rays over the long stretch of arid land. What solitude, what loneliness!

When we got back to Alice Springs, Tony gave me a quick tour of the town and pointed out some places where the Aborigines were moving in. Some of the white townspeople were beginning to fear the fast-growing Aboriginal population.

Canberra, June 18

After finishing my lectures and film screenings in Alice Springs, I was off to Sydney, where I was warmly taken under the wing of Frank and Joan Marryat. Joan had lost her hearing at the age of ten and later married a hearing man. Joan and I had met through a mutual friend in Trinidad, and our friendship quickly blossomed. During their first trip to America, she and her daughter Marelle had attended the Maryland Association of the Deaf Convention two years earlier where they were astonished by the independence and capability of the deaf people who had organized and participated in the meetings. Joan invited me to come to Australia, not only to promote Total Communication, but also to prove that deaf people could be independent citizens.

During their trip to America, Joan and Marelle had stayed with me. Both were excited to see America; they found the people and the food to be similar to what they were used to in Australia. However, at one point, I found myself waiting for half an hour while Joan watched, spellbound, as squirrels darted up and down trees. Now that I was visiting her in Australia, she smiled and nodded understandingly as I raved about the food. And she patiently waited while I stared at a platypus swimming in a huge tank at the Tarafone Zoo in Sydney. What a fascinating creature, with its beaver-like tail, webbed feet, and duck-like bill.

Since Joan's husband was an Australian diplomat to the United States, she was able to convince her country's ministry of education to fund my sojourn in Australia. I had a very full schedule in front of me, particularly in Sydney, Melbourne, Adelaide, and Perth. I visited, lectured, and was interviewed by dozens of newspapers and radio and television stations. I presented demonstrations, held parent talks, and spoke with teachers, principals, audiologists, speech therapists, public service inspectors, school authority officers, special education departments, four Quota International clubs, several teacher-in-training programs, three clubs for the oral deaf, and eight clubs for the deaf.

Though I had been warned to expect resistance to signing in Australia, I found very little from educators. In fact, many teachers were questioning the effectiveness of the oral teaching method and were receptive to other means of teaching. Cued Speech was quite popular in private schools. I was astounded to find so many parents participating in the education of their deaf children, though many were often reluctant to accept Total Communication, saying they felt that Total Communication was for slow learners or mentally retarded children. When people offered that opinion, I raised my eyebrows and said, "Look at me. I was rigidly taught oral until I was nine, then learned Combined Method from teachers and American Sign Language from school mates. Reading, writing, fingerspelling, speaking, lipreading, signing, and wearing hearing aids are Total Communication. Once you eliminate any of these, then this is not Total Communication. Now am I mentally retarded?"

During newspaper interviews, I tried to be very tactful, remembering the incident with the Hong Kong reporter. Joan looked at me defiantly and said, "You are in my country. I want you to speak out for our deaf children. You have to make it strong to wake up those selfish

parents who want their children to talk." She tearfully recalled years of anguish over her profoundly deaf daughter. Every school in Canberra was strictly oral. She wanted to enroll Marelle in a school near Sydney that used manualism, but because of her residence, she was denied the transfer. Marelle went through years of frustration, tantrums, and tears at not being able to adequately communicate with those around her, and she was often hysterical enough to claw her own arms until they bled. Joan had seen many other deaf children shattered by similar frustrations in communicating. She told me, "I spent hours writing letters all over Australia and made long distance calls as far as Darwin and Perth. I convinced the government educators to work with you and made sure you are well taken care of! If Gallaudet objects to what you say, we'll write them letters! Use your guts all the way through!"

Once, when an interviewer from a TV news station visited me at Joan's home, he talked slowly enough for me to lipread his questions during the filming. But I didn't have a chance to answer before Joan barged in and spat verbal bullets at him. She did the same with other interviewers during that week. I asked her what she had been saying. She smiled coyly and answered, "About you and nothing else!" So that was how such strong remarks had been printed! The reporters had taken her comments and attributed them to me! Many Australians did hear me on the television, saying, "Putting hearing aids on deaf people and expecting them to speak perfectly is like putting a pair of glasses on the blind and telling him to read."

Sydney, July 4

While in Sydney, I stayed with Merle Coppell who helped me treat a case of laryngitis that I had developed. I had met her a year earlier when she was visiting Gallaudet, and she lost no time inviting me to Sydney. While I was in Australia, Merle, too, implored me to speak out on behalf of deaf people and forget diplomacy. She told me it was about time for everyone to hear from a person who knew what being deaf was like. At a reception following one of my lectures, a hearing aid dealer told me he was not happy about some of my remarks, which he read in the newspapers. Ironically, his deaf wife found it impossible to use a hearing aid, but used her during a demonstration of a hearing aid at the Australian Association of Speech and Hearing Convention.

During a parents' meeting, I was fortunate to have Mr. Ferris, a counselor of deaf adults, fingerspell using the American alphabet to help me understand what was being said, as I was still having difficulty lipreading the Aussie accent. As we entered the huge reception room, he fingerspelled to me, "Wow. This is the largest attendance I've ever seen!" Many deaf adults hugged me vigorously or pumped my hand up and down, thanking me for coming and saying how happy and grateful they were. They had spent their lives battling against hearing people's disregard and contempt for the challenges deaf people face. After my presentation, I heard comments like the following: "What you said is the very thing the hearing need to realize"; "I agree with you 100 percent"; and "We are grateful!" One mother flew in from Chico the night before and told me how thrilled she was to see me in a recent television interview. Mr. Roger introduced himself and admitted that he wouldn't relent to signing, and he and his deaf daughter quarreled over speech. She had eloped with a boyfriend against her father's will, and they had only recently been reconciled. After seeing my presentation, Mr. Roger tearfully apologized to his daughter. I met a teacher from New Zealand who begged me to visit her country because the speech training in New Zealand was so rigorous that more than 60 percent of deaf pupils ended up in mental hospitals. I told him I wished I could, but my schedule was already full.

When I returned to Merle's home, she showed me the newspaper articles about Dr. Daniel Ling's arrival and his theory for why teaching speech to deaf children was better than signing. Dr. Ling was a famous oralist from Canada. One radio station wanted us to debate the pros and cons of signing versus speech. Merle encouraged me, saying, "Do it! Spare no diplomacy. Speak out!"

I agreed to do it and the interview was scheduled for July 7. A chauffer from the station picked me up, but we got caught in traffic. The chauffer turned to me three times, saying, "The radio is asking everybody to stand by. Professor Parsons is stuck in traffic." I shivered to think that people thought of me as a VIP. When we got to the station, Holly, the radio assistant, was outside, waiting to rush me upstairs. There was no time for either a pre-interview or a review of written questions that were to be asked. I kicked myself for not thinking to ask Mr. Ferris to accompany me and interpret. To make things worse, Bill, the radio commentator, wanted us to take turns answering his

questions. I rebelled, arguing that, without an interpreter, I would have no idea what he was saying.

Dressed in an expensive suit, Dr. Ling smiled and smooth-talked. He deliberately mumbled in a tight-lipped fashion, expecting me to lipread. He raised his eyebrows with surprise when I didn't understand something he said and replied, "There are many deaf who can lipread well and speak well!" Sarcastic words volleyed back and forth between us until Bill herded us into the soundproof room. I was far from myself, thinking wistfully about all those wonderful American interpreters thousands of miles away. Instead, I had Holly sit next to me so she could scribble Dr. Ling's presentation on a piece of paper for me to read.

The light was on "Air." Dr. Ling talked lengthily and knowingly. "Where did he get all his incorrect information?" I asked myself. Holly wrote summaries of what he said:

> Doctor Parsons is advocating—all deaf should learn to sign—that is simplistic—all deaf go to special schools—all deaf stay in residential schools—worry that children will be isolated in deaf schools—some children can operate normally in normal schools—oversimplification needs correcting—all deaf people are deaf, deaf, deaf—Some people have residual hearing, which can be supplemented by aids and lipreading—very few profoundly deaf—children in first year of life with hearing aids and be taught to communicate normally—fear that teaching sign will isolate people—in Total Communication, tendency of people to rely on signing, whereas people taught orally even profoundly deaf can become linguists, can even be taught to sing in tune—incredibly little hearing—can sing in a normal voice—both manual and oral schools have advanced (battle between two—100 years old) but advances in oral education as great—the deaf are poor advocates—not experts in advances in the oral methods—If he is mentally retarded, don't go to mental retards, so don't go to the deaf for expertise in deafness.

Bill turned to me, asking for my comment on Dr. Ling's remarks. Those remarks! After reading them, I was ready to go on a long tirade. Controlling my voice, I said, "I wish you were profoundly deaf for only one month, and then you would be singing a different song. I am deaf and I know what it is like to be deaf. I know what it is like to lipread." Dr. Ling threw up his hands and opened his mouth to interrupt. Bill signaled for him to stop and told me to continue. I explained that many

deaf people find lipreading difficult. It is also impossible to lipread in many instances, such as when someone is speaking into a microphone. Bill wanted Dr. Ling's answer to the microphone problem. Holly scribbled his response:

> I know hundreds of very profoundly deaf from birth have opposite view. President AG Bell Assoc.—profoundly deaf—hundreds of deaf advocate oppose to what Prof. Parsons advocated—isolation—In recent article—are hundreds of children who are integrated into ordinary classroom—are doing well academically.

I answered that deaf people should use everything—sign language, lipreading, speaking with or without voice, and hearing aids when needed. Bill asked me, "Do you mean all kinds of communication are put in one box—just one box?" I said, "Yes." Dr. Ling and I continued to argue. The last straw for me was when he said, "The deaf should not marry the deaf." Then I saw the "Air" light go off and all hell broke loose. I screamed loud enough to pierce eardrums as Bill and Holly grinned. I shouted at Dr. Ling, "Mr. Gallaudet and Dr. Vernon were the national heroes of the deaf, and you are the villain!" He smirked and said that he would never change his mind. I continued to shout as we went down the hall, then down the elevator, and unleashed my final fury as we parted on the street. I turned to Bill and Holly to apologize for my awful behavior but they said, "Your talks are exciting. We're happy."

Principal Walter Parr, a lecturer of special education at Sydney University, came to fetch me from the station. He looked at me timidly as he opened the car door. "I won't bite you," I said with a controlled voice. He replied, "I heard you on the radio. Your voice was dynamic!" He took me to a large auditorium packed with student teachers waiting to hear my presentation. At first, they were shy about asking me questions because they, too, had heard me on the radio. My throat was hurting again, so I asked a young student to record my mispronunciations. At the end, she counted seventeen, and I said to the room, "I guess I have Indian, Ceylonese, Malaysian, and Thai accents. Ironically, I will need a speech therapist!" A roar of laughter went through the room. After that, the audience overwhelmed me with enthusiastic questions. They were disappointed when it was time to go, but I was happy to leave because the sharp pain in my throat was mounting.

Merle told me later that her phone rang off the hook with people say-ing how glad the radio debate had happened. Everyone felt that the publicity it generated would help raise deaf awareness—the very thing I'd been suggesting. Many people advised, "Talk as strongly as you can. We need a bombshell to wake up the public; don't apologize to that ugly Canadian!" Most importantly, the debate generated numerous newspa-per articles about deaf issues such as the acceptance of Total Communi-cation in Australian schools. As I waited at the airport to leave Sydney, Mr. Roger approached me and pressed something into my hand, saying, "Please accept this as a token of my happiness; you have saved me and my daughter." Then he abruptly left with tears in his eyes. The gift was a beautiful ring with an Australian deep blue sapphire and two small di-amonds with platinum prongs set in 18-carat white gold. Three months later, I learned from Joan that Mr. Roger had passed away.

Melbourne, July 11

In Melbourne, I had standing-room-only crowds at every lecture or presentation I gave. Parents listened, teachers nodded their approval, and deaf people rooted vigorously. One newspaper wrote that I was "the deaf Florence Nightingale."

Mr. Flynn, the executive director and secretary of the Adult Deaf Society, was stunned to find that I had very limited time for sightseeing in Melbourne, so he arranged for me to visit a new, ultra-modern art gallery. I also spent my spare time getting to know some people in the deaf community. One deaf couple, Mr. and Mrs. Peters, who had all hereditarily deaf children, invited me over to dine with them at their home. Astounded, Mr. Flynn said, "They invited you to their home! Do you know they belong to the Brethren religion, which doesn't allow them to have guests in their house?" I answered, "Their son, Graham, is at Gallaudet. And because I helped him there, he wrote his parents a letter, *ordering* them to host me."

At the dinner, I was dazzled to see books in every room of their house and realized why their boys were so far ahead of other deaf chil-dren in reading. They served me a country dinner and then they took me to a zoo. Being in the car with Mr. Peters was a bit frightening since he used the British two-handed manual alphabet while driving. At the

evening's end, I thanked them for their wonderful hospitality and they thanked me for helping Graham.

Adelaide, July 17

In Adelaide, I stayed with Mr. Barry, the principal of the South Australia School. He had dared to implement the Combined Method in his school and experienced great success. When I learned Dr. Ling had been at the school, I asked for Mr. Barry's opinion about him. My host shrugged his shoulders and said, "Another Dr. Ewing." (Dr. Ewing was a British Alexander Graham Bell—a staunch oralist who taught at Manchester University in England.) He also said, "You are awakening the sleeping giant—Australia!"

One day, Mr. Barry rushed me to the local ABC TV studio. He was excited and told me how impressed the Adelaide people were since they had never seen or heard a deaf person stand and talk to a hearing audience. During the pre-interview, the TV commentator wanted my real opinion on deaf education. I refused to answer at first, wanting to be diplomatic. "Drop a bomb!" Barry mouthed, banging his fist. "Drop it hard!" When asked the same question on the air, I commented, "Australia has an emblem of the emu and the kangaroo because they can only move forward. Well, there are too few schools that live up to that motto!"

To relax, Mr. Barry and I walked through a beautifully landscaped park along a river filled with ducks and swans. He admitted to me that keeping up with my tight schedule left him exhausted, and he couldn't imagine how I had endured the pace for weeks. I said, "I use sheer will power on behalf of deaf children whom I regard as my children!" During our walk, we passed the modern opera house with cantilevered balconies and red-orange paneled wood walls. On the last day of my stay, I visited Mr. Barry's old Gothic school. I showed the pupils different American Signs and gave them a pep talk about reading and writing more. As we left the classroom, he said with awe, "Their faces! They looked different!" At the airport, Barry asked if there would be any chance I could return to Australia and to Adelaide. I answered that I certainly hoped so.

Perth, July 21

The first thing I saw when I got off the plane in Perth was a group of red-billed black swans paddling languidly in a nearby pond. Mrs. Donovan, the principal of the Mosman Total Communication School, approached and covered me with her heavy coat. Then I was interviewed by newspaper reporters in a private reception room at the terminal. I looked at my busy three-day schedule and said to myself, "I will survive." As soon as we reached Mrs. Donovan's home, I went straight to bed with a splitting headache and throbbing throat. She had her own remedy to help me heal my voice.

Mrs. Donovan briefed me about Mr. Fisher, the head of the government's special education department and a strong oralist, and the assessment team who determined the method of education for Perth's deaf pupils, separating them into oral method, Total Communication, and Cued Speech classrooms. I was irritated to find that the oral unit was created specifically for the profoundly deaf. Mrs. Donovan claimed that the children at her school learned more quickly through Total Communication and were happier than those at any other school in the unit.

I had a long meeting with Mr. Fisher and, like a cracked record that had been going on for six months, I pointed out the advantages of Total Communication and the disadvantages of oral education. He liked the American one-handed alphabet, preferring its safety and convenience when a person is driving or carrying a grocery bag. And he was receptive to moving the profoundly deaf students to a Total Communication school.

I visited a purely oral kindergarten class, which depressed me. The students that I have seen in American Total Communication preschool classes are generally happier and more talkative than those in oral-only classes because they are allowed to express themselves by signing. I visited the local high school unit for hard of hearing students. After I spoke to the class, a student exclaimed, "Her speech is so good!" What a nice compliment from the mouth of a girl who was hard of hearing.

I also visited the Speech and Hearing Center, which specialized in Cued Speech. Principal Venard, an American from Wisconsin, surprised me with her flying arms and hands, signing in Amselan (ASL)

with her lips shut. I asked her to speak while she signed, but she replied, "I can't speak and sign in Amselan at the same time." She was lively and piquant but I couldn't read her signs because they went by in a blur. Ironically, she wouldn't permit signing in her school, but she did allow the pupils hear me talk and suggested that I demonstrate some signs. Afterward, she asked them, "What do you think of Ms. Parsons?" They were surprised to see my waving arms, and a few said that signing looked awful. I asked, "Have you ever seen Hawaiian hand dances? I am signing like the Hawaiian *vahines* who weave their hands and arms in the air." They then changed their minds and thought signing was nice. In spite of my strong disagreement with Principal Venard's teaching method, I liked and admired her. She and I discussed our respective trips to Russia and how we were both impressed at the Russian children's ability to speak and sign or fingerspell simultaneously.

The Mosman Park School was located a short distance from the beach. I asked if there were sharks in the water. Mrs. Donovan replied, "We go in the water just the same! We don't think about them!" She also told me that rubella had been striking every three years, and each year, the virus seemed worse. Thus there were more children with multiple handicaps who needed to have signing added to their education.

During the last day of my visit, I managed to grab an hour's rest, and then Mrs. Donavan took me to the school auditorium to find an overflowing crowd of parents, teachers, psychologists, social workers, representatives from the Deafness Council, and members of the Lions, Rotary, and Quota International clubs. During the question-and-answer session, someone asked if I identified as a normal person. My emphatic "Yes" had them applauding. During a "raise your hand" game, I asked the parents, "Do you want your deaf child to talk?" All hands went up. "Do you want your deaf child to have knowledge?" All hands went up. "Then which comes first? Should it be talking?" Only two hands went up. They asked if I thought it was necessary for deaf children to be taught by deaf teachers. My answer was a big "Yes!" The president of the Quota International club, a women's service organization, asked how they could help the school. Knowing that Quotarians from all over Australia had been donating hearing aids, I answered, "Send lots of books!" They were stunned, but eventually shook my hand. Mrs. Donovan gave me a Cheshire grin and exclaimed, "It was successful. Thank you!"

Later, I had a conversation with an Australian teacher that deeply troubled me. She said, "I deeply honor and respect you. The world needs more like you. What do you think of American Sign Language?" Her question caught me by surprise. I answered, "Of course I use Amselan with my deaf friends everywhere, but in a large classroom, I codeswitch to keep my students awake, and I use English signs for note-takers. I speak without voice and sign with people who are late-deafened or hard of hearing, as well as with students in a small classroom." She replied, "I see your point, but I've been in America for two years. There is a growing breed of the Amselan-using deaf. They don't believe in following English and are likely to resent hearing people. They believe Amselan is mandatory for small children to start with. I am most concerned history will repeat itself in Australia." Chills ran up and down my spine and I couldn't sleep that night. I hoped she was wrong.

Feeling more dead than alive, I decided not to go out to dinner and cancelled a visit with oral deaf adults scheduled for that evening. I relaxed and watched *Seven Brides for Seven Brothers* on television, without closed captions. The next day, Mrs. Donovan took me to the airport where we bade each other a fond farewell. She said, "I expect more calls next week. Your talk has been successful. Before you came, there was strong opposition to sign language. Now it's different. It IS successful."

She, like everybody else, expressed her wish that I would return someday.

Singapore

July 24

My faithful deaf Asian friend Heng was at the airport to welcome me and whisk me to his home. After weeks of using seat belts, as is lawfully required in Australia, I felt naked without one. As we drove, the cool sea breezes tranquilized me. When we got to Heng's house, everyone exclaimed that I looked well fed. I also found a letter waiting for me with a plane ticket to Penang. According to the letter, it was urgent that I go back

at once. I also received a registered letter with a special governmental permit from Ceylon to permit my passage. I had had to apply for special dispensation because foreigners had been forbidden to travel there after recent political upheaval.

During my first day in Singapore, I slept off and on and relaxed. Then Heng caught me up on the current situation with the schools for the deaf in Singapore. Mrs. Neo, the principal of the oral section who had strongly disagreed with my views during my earlier visit, and Mr. Lee, the officer of the Singapore Association of the Deaf, had changed their minds and once again opposed using sign language in the classroom. They boycotted the NAD's ABC manual language book and Mrs. Neo went so far as to call it trash. I protested, explaining that it was a best seller and the most popular method for the international deaf to communicate across borders. I was beginning to regret cutting my stay in Australia short.

When Dr. Goh learned that I felt like an intruder in Singapore since there was such opposition, he exploded in anger. He declared that he and his committee members supported Total Communication and were unaware that plans to implement it had been cancelled. I could actually hear his thundering voice as he phoned, demanding an emergency meeting of the administrators at 5:00 in the afternoon right before my lecture at 6:30. He ordered the schools to start using the Combined Method on Tuesday morning. When Heng heard the news, he turned to me and said, "You have dropped a bomb!" I joked, "But I didn't do it intentionally."

During the emergency meeting he had called, Dr. Goh asked Mrs. Neo to make an announcement that Total Communication was to be freely used in school. With great reluctance, she agreed. Then at a meeting with the teachers of all the schools for the deaf in Singapore, Dr. Goh told her to make the same announcement to the teachers. She protested again but unhappily made it. The teachers rejoiced. I asked if they had any questions. Mrs. Neo demanded answers to her negative questions such as "What would happen if Total Communication completely discourages speech?" and "What if Total Communication slows down the students' learning?" The teachers shook their heads in disgust behind her back since they supported this new teaching method. She

ordered me to demonstrate Total Communication in all the classrooms during the following day. In spite of my extreme fatigue, I accepted. She was very concerned that the students would not develop speech. I replied that it was more important to instill knowledge. Many teachers nodded their heads approvingly.

The next morning, with all the teachers following me from one classroom to another, I asked the first teacher to demonstrate her teaching method. She had all her children talk, or rather shout, unintelligibly. Then I took over, talking and signing. They responded like ducklings taking to water. By the third day, I bowed out of teaching and stayed in bed.

I enjoyed talking to Heng, who, over and over, gave Gallaudet credit for making him who he was. Until he was sixteen, he was withdrawn and quiet. His oldest brother made the decision to send him to an American school. He learned grammatical English, then sign language in English form, which gave him a quick passport to mental development and enabled him to improve his command of written English. At Gallaudet, socializing with deaf people and hearing people using English sign language helped him to overcome an inferiority complex, build leadership skills, improve his decision-making skills, and develop his sense of independence. While he was at Gallaudet, he became highly motivated to challenge speech training for the first time and learn to talk. He got a hearing aid and was given a list of idioms to read out loud. He realized his zest was squelched with this erroneous move because he could not speak or understand spoken words. He said, "Never mind. I tried and will try anything."

I spent the latter part of the day resting in my bed and writing thank you letters to Australia. Ever since Iran, I always wrote such a letter to every host, principal, or teacher who helped me to thank them for their wonderful cooperation in helping the children to have a better education through Total Communication. I usually wrote these letters the night before I was to leave a country so I could send them locally and save overseas postal expenses. But I was so busy in Australia that I didn't have the time to write them there.

I survived those three whirlwind, busy days, and then I flew to Penang. I promised to return to Singapore for the last stop in my tour.

Malaysia

Penang, July 27

In Penang, I stayed with Saleena again. She was concerned because a professor from the University of London was coming to Penang to try to revive support for oralism as the main method for educating deaf children. Dr. Mahathir had announced, but not written, that the law allowing Total Communication in all the schools for the deaf should be passed. We were told the next morning that the teachers from all the schools for the deaf would be convened in a swanky hotel with a gorgeous air-conditioned hall. Saleena and her staunch allies reserved a suite in the hotel in the afternoon. It turned out to be a small hall with uncomfortable chairs, no air-conditioning, facing the blazing hot sun. My session was not even included in the program.

When I woke up the next day, I was so sick with chills I missed the morning session. I had to drag myself to the hotel on wobbly legs to make the afternoon session. The room I was to give my lecture in was full and intolerably hot. I had to grip the podium to balance myself, and it took all my willpower to look composed. I first used my voice, then slowly introduced some gestures, and then began to sign.

Some militant oralist teachers and principals deliberately fanned paper above their heads, blocking other teachers' views. They stood up and sat down, refused to look at me, put their heads together and whispered loudly, and did everything they could to disrupt my demonstration and speech.

After the meeting, I almost collapsed, wailing to Saleena, "I am so, so sorry. I failed." Surprised, she looked at me and exclaimed, "You did beautifully! I didn't know they upset you!" When she realized how sick I was, she rushed me home and put me to bed. I was shaking and running temperature. I refused to return to the convention that night. Voting on whether or not to implement Total Communication in Penang's schools ensued. Saleena came home late in the night, tapped me on my shoulder, and said, "We won!" I pulled the sheet over me and let hot tears of victory scald my face.

Just before I left for Singapore, a father and son approached me. "Do you remember me?" he asked. Of course, I did. While at the meeting in Kuala Lumpur, he had desperately asked me if he should continue oral communication with his son who never responded to speech. At the time, I didn't have the time to conduct a sign class, so I suggested he take one up under Tan Yap and Dr. Dora Tan. I also suggested trying to fingerspell to his son. So, I hurriedly showed him how to fingerspell from an alphabet card.

I was overwhelmed to see how he and his son now fingerspelled to each other at a blue streak. He said, "Now my son loves me as much as I love him!" He then slipped a small box into my small handbag and left. That night, I opened it and found an 18-carat gold ring set with a fire opal—another token of heartfelt gratitude from a father.

Singapore

August 3

I returned to Singapore and had only two days to attend all the meetings with teachers and government personnel. One of the issues that we discussed was whether to support Total Communication with the inclusion of Signed Exact English (SEE 2). Astonishingly, they chose SEE 2 over all the other different sign languages! I could not believe my eyes—this decision was approved by deaf people along with hearing people.

They explained their reasoning: The Singapore government was mandating excellent command of English for the sake of world trade. Singapore has no factories, farms, or industrial plants, but does have fishing and shipping industries and other businesses that demand their employees understand English in order for them to compete in the global marketplace. English is the international spoken language of business. The Tower of Babel of Chinese, Hindi, Malaysian, and English—all the languages spoken in that country—was weakening the Republic of Singapore.

Mr. Peng, the principal of the Chinese School for the Deaf in Singapore, used Chinese Sign Language, but he noticed that the students used unstructured signing (natural signs) at all hours but had only a few hours of reading and writing in Chinese in the classroom. He decided that the

students in his school would only use the structural sign language that followed the official written language of the nation—English.

Until he attended Gallaudet, Heng, like most of his fellow deaf children, used natural signs that he picked up from his peers. At Gallaudet, he was astounded to see students communicating using the Simultaneous Method. He told me, "Although I cannot speak, it is discernible. I should have started the Simultaneous Method when I was very young. I can read lips when signing, and that is the best method of learning English." After his second trip to Gallaudet as a graduate student, he took a course in SEE 2. He realized fingerspelling after each word reinforces letters that could not be seen by lipreading alone. An addressee could understand the sign TWO DOG but miss out on the plural "s." Being a teacher, Heng began using this method to test his older students and found that it accelerated their learning and gave them a better command of English. "I have been trying to prove this method to Mrs. Neo and Mr. Lee, but they wouldn't believe me," he said. Another deaf adult suggested that after SEE 2 was implemented, someone should track the children's progress in the three core primary education subjects: English, mathematics, and science. Then they would have evidence demonstrating that Total Communication was the best method for educating deaf children. This group of Singapore deaf adults voted and passed the SEE 2 measure with acclaim from the government.[10]

Ceylon

Colombo, August 5

Plantations thickly carpeted with green palm trees, red-roofed houses, and hectares of rice paddies were a familiar sight as the plane came into Colombo for a safe landing. The unstable political situation meant soldiers were everywhere. Fortunately, I had the ambassador's special permit, so I breezed through customs until one inspector looked at me balefully. I was afraid that my films might be confiscated, but Lady Luck walked with me. When I opened my suitcase for inspection, the inspector's eyes were arrested by ten copies of the NAD's book, *A Basic Course in Manual Communication*. He picked one up. He began to slowly flip through the pages until I explained that these books teach the signs used

by deaf people. He looked at me and asked, "You deaf?" I nodded. "My little son is deaf," he answered with sadness written on his face. "Then have him learn sign language and he will be happier," I suggested. He simply told me to shut my suitcase and officially stamped my luggage without inspecting anything else. Another officer confronted me, knitting his eyebrows in a frown as he pointed at the listed occupation on my paperwork: university lecturer. I had been warned not to use the words *teacher* or *professor* on my paperwork because teaching was viewed with suspicion in the then-current political climate, and college was unheard of in many countries. After showing him my permit from the ambassador, he suddenly changed into Sir Galahad. He stopped the taxi drivers from mobbing me and helped me to get an air coach ticket.

As I had promised during my earlier trip, I traveled to Little Woodford, a private oral school in an old mansion run by Mrs. Sita Wijetilaka. She had four teachers with five pupils each. When I arrived, everyone I met was stunned to find that I had lost my voice once again due to my extensive lecturing so Mrs. Wijetilaka cancelled the first part of my heavy schedule and arranged a private tour to some out-of-the-way places as a token of thanks for enlightening their deaf children. But there was a restriction on sightseeing by foreign tourists. Fortunately my hostess Vijitha's son Rohan had three free days, and he borrowed a car and a chauffeur.

Of all the exotic places I've been, Ceylon, despite its small size, was one of the most richly laden countries I've seen, with ancient monuments, isolated villages, and gorgeous tropical landscapes that outdid Tahiti, Trinidad, and Bali combined. Remote villages retained old customs and cultures. Ancient cities, such as Polonnarupua, Danebella, Anuradhapura, and Mihentale, were dotted with temples, stately palaces, and public baths. Stone bridges and roads wound their way through the cities and were lined with intricately carved guard stones, statues, and gorgeous frescoes. Cisterns and dolmens told of life in prehistoric times. One stone temple had three mammoth Buddha images carved out of living rock and a colossal recumbent figure of Buddha.

The rock fortress of Sirigriya was completely isolated from other cities and was unique architecturally, politically, and spiritually. It was built by a fifth-century megalomaniac king as a place to hide from his enemies after he murdered his father and escaped to this towering crag.

The thought, however, of climbing to the top reduced me to a bag of shakes. But Rohan and Siri, the chauffeur, argued that they had driven a long way to come here and this would be my only opportunity. I had already spent nearly two days climbing up steeps steps and hills, walking barefoot on sun-blistering sacred grounds until my feet became tender and raw. So, at my own slow pace, I began the long climb. We made it two-thirds of the way up, but were stopped by very poisonous wasps that came dangerously close to the cliff stairs. In fact, a guard was positioned there in a cage with heavily meshed wires to protect him from the wasps. At one point, a group of Indian tourists began stampeding down when one woman screamed that a wasp had gotten in her hair. Rohan, Siri, and I walked very quietly and cautiously and managed to avoid the wasps. We did get to see a cave that was richly and gloriously covered with frescoes of women that had been painted more than 2,000 years ago.

I first encountered a giant python in Ceylon. The chauffeur stopped the car when he spotted it slithering alongside a narrow dirt road, but I screamed for him to move on. I asked Rohan if there were any more snakes lurking about and he shook his head. A short time later, however, the car ran over a big one. After that, I had either Rohan or Siri walk ahead of me everywhere we went.

The hotels were cheap, but not always restful. I paid 75 cents for a room with a window that faced a verandah full of men drinking their idle hours away. And if I wanted to use the bathroom, I had to walk through those rowdy men. After that, I splurged on better hotels that charged $2.00 for a night.

Jaffna, August 10

When Sita learned that I wanted to meet with the astrologer, Mr. Pundit, who had remarkably predicted my overseas work, she made a long-distance call to arrange a rendezvous. He, in turn, scheduled my three-day visit to the Jaffna School for the Deaf and the Hindi Women's Association, which supported the school and recruited wealthy donors. Due to my dwindling money, Sita asked if I would be brave enough to ride on a third-class train that would take seven and a half hours to reach the astrology center but cost only $2.60. I told her that this would not be a problem as I'd been on worse trains in the past.

The train's wooden seats were so narrow that I had to turn my knees sideways. Sita had warned me that all train station signs were printed in Hindi, so I needed to pay attention to the time and get off the train at 7:40 p.m. When I arrived, Mr. Pundit quickly picked me out of the crowd as I was the only white foreigner and asked, "Ms. Parsons?" Knowing my financial difficulties, he and his stately wife Lakshni welcomed me to their humble but warm home. Unable to lipread their British accents, he spent hours scribbling notes to me.

I told him I was astounded at his accurate horoscope, but I did point out his error in predicting that I would be a highly religious during my year abroad. He wrote, "You are a greater divine person than us. Work is worship. Duty is your God. Service is your deity." He added, "Beware of reptiles. These are vicious people who attack your noble services to the world." He showed me letters from all over the world from people who were impressed by his accuracy.

I met with teachers and principals from two deaf schools in Jaffna who were very receptive to Total Communication. I emphasized that copying words written on blackboards was not considered to be part of Total Communication but that reading books was. Then I went back to Colombo for a brief stop at Sita's; I assured her that her twelve-year-old daughter Thushara had the strong potential to attend Gallaudet.[11] She, however, needed to practice more in English, algebra, and geometry, and she needed to read more books. When Sita's husband learned I was going to Africa, he warned me to avoid Uganda and Mozambique. He said, "You will be taken prisoner, and other deaf children all over the world will lose your able guidance."

India

Bombay, August 15

What a tremendous welcome I received in Bombay compared to my first arrival! This time, all but a few educators attending my lectures were for Total Communication. There was still, however, a heated discussion about which sign languages should be adopted, as India has many regional languages. Some deaf adults refused to share their language with others and didn't want to learn other regions' signs. Attendees finally

agreed to accept at least 500 signs from NAD's ABC book and kept the rest of their local signs. Teachers, hearing volunteers, and deaf adults had set up morning and evening classes for a three-week crash course. I had a good excuse not to use my voice but whispered and moved my lips while teaching. I saved my voice for presentations and lectures as well as magazine and newspaper interviews.

The people who attended my lectures were astounded to learn about the advantages and disadvantages of oralism and Total Communication. And all but one of the educators at my presentations was enthusiastic about allowing signing in classrooms. The die-hard oralist believed that using too many methods would confuse a deaf child. All my self-composure and discretion flew out of window. "Who gave you that idea?" I said angrily. "I'm fed up with hearing teachers telling about the problems of deafness to other teachers. To conquer the problems of deafness you must ask the deaf people themselves!" A stunned silence ensued. Then pandemonium broke loose. The previous March in Bombay, Mrs. Ghata, another ardent oralist, had vehemently defended speech as Dorothy Souza argued for the benefits of sign language. Now, this very same principal began hotly defending Total Communication as the best answer for deaf children. My jaw dropped at Mrs. Ghata's drastic turnaround. Another true friend of the deaf! I felt like a contented cat licking milk off its paws. Now the Total Communication supporters wanted all of my articles, lectures, and newspaper clippings bound and presented to the University of Bombay. Many teachers wanted copies of my journal.

During my free time, Dorothy again took me to out-of-the-way places not seen by tourists. She told me that the gorgeous white horses that pulled the child prostitutes' buggies, which I had seen on my last visit to the Street of the Slave Girls, had all been burned to death when their large barn accidentally caught fire. She took me to two different funeral pyres on a northern beach. She explained that when fire reaches the corpse's brain, the brain explodes like a shotgun.

Dorothy introduced me to two deaf Hijra, who I thought at first were gay men because they were dressed in women's saris. No. Effeminate men? No. Dorothy explained that they were either castrated men or hermaphrodites. The Hijra cult was a holdover from the days when eunuchs guarded harems. Now they mostly lived in groups; made money

by begging, dancing, and singing; and had their own folklore, myths, and traditions. They created their own families by adopting children. They all went through a castration ritual, which involves the quick slashing of the entire genitals. About 5,000 Hijras were believed to live in Bombay. I was told that the cult originated from the story of an unhappy king who had no son. So Goddess Bahuchara blessed him with a son who was "born impotent." The child Jethos dreamed that the goddess ordered him to cut off his genitals and dress as a female. According to folklore, since then, all initiated Hijras have followed his example. I asked the deaf Hijras if they were happy. They said yes, although it took me quite awhile to remember that head-shaking from side to side meant "yes."

One night, while dining at the home of a well-to-do principal and owner of an oral school, I sat across from a deaf teenage girl, who was sitting quietly while six teachers chatted a blue streak around her. I got her attention and began to speak voicelessly with simple gestures. Her eyes brightened and she responded timidly. Her mother noticed our conversation, banged her fist on the table, and shouted, "We can't hear you talk. You are rude!" I slammed my hand on the table and brayed, "We can't hear you talk. For years, we the deaf can't hear people talk at the table and are left out. My hearing mother was a teacher and a principal, but she had her guests speak slowly for my sake. And she fingerspelled when necessary. Now it is high time for you to sign and *include* us in your conversation!" Silence enveloped the room. I added, "Parents give a gift of life to a child but do not own it."

❧

Before I left for Africa, the American embassy in Bombay warned me of the great dangers I might encounter in Uganda, Ethiopia, and Mozambique and advised me to cancel my visits to those countries. I decided to visit Ethiopia since I already had contacts established there. During my last night in Bombay, my hostess Behroz came to my room and said with a very serious look, "I worked in Africa for three years. Danger was everywhere. So if you are raped, try to keep cool and 'cooperate.' Don't scream or fight. You will have a better chance for them to spare your life."

Ethiopia

Addis Ababa, September 19

There had been a great deal of unrest in Ethiopia since the death of Emperor Haile Selassie the previous year. He had been deposed and arrested in 1974. He died a year later under questionable circumstances. Most people thought he'd been smothered with a pillow. The lives of all the Ethiopian princesses were spared, and they were placed in custody for their own safety in the Ethiopian capital of Addis Ababa. The long line of Selassie claimed they were the descendents of the Queen of Sheba.

When I arrived in Addis Ababa, my first impressions were how delightful the mountain air was (the city is 8,000 feet above sea level) and how shy the Ethiopians were. They didn't respond to my smiles. I learned from Haile Bokure, my interpreter in English signs, that I was the first white deaf person they had ever encountered.

Among those greeting me were the beautiful Ethiopian princess Yenealem, Anya for short. She gracefully approached and handed me a bouquet of flowers. Princess Anya had been adopted and reared by Princess Sophia, a relative of the late Emperor Selassie. She grew up in the royal family until the emperor was overthrown by the army in 1974.

The socialist government, which paid for my hotel expenses and gave me the occasional use of a chauffeured car, was already receptive to signing in classrooms so, much to my relief, I didn't have to lecture. The main problem for deaf people in Ethiopia was that blind people were the first priority. What the deaf Ethiopians wanted was to establish a government school for technical assistance in administration and curriculum development, as there were already two government schools for the blind. Confronting the ministry of education, the members of the Ethiopian Association of the Deaf asked, "Why do you neglect the deaf? They are Ethiopians. They are our own people." In Africa, it was customary for Africans to prefer blindness over deafness because blind people used speech. Deaf people were ridiculed and mistreated. However, two officers from the ministry enrolled in my sign class. They were courteous, attentive, and enthusiastic. I advised the officers to try generating a lot of publicity for deaf awareness. For the first time, newspaper interviewers met

with us to write about deaf issues. The international labor organization arranged to see me. Mengistu Haile Mariam, the country's new ruler, gave orders to the government workers to give first priority to the needs of the deaf. One door after another opened.

The threat of revolution hung in the air. Every time I went to the bank, policewomen or female soldiers, regarding me as a white alien, would roughly search me by squeezing my bust or between my thighs. I learned afterward that they did this because explosives could be hidden in thickly padded bras or underwear. They took their time searching my purse while a queue of women and children lengthened behind me. Sometimes the guards made me leave my camera with them while I did my banking. One took away a small bottle of my perfume and kept it. One time, I wanted to cash a traveler's check at the bank, and I started to walk in the door. Unable to hear the soldier yelling at me to stop, I found myself with a bayonet-tipped gun pointed at my stomach and a soldier snarling at me. He prodded with his weapon and I snapped, "Young man, I only want to cash my check. Conduct yourself like a gentleman." He gave me a lopsided grin, touched his helmet with downcast eyes, and said, "Sorry, the bank is closing up."

Soldiers with guns constantly patrolled the streets. Trucks full of soldiers with machine guns were on guard at the city's entrance and exit gates. Several times, I was warned not to go out alone after 6 p.m. and to never ride in a taxi after dark.

One day after class, I took a shortcut back to my hotel, and two different boys tried to wrest my purse from me. I gripped it and stubbornly held on. I used the same street the next three days, but they left me alone. I thought to myself what I needed was a bullet from an elephant gun to go through my thick skull before I was going to be intimidated or afraid. A week later, an illiterate deaf man recognized me as a deaf American. Luckily, he had been following me back to my hotel when a well-dressed man tried to attack me from behind and nearly knocked me down. The burly deaf man leapt into action, bellowing and snarling, and fearlessly threatening to flatten my assailant. We spied a policeman across the street, so I ran toward him. The assailant saw the policeman and fled. I thanked the deaf man for so valiantly defending me. He answered with gestures and sign, "You me deaf. You me same. Friends." Throughout my stay, such warm hospitality and humility as shown by

Meeting the deaf umbrella factory workers in Addis Ababa, Ethiopia.

the Ethiopians overwhelmed me. They were very protective of me. The color of their skin might be dark, but their spirits were pure white, and their hearts, gold.

Deaf and hearing Ethiopians of the Rehabilitation Center, an umbrella factory, a textile firm, and a missionary school had enthusiastically enrolled in my class, so the government sent me a car with a chauffeur in the evening for my safety. The umbrella factory, the only one of its kind in Ethiopia, was also the only company that hired blind, disabled, and deaf people. As a token of appreciation, I was treated to long drives to villages in the Rift Valley, passing by the beautiful countryside with its flat-topped, crooked acacia trees and hectares of *teff* (an Ethiopian grain). *Injera*, the traditional Ethiopian bread, is made from ground teff and then baked into porous pancakes. In the Rift Valley, people live in round *tubuks* made from branches stacked together to form a family compound. Snakes were everywhere, so I couldn't walk alongside the river. In Nazret, there were horse-and-buggy taxis.

It is customary in Ethiopia for hosts to hand-feed guests, so it took a great deal of willpower for me to smile and let friends each taking a turn to feed me. My thoughts tunneled through my head, asking, "Did

they wash their hands? I never saw a wash basin in a toilet room." A number of times I needed to go to the restroom at a restaurant and found that a toilet with no top cover was inside the kitchen. It reeked and drew flies that buzzed over the food. After that I refused to eat at shoddy cafes. I could write lengthy pages about their strange foods and strange theories. I could not stomach their custom of eating bloody raw meat that had been doused generously with hot red pepper sauce. The sauce was supposed to kill the microscopic worms. I averted my eyes while they voraciously gnawed that meat.

For months I had graciously avoided certain foods that I couldn't stomach. When hosts served me foods such as gigantic cockroaches, eggs cooked just before the chickens within them were hatched, or cooked intestines stuffed with blood, I avoided hurting their feelings by saying graciously, "Oh, your food looks so delicious but I am so sorry I cannot eat because it is against my doctor's orders (or against my religion or against my beliefs since I am a vegetarian)."

While attending a wedding feast at a family's home, a newly wedded couple went into a bedroom. Everybody stopped merry making and listened. After the bride screamed, the husband came out, carrying a blood-stained napkin. All rejoiced for it was a symbol that her virginity being broken. Her parents were tremendously relieved. It took a lot of control for me not to look shocked.

For five weeks I volleyed back and forth from classes, lectures, and relaxing breaks in the countryside. Although some of my students used American signs (which had been brought to Ethiopia by the Church of Christ in 1968), they wanted advanced lessons in structured English to improve their English literacy. They felt the NAD's ABC book was the best basic way to start learning. So my schedule, with yet another class, got heavier. It was touching to witness how earnestly and diligently they learned sign language. One said, "Now I would rather be deaf and I have been teaching my family who now are not ashamed of me." Others agreed with him.

I did have problems sorting out the Ethiopian calendar. Its year, month, date, and time were different from the Western calendar. For example, the Ethiopian year is seven years and eight days behind the Western year. For example, if the Western date is September 23, 1976, the Ethiopian calendar for the same day would be September 15, 1968.

My last week in Ethiopia was spent traveling to Harar, Jijiga (Ogaden Desert), and Dire Dawa with Princess Anya and Haile, my host and interpreter. One night, we tried to find a hotel room but because of the curfew, all the respectable hotels were booked. We had to get a room in a cheap hotel near the bus parking lot. Princess Anya lent me her *shemma* (a woven shawl) to cover the dirty pillow and reeking mattress.

We were up before dawn and walked by rows and rows of buses with no signs and no directions under the full moon. All kinds of Ethiopians from different tribes milled around, showing their tickets on the right buses. We found ours and got on. The bus rattled and shook on the dusty bumpy road. We were frequently stopped by guards searching for explosives. As we left the city, the scenery changed to picturesque valleys and beautiful mountains. The journey to Harar took nearly fourteen hours, so at each bus stop passengers dashed out to buy peaches, bananas, and other bits of food. We all shared it. Since there were no restrooms on the bus, I had learned not to drink water before beginning long rugged drives. The women had to suffer in pain and silence while the men had easy access to nature. Christian men stood while Muslim men squatted.

We finally arrived at the walled city of Harar, which resembled Jerusalem. We couldn't find a hotel room and finally settled on rooms in a dilapidated house. We were too tired to care when a heavily painted and flashily dressed prostitute sailed into the room and glared at Anya icily. Anya stood up with her royal head high and glared back. She then turned to Haile and said, "Are you aware we are in a house of prostitution?" He didn't care and was more interested in finding food. Since it was late and the restaurants were closed, we managed to buy a can of tuna, a can of pineapple juice, and a bottle of orange drink from a street vendor and sat down to share our meager supper. A pimp took pity on us and advised to use a room set apart from the main house. Bed bugs gleefully shared the room with us.

After half a day walking tour, bargaining for antique jewelry at a Muslim market in an old part of the city, we rode on to Dire Dawa. Naked men worked in the fields knee deep in water. A car nearly collided with our bus by cutting in front of us. Our enraged bus driver took off in hot pursuit, careening down the mountain side with its hairpin curves. Everybody screamed, yelling for the driver to slow down. It was

a miracle we arrived at our destination safely. We spent a day in Dire Dawa, walking and seeing donkeys and camels loaded with hay; women with colorful attire, jewels, and braided hair; ancient patriarchs in skull caps and baggy trousers. We meandered over the border to the neighboring country of Somalia, which was more primitive and also more picturesque. The natives gaped and groups of children followed, gathering up the courage to touch my white arms or hands. I said to my companions, "Watch them disappear," and I whipped out my camera and aimed it at them. They ran away pell-mell and suddenly the street was bare.

We also visited the remote city of Jijiga, which also bordered the more aggressive country of Somalia. Anya wanted to visit her uncle so we crossed the border. She also showed me the fantastic rock formations with huge boulders balancing precariously atop one another in this desert land. After we arrived, we were dismayed to learn there were no return buses to Harer for two days.

The more I got to know Princess Anya, the more I admired her. She was an exquisite, delicate beauty who was born deaf. She was a rare Ethiopian deaf woman because she spoke verbally to everyone. Amharic was easier to speak than English. I was amused to see how men flocked around her, spellbound, and listened to her talk with their eyes roving up and down. Never once did they attempt to touch her.

Instead of waiting for the return bus, we took a train, traveling third class to save our dwindling money. By a stroke of luck, Anya's cousin wriggled through the mobs of ferocious Afar men and held a seat for us inside the train. The cousin yelled for us to hurry up. In the melee I crammed myself on the seat next to the nearest Afar man. I had been warned that these men were known to carry carved knives and kill men as a token of courage prior to their weddings. During all day until late in the night, I endured the hard bench in the hot car and suffered the odious body smell of those tribal Afars. At first they resented me as a stranger but I learned that if I treated them well, they would fight to the death for me.

At each stop, passengers would lean out of windows to buy bananas and other fruits. The Afar by my side simply leaned over and swiped fruit from the tray on top of the vendor's head! The longer my companions and I gestured to each other, the more curious and friendly the Afar men became. One flashed a long, curved knife in a waist scabbard.

I marveled at the exquisite leatherwork of the scabbard. Every time after a train stop, conductors in uniforms with guns over their shoulders yelled, pushed, and shoved the tribal men. The Afars were terribly afraid of guns so the bedlam soon quieted down. I sighed with relief when they got off, but at the next stop another group of Afars poured in and packed the car again. We arrived in Addis Ababa past the curfew, and were told it would be wise to find a hotel. I replied, "Forget it. I have enough of bad smell and bed bugs. I'll walk." Soldiers confronted us but apparently they recognized me from publicity so they let us go.

Dr. and Mrs. Mundel invited me to their house on embassy row to meet their partially deafened daughter Stephanie. She was a peppery, defiant, and energetic bombshell. Mrs. Mundel had wisely seen to it that she had not been coddled or sheltered, but gave her a sense of independence. Mrs. Mundel said, "I want Stephanie to associate with the hearing and the deaf."

Kenya

Nairobi, October 26

I arrived in Kenya only to find out that I needed to have a visa to enter the country. So I had to wait for an hour at the airport until an attractive, lithe lady in a stylish yellow suit approached me with a questioning look, and asked "Mrs. Parsons?" She introduced herself as Mrs. Katherine Abilla from the ministry of education. Mrs. Abilla took over smoothly and professionally and straightened everything out with the visa. I gratefully followed her through the airport like a tired puppy. My baggage went through customs undisputed.

Mrs. Katherine Abilla was the chief inspector of schools at the Kenyan ministry of education. She had taken some of her time and driven her car to the airport to meet me. Katherine was my constant hostess, sponsor, and guide while I was in Kenya. The programs she planned were jam-packed. "I wish you could stay longer!" she lamented. The year before, when word got around Gallaudet College that I was going on a global journey to campaign for Total Communication, Michael Ndurumo, an African student who was then attending Gallaudet, begged me to include Kenya in my itinerary. He also introduced me to

the government's department of special education through the mail. Then Katherine read about me in *Gallaudet Today*. At a deaf education conference in Tokyo, she met Mrs. Behroz, a principal in Bombay and Mrs. Saleena Yahaya-Isa, who had both highly recommended me.

Nairobi had quite a pleasing climate, though it was somewhat hotter than Addis Ababa because it was only 5,800 feet above sea level. I also noticed the difference in atmosphere between a country under a socialist government and one under a democratic government. Guards, guns, security men or women were nowhere seen. I was amazed to see so many white people here. The landscape was dotted with jacaranda trees with lilac flowers that bloomed luxuriantly prior to the onset of the monsoon season in November.

I first had to go to the American embassy to see if there was a letter from the Gallaudet College Alumni Association (GCAA). Because my money was running very low, I had sent a letter from Bombay to Donna Chitwood, the editor for GCAA, explaining that I would have to cancel my work in Africa if I didn't receive additional funds. She catapulted into action and sent out mail to those who had previously supported my global work. Many people who enjoyed reading my journals lost no time contributing to the Parsons Fund. GCAA had raised $800 and was sending the check to the American embassy in Nairobi. So I was able to inform Tanzania, Swaziland, South Africa, Nigeria, and Ghana that I would be visiting them as well.

I began by visiting the government's department of education before visiting the city and country special schools all over Kenya. I met Kristina Kenyatta, daughter of His Excellency Mzee Jorno Kenyatta, the first president of the Republic of Kenya. As an education officer in the special education department, she had a keen interest in the deaf children. With Kristina's help, Katherine had blazed the way, and opened door after door as she gained access to people with influence over deaf education.

Katherine confidently explained why she thought deaf people should be trained to speak and lipread in order to fit in to hearing society. I likewise explained lengthily about the difficulties and disadvantages of educating deaf children through oralism. I talked about how through Total Communication, deaf children could gain knowledge and self confidence. I told her about the rights of deaf people, the policies of

Manchester-trained teachers, and the problems of Commonwealth countries who followed the oral method in educating deaf children. It was my longest talk in a long time and I was careful not to strain my voice. She listened attentively and commented that she looked forward to hearing my lecture and seeing the films.

Katherine explained that in Kenya many schools were founded by voluntary or religious bodies such as the Catholic Church, the Salvation Army, the Peace Corps, or the Rotary Clubs of Kenya, but due to recent financial difficulties and some local revolts, the government was taking over all private institutes. She and others employed at the ministry of education were trying to ensure that programs for the handicapped grew. They also helped in educating the public about people with handicaps.

Most schools for the deaf had dormitories and were self-supporting with gardens and chickens tended by the children. Each classroom had earphones and a microphone. I asked how the children communicated with each other and was told "They gesture." "Then why don't they use proper sign language?" I asked. "No, they must be taught to talk and to lipread hearing people."

At each school, Katherine introduced me to a group of teachers. I then gave my lecture, which often left them speechless. They usually resisted my ideas but after much discussion most eventually asked how they could get help in learning the Total Communication method. It was obvious that the more the teachers didn't communicate with their pupils, the less the children learned and the less contact between teachers and pupils, the less those children gestured.

Headmaster Mathenge of Tumutumu School asked if there was any way to help one of his students, Michael Ndurumo, learn to lipread English since he was able to lipread Kikuyu. I told him to not bother—so many foreign deaf people I had met said lipreading Hindi, Marathi, Malaysian, Amharic, Italian, and so forth was very easy, but English was the hardest.

When visiting various schools across Kenya, I enjoyed long countryside drives through fields and hills with modern farmhouses and a few *tukuls*. I beheld the lovely sight of Mount Kenya's jagged snow-capped peaks. We stayed at the Outland Hotel that the ministry of education had reserved for Katherine and me. I was happy we were going to be staying in a first-class hotel with no bloodthirsty bed bugs.

In every school I visited, Katherine listened to complaints from headmasters and teachers about their financial needs. I began thinking about getting the Peace Corps volunteers involved with teaching the deaf children in this country. At the schools, some people continued to resist my ideas but eventually most accepted the philosophy of Total Communication. I was even asked to return the next year for a month-long seminar for teachers from all over the country.

At each school, I restrained myself from stopping the children from carrying my bag full of visas, my passport, and I.D., traveler's checks, and appointment books because they only wanted to welcome me. I kept one eye on the little bag-carrier and the other on the teachers' incessant questions.

Some deaf Kenyan people had a white streak in their hair and the lower half of their eyes were bright blue—signs of a genetic condition called Waardenburg syndrome, which had originally been brought by Danish merchants years earlier. I was told that the common causes of deafness differed from Ethiopia to Kenya. In Ethiopia, most people were deaf due to epidemics, birth accidents, and "accidental falls" as a cover-up for venereal disease. In Nairobi, where the Muslims and Indians predominated, the cause of deafness was hereditary. There were many albinos. Some people lost their hearing due to otitis media during their teens. No wonder so many Africans went to Gallaudet with a high command of English—they were adventitiously deaf; in other words, they became deaf after they had already learned spoken language.

It was customary for every child to shake hands with adults in Kenya and Ethiopia. I met one little boy of six, who, with an air of loneliness, held out his hand and then clung to me steadfastly. With no teachers around, I jumped on the opportunity to experiment with him. I signed and moved my lips simultaneously as I pointed at his t-shirt "Pink and orange," and at mine, "green." He gazed at me and parroted the words back perfectly. Walking toward a classroom window, I pointed at an orange ball inside and signed "orange." His eyes lit up as he copied me, and then he pointed at the red ball and signed "Pink." I corrected that it was red. He pointed at the grass and signed, "green." His lip movement was almost accurate. Gripping my wrist firmly, he touched my watch with tender care. "It's 3:15." He replied, "3:15," and spoke "three" precisely and voicelessly. As other children followed me back to the

waiting car, the boy held my hand firmly. He gestured, "You born deaf?" His knowledge of the sign for "born" surprised me. I nodded. He gestured, "You me same" and kissed my hand. Our meeting was brief, but we felt a deep bonding, and I thought of him for the rest of the day.

Mumias School was run by four dedicated Ursuline sisters. They found, however, that the more they followed the oral Manchester teaching method, the less successful their teaching became. They were dismayed over the frustration, rage, and fighting among the pupils. I replied, "You have to be deaf to understand." Although they resisted at first, they decided to try Total Communication. The following day I met with more than fifty teachers, teachers-in-training, and Manchester-trained lecturers. I was so weak from extreme fatigue that I had to lean on the back of a chair and twice had visual blackouts as I spoke. The afternoon seminar's discussions were so heated and electrifying that it didn't end until 5:00. They had the same fear that deaf people would stop talking if they used sign language. I pointed out that each person differed about how much they used their voice while signing and added, "It's knowledge and learning that are accounted for through help of signing." They then objected to deaf people communicating to each other voicelessly. "Whoa!" I answered, "I'd rather drop dead than using my voice with a deaf person. They can't hear my voice and I'd feel silly." One demanded why I couldn't lipread all people instead of a few. "Not all people move their lips correctly, like not all deaf people speak correctly." I answered. One asked obstinately why signing should be added as part of Total Communication. I replied, "If a person's head is cut off, would he be considered as whole? Sign language is the head of Total Communication."

After returning to the hotel I went straight to bed but was woken an hour later by Katherine. Frank Williams, the head of the Manchester teaching program at Sirbira College, was waiting downstairs because he had missed the seminar. He spoken to some of the teachers who attended and felt he had to try to get me to see his point of view. What a character he was! Witty but stubborn. Tough yet gentle. Generous yet shrewd. Polite yet frank. I've never seen a man who could consume so many bottles of beer without getting drunk. He chain-smoked four packages of cigarettes. We had amiable head-on clashes over the Manchester philosophy and Total Communication. He disliked the look of

sign language whereupon I admonished he was insulting my language and added, "How would you like it if a foreigner told you he doesn't like the sound of your English language?" His eyes widened, and he apologized. He also believed in segregating deaf people by their hearing status: partial hearing, hard of hearing, and deaf. I retorted that his system was like dividing cattle into groups for breeding, grazing, and slaughtering. He stubbornly insisted that deaf students must be educated orally in order to be a productive member of a hearing society. I pointed out that American deaf people had equal opportunities for jobs. He fired back, "It's not the same here and Michael will not be able to have an office job because he can't talk!" I suggested Michael could become a teacher of the deaf. He shouted "Never!" and I screamed, "You Englishmen are selfish! There are hundreds of deaf teachers who are great inspirations to deaf children." He smiled, "You plant in your garden and I plant in mine. Don't come to my garden." I purred, "Don't go to the garden of the deaf. Die-hard oralists are like weeds and are not welcome!" Katherine sat there amazed at how we argued ferociously but with grins and laughter. I liked him, but wished he would be more flexible. I promised to mail him more information about Gallaudet.

The last day was hectic. The check hadn't arrived yet from Gallaudet and with what I borrowed from the Mundels, no one thought I could live on such a small amount. Katherine offered to lend me some money, but I refused for fear of not being able to pay her back. She gasped, "But can you live on this amount?" "I've survived so far!" I assured her. Then suddenly, a secretary at the Kenya Society received a phone call from the American embassy that a money order telegram had just arrived for me. I hurried over before the bank closed. I exclaimed, "My angel is still watching over me!" Through the quick action of Donna Chitwood, my wonderful Gallaudet friends had contributed $800 so I could extend the journey through Africa.

I then learned that Rhodesia had attacked Mozambique. The American embassy strongly advised me not to go there. A letter from Swaziland was forwarded to me from Ethiopia full of welcome and heartfelt thanks from the Mbabane ministry of education. Its director had heard my presentation in Australia and afterwards had asked if I would do his small country a great honor by visiting. Since I would

return to Nairobi as a stopover to Nigeria, I left half of my baggage with Katherine so I could travel light.

Mozambique

Maputo, November 5

I was stranded! The weather was bad as our plane circled to land and almost nose-dived because of an air pocket. The Maputo air terminal as well as the airport was almost empty of passengers and planes. I asked a terminal officer for a transfer to Swaziland. She stared at me stonily, snatched my ticket, and sauntered to a counter where a long queue of passengers waited to show their passports and visas to a lone officer. He, too, was sullen and arrogant. In spite of the heavy humidity, their icy attitude chilled me to the marrow of my bones. What a contrast to the courteous and friendly Ethiopians and Kenyans.

I questioningly pointed at my watch. I needed to hurry because my next plane would be leaving for Swaziland in half an hour. She shrugged her shoulders as she slowly walked toward the snapping officer. He barked something. Acting like a typical deaf person, I pointed my finger at my ear. That threw him off at first but he regained his composure, and impatiently scrawled, "Visa." "But I'm going to Swaziland!" I answered. He shook his head curtly and glared at me as though I were a stupid bovine. They reluctantly let me through without a visa and were startled that I had no baggage claim. But then the plane was canceled due to bad weather in Swaziland. As a transit passenger, DETA Airlines arranged a free booking at a hotel as well as a free taxi ride. My next plane would leave at two the next day.

I noticed billboards outside the terminal entrance with "WHITE GO HOME!" in large print. A middle-aged man asked me which hotel I would be staying. I refused to answer. He scribbled, "You Français?" I shook my head. "You Deutsch?" No. "You Swede?" No, and I added, "American." He looked alarmed and hastily wrote, "Don't wear your jewelry, especially gold!" He was staying at the same hotel and asked if he could take me to dinner. Again, I answered no. He wrote, "Don't walk alone in the dark!" with heavy underline under "don't."

After I had checked into the hotel, I had a big lunch and then decided to take a brisk walk. Everywhere I looked felt depressed and desolate. Signs were posted emblazoned with "Support the people's fight against the imperialism!" I didn't know Mozambique was a communist country. After meandering through a number of bare-looking department stores, I stepped through a wrong exit into a narrow alley and before I knew it, I was surrounded by three sneering young men. Tribal scars crisscrossed their faces.

I first thought, "My angel's wings are finally tired!" Remembering Behroz's warning, I spoke, then gestured when they appeared not to know English. I offered to let them take my purse but asked to keep my plane tickets and passport. One pulled out a knife, pointed it at my stomach as two others gripped my arms to drag me down. The one with the knife spoke, but I pointed at my ear and shook my head. Then I got the biggest surprise in my life—he signed in a manner that was similar to British signs. "You deaf? Me have deaf sister." He was not speaking English, but he spoke rapidly to his companions who momentarily hesitated and disagreed. Then they slowly released me and slinked away. I all but crumpled to a heap. He helped me up and propelled me back to the street, asking me what I was doing. With trembling fingers I hastily explained that I was traveling around the world to help deaf children. He knelt and kissed my hand, signing, "You saint. No go alone." My life was spared because of his deaf sister.

Making the straightest line back to my hotel room, I broke down and cried. I napped fitfully and cried again and again for nearly two hours before deciding to have some fruit salad for a light supper. I stepped into an elevator to ride up to the twelfth-floor restaurant and again met the man from the airport who decided to join me for dinner. His eyes lit up with gladness and he gripped my arm pleading, "I must talk with you." "I'm tired!" I warned him rudely. He scribbled out his plan without being overheard, saying I had long tapering arms. He wanted me to wear seven Indian bracelets into Swaziland. "You are an American and you'll go through duty free." "No!" was my brusque reply.

I ordered fried prawns. When they came, I nearly gagged at the sight of their shells, black eyes, and spindly feelers. He gladly snatched my plate and greedily cleaned up every morsel from the shells. I had no appetite—I was still in shock from the close call that afternoon. Again

he asked if I could at least carry a portable radio. "Illegal?" I asked suspiciously. He explained he had been a "timber king," selling wood all over the world and commuting every few weeks to New York, Lisbon, Nairobi, Maputo, Manzini, and Johannesburg until the communist government of Mozambique confiscated his vast trade. Now he couldn't get luxuries through customs. With me as a transit American passenger, there would be no obstacles. I asked in exchange if he would find me a cheap hotel without bed bugs in Swaziland. He asked, "Which city? Mbabane or Siteki? Tomorrow will be Saturday. The ministry of education in Mbabane will be closed." He added with a serious expression, "In Africa, a white woman is *a white woman.*" Many Africans were so angry over the oppression they had suffered under white colonists that they would not consider sparing a woman's life because she was white. I realized now that the Timber King was my live guardian angel!

Shortly before going to the airport, the Timber King brought me an overnight case covered in zebra fur and a purse made of gazelle instead of the portable radio. He suggested I pack my meager belongings in them in order to get through customs more easily. I took out my money, rolled up the hard cold cash, and tucked it inside my bra. I also tucked my gold necklace inside my shirt, otherwise it could be yanked off by a thief.

Back at the airport, the terminal officer from the day before recognized me, led me to an inspector's stand, and told me to wait. I waited for nearly an hour. The Timber King found me and pushed me to a ticket counter to get a seat reservation. I was almost denied booking because I didn't have the proper paperwork. The Timber King barked at the man until he booked me a seat. If he had not been there, I would have never heard "All boarding for Manzini." He grabbed me to the departure room. The insolent woman inspector turned my purse and wallet inside out. No visa! She wouldn't let me through. The Timber King came to my rescue again telling the inspector that I had never been given a visa form. Another policewoman frisked me and found the roll of American dollars in my bra. She went livid with rage, snatched the dollars from my bra, and yanked me to a policeman, waving the dollars under his nose. He, realizing I was deaf, showed me a card I was supposed to have filled out declaring my money. Of course, I had never been given that as well. He simply tucked my money in his pocket! I

was ready to explode—that was all the money I had. I began to scream like a banshee. The Timber King, my good Samaritan, again came to my rescue by showing the guard my plane ticket with the immediate transfer. How could I get American dollars in so short a time? Sneering, he reluctantly returned my money. The Timber King signaled me to go immediately to our little plane on the airfield by myself because he was being held up with problems with his own plane ticket. The door was about to shut when he made a mad dash, banged on it, got in, and sat next to me. I said to myself, "Brudder, I'll never want to set my foot in Mozambique again."

Swaziland

Manzini, November 6

The little plane landed on a small airfield and stopped in front of a tiny terminal. No one was there to meet me. Putting all my belongings back to the knapsack and returning the exotic bags to my friend, I bade him farewell and thanked him for his help. I assured him I would find my way but he shook his head at my overconfidence. He explained that Swaziland had many casinos between Manzini and Mbabane and people flocked there to gamble. He reminded me that he had promised to find me a hotel so we went off together.

After going to three expensive hotels and being told they were booked solid, I was crestfallen to find at a fourth that they only had one room available "O.K. we share a room," I conceded. "Are there twin beds?"

He invited me to accompany him to a casino, so I tagged along. As we walked down the pine-tree lined road, I suddenly exclaimed that the scenery reminded me of northwestern Switzerland. The casino at the other hotel was a glittering, swanky showplace. Women glided gracefully by, richly gowned, heavily bejeweled, and stylishly coiffed. I sat down to watch the fancy European women parading through the majestic lobby. I marveled over Swaziland's contrast to Mozambique. What prosperity there was in this tiny nation formerly called Zululand!

All the next day my Samaritan was away on business so I sat on a lawn chair, drinking in the beauty of the mountains and the dark green forest. Yet my mind kept wandering back to the deaf children, to the

schools, teachers, and principals I wondered what lay ahead of me in Swaziland and South Africa. I also caught up with my journal entries and wrote letters. I spent the afternoon meandering through the three different hotels and their beautiful grounds. I passed many *tukuls,* whose thatched roofs were artistically and precisely designed. I also saw several huts, or *kraals,* owned by polygamous Swazi men. The huts are clustered together, and each hut is for a wife and her children.

At our last breakfast together, the Timber King told me to eat as much as I could because my clothes were too loose on me. He asked me if fingerspelling and signing made my fingers exceptionally graceful like a ballerina's. I chuckled, "That is a compliment, but fortunately I was born with it." He asked why I had come to Africa and I told him of my global campaigning on behalf of the oral-trained deaf. He was so impressed that he took care of all the bills as a token of admiration and as part of his contribution for my volunteer work with international deaf children. He added that he hoped I would go to Portugal where I could assist the deaf children of his country. I said, "I'd be glad to, provided you give me a letter of introduction to the ministry of education or a principal." He shook his head, and told me "No, just find the information and go." I never learned his name.

Before he left, he made a phone call to Swaziland's ministry of education and arranged for someone to come pick me up since he wouldn't let me stand on the highway and wait for the bus that came every hour. I was at a loss as to how to thank him. The King of Timber, my guardian angel and friend, remained a mystery to me. He was a gentleman with aristocratic manners and a commanding confidence in public but he was considerate, gentle, sincere, and generous with me. He was highly intelligent and multilingual. He had an eccentric English way of carrying his umbrella. In the short time we spent together, I enjoyed being a bit dependent on him for awhile. He had chided me for being too independent and warned that I could get in some dangerous situations if I weren't careful.

I had the Timber King call Mrs. Anne Leng, a British social worker and advisor to the ministry of local administration, and she arranged to pick me up at the hotel. She had searched for me at the airport over the

weekend but couldn't find my name on the passenger list. Undaunted, she checked with the three hotels to see if I was staying with anyone of them but did not go to the fourth where I stayed. She then asked whether I wanted to stay with her at her apartment or book a hotel room. I preferred the former.

Mr. Mabuza, who invited me to Swaziland after hearing my talk in Australia, turned out to be a principal of a secondary public school and knew that the school for the deaf was under construction. I met him again in Swaziland—he was surprised to learn I was deaf!

Mbabane was a lovely little town tucked cozily into a petite valley with beautiful pine trees cascading over the nearby mountains. It strongly reminded me of Switzerland. Visitors could swim in the rivers only if signs had been posted declaring the water bilharzias-free. Bilharzias are flatworms that cause a fatal disease known as "snail fever." Drinking, washing, fishing, or swimming in infested water allows the worm's larvae to enter the human body where they can cause damage to the liver and urinary tract. Anne Leng came to Swaziland four years earlier and became interested in cases of handicapped children. For a long time, the government had discussed building a deaf school, but nothing had really been done. She took up the project and began fighting for financial aid for the building expenses. Through delays, the cost of the building eventually doubled. The facilities were for twenty deaf children. Unfortunately parents were not enthusiastic about sending their children to school so only three boys and three girls enrolled, leaving the rest of classrooms, dormitories, and dining room almost bare. She was excited about my visit and was confident that my radio interview would inspire popular interest. She contacted the Dominican Order in Capetown and two sisters were sent to teach. Both had experience teaching deaf children all over South Africa. Sister Madeleine, the principal and Sister Gilbert, a Manchester-trained teacher, were open-minded about communication. We spent all afternoon discussing Total Communication and pure oralism. In fact, they asked me to talk and sign with the deaf children. The children had the familiar stony expressions of many orally educated children. I started out with finger-counting to ten, then I signed a short tale about how I came on the plane, and explained the lesson in this classroom. The sisters were stunned to witness the children's metamorphosis—they smiled, their eyes lit up with knowledge, and their hands flew. Some even moved

their lips accurately. They begged me to come back to teach but I suggested that they try to get a deaf volunteer teacher through the Peace Corps. Throughout my stay, Anne and I had a whirlwind schedule: I met with officials at the ministry of education, the American embassy Prince Masitsela, a minister and a son of the king of Swaziland. I had an interview at Swazi Radio and I lectured at the United States Information Services office. Many people were at first coolly polite, which soon gave way to interest, and ended up enthusiastically listening to me. Prince Masitsela, upon learning that my hearing children and grandsons knew sign language, asked if I would bring my grandsons the next time I visited because he believed deaf children would learn faster from hearing children their own age. I felt my lectures and interviews were successful and well received. Anne told me she had planned everything in advance, and she had every reason to be pleased that people came to listen to me.

꽃

I visited St. Philip, a training school for weavers, which had fifteen deaf girls in their late teens enrolled in a four-year course. They were illiterate, but they had been taught enough reading, writing, and math to understand the instructions for sweater weaving. Their communication was acutely limited. I was amazed at the code that they developed. A quick twist of a head, a flick of an eyebrow, and a few jumps of their fingers across a cheek, chin, nose, or forehead was their conversation!

The sisters and I were dismayed to learn I did not have a visa for South Africa. I couldn't get a refund for my ticket and would have to get a flight to Nairobi from the South African airport once I arrived. The nuns faxed Father Cyril Axelrod, a deaf Catholic priest who ministered to deaf people, and asked him to meet me at the Johannesburg airport where we could perhaps talk during my layover.

Johannesburg Airport

November 13

I was astounded to see so many skyscrapers in the city of Johannesburg. While waiting for the next plane, an agent told me that there were people upstairs who wanted to see me. They were the Ordmans, who

received a telegram I had sent explaining why I couldn't visit South Africa, and Father Axelrod. They were stunned I was here and disappointed to find that I couldn't enter the country—so near yet so far. They begged me to return in the near future. "Money for the plane speaks," I said. Being able to sign was an advantage—we signed to each other through the glass wall for nearly an hour. They asked me why I didn't notify them in advance, or come to stay a week or two, or at least three months. I told Mr. Ordman I had mailed him twice but never got an answer and I wouldn't come uninvited. He admitted he thought it would be impossible for me to fly so far south.[12] Father Axelrod wished we had corresponded. He and others had been fighting in vain to introduce Total Communication. Two years earlier a hearing man from America had come to lecture about it but failed to change any minds. A law mandated that every deaf school, even a new one, should automatically be oral all over South Africa. Too many Manchester-trained people held the upper hand; three Manchester-trained educators, in fact, had positions at the ministry of education. There were a few schools that used sign language outside the classrooms but they were all for black people and the Indians. But the teachers came from different countries so the deaf adults used different sign languages. When they met, they were unable to communicate. "Just like Australia!" I exclaimed. Of all the five sign languages Father Axelrod used to preach all over different domains, he declared, "l'Epée's signs are the best and the most logical."

Kenya

Nairobi, November 14

Fortunately I had the airline agent call Katherine to meet me just before she went out with her husband and friends. She met me at the airport dressed in evening attire and I felt like a heel for breaking up their party. Katherine was delighted to have me back and lost no time arranging for television and radio interviews, more lectures, visits to the Kenya Society for the Deaf, the American embassy, and more schools for the deaf. I began to demonstrate to teachers how quickly children picked up language and knowledge by using the simultaneous method.

I awoke one morning with a splitting headache, but I sallied forth with a scheduled interview. I began to falter, however, when I noticed the interviewer's passive and stony face. I asked myself "Am I boring him?" and suddenly had another attack of a sharp pain in my head. I ended the interview abruptly, much to everyone's surprise. Katherine chided me for thinking the interviewer was bored. She assured me that everybody was fascinated and were thoroughly disappointed with my brief talk.

She voraciously read my reports on Swaziland and was astounded that my attacker spared my life just because he had a deaf sister. She, as usual, prepared special dishes for me since she and her family ate typical African meals, such as *ugali* (cornmeal mush) with a fish stew that had everything in it—eyes, fins, and bones. Every time I felt blue and despondent, I lost my appetite but Katherine would sit beside me to make sure I cleaned the plate. She said she hated cooking but did it especially for me so I just might as well eat it.

For four days I squeezed in spare time to haunt airline offices and the Madagascar and American embassies to get a Madagascar visa. Those people in that island country had waited for months for me to visit ever since I met them at the meeting of the World Federation of the Deaf. We had a special Peace Corps meeting where I met Melle Soa Rasoamanpionone who wanted me to come to Madagascar. She had the director of the Antsirabe School for the Deaf write me a formal letter of invitation for a three-month stay. Since I received his letter at the last minute I was only able to squeeze Madagascar in my itinerary for a one-week visit. But without a visa, I wouldn't be able to go. The visa finally came through on the morning of November 17. Katherine took me to the airport and insisted on staying with me until I safely boarded the plane.

Madagascar

Tananarive, November 18

The Madagascans are a multiracial society—When I arrived I saw Indians, Asians, French, Africans, Turks, and Arabs. I also saw people who looked like they might be Burmese, Thai, Filipino, Tahitian, or South American Indians.

I had to go through a slow and tedious health inspection before I could officially enter the country. When it was over, I found that the American embassy had sent a car for me. Jack Raobelina, the Madagascan employee from the embassy who met me, warned me to state the exact amount of currency I possessed, otherwise extra money would be confiscated at my departure. We reached the embassy just before it closed. I learned that every African country demands visitors have a visa. I didn't have one for Tanzania nor Nigeria. Jack roared, "What! Don't tell me you have been traveling in Africa without visas!" I griped I never had met so many obstacles and he replied, "Only in Africa!" and added, "Do not walk alone in the dark, and do not ride in a taxi alone. Problems! Problems! You must watch the official stamp on money declaration at money exchange." I stayed overnight at a French hotel.

The next morning, Jack took me to the train station and assured me he would fax the principal of the school for the deaf in Antsirabe that I was coming. After I arrived, Soa, the principal, and others rejoiced that I had made it and thanked me for coming. Several people from the ministry had come to the school a week earlier and were disappointed to not find me there. I was just as disappointed that the school children were away for a three-month vacation. All the residential teachers, however, remained. This school was the only one for deaf children in all of Madagascar and could accommodate only 56 deaf pupils. There must be over 3,000 deaf people who remained illiterate.

I met Goel Do, a deaf Malagasy teacher of nine years. He was enthusiastic about structural sign language and agreed it would be better for the deaf pupils. Of all the teachers at school, the other deaf people looked to him as inspiration and a common confidant. I had a long talk with Goel and the director of the school about international signs, gestures, and structural signed language. They started out as strong advocates for gestures as "natural signs" and ended up realizing the importance of teaching a sign language that followed their country's written language. At first they argued that would be impossible since some words had several meanings in Malagasy. I explained that English had similar words such as "right" but had different signs for the same word. "I am right," "I am on the right," and I have "right of way." Then the director said he thought simple gestures would be enough for deaf children. I asked him to demonstrate various signs for "here,

now, today" and he could only point downward for these three words, while moving his lips to form the words. "Yes, but do those children think or move their lips to specify the different meanings of the same gestures?"

I showed how to vary signs for "know, think, idea, imagine, concept, create, dream, and suspect." Goel slapped his hand on his lap, broke into a broad smile, and nodded in agreement. For years he wondered why the children he taught missed out on so many words in writing. He fully agreed that the different and more complex signs would reinforce their thinking, speaking, and even writing. Both he and the director insisted that I explain the importance of structural signs to the teachers. I gave them the brief history of how Mr. Gallaudet brought l'Epée's signs to America from France. He added, "Now you bring it here! We speak French. Madagascar won its independence from France in 1960 but French influence strongly reigns here."

For the next five days we had meetings with teachers, the president of the school association, and the vice minister of Antsirabe. In the city, there was a banner in Malagasy that read, "Help deaf to speak." I suggested changing it to "Help deaf to learn."

I soaked up the French atmosphere, which lulled me into a tranquil state of mind. The French language, however, had been discontinued and the populace had reverted to Malagasy, their own national language. After a week of paradise with the friendly staff, I felt reluctant to leave. They wouldn't let me return by train so Soa accompanied me in a car. She explained Madagascar was a red island consisting of red soil, so houses were all built from red bricks or red-brown clay.

Soa and I said our sad good-byes. But a surprise awaited me. The British High Commissioner had arranged for my visa to Nigeria! The embassy limousine brought me back to airport. I had taken Jack's warning about extra money to heart and had hoarded the receipts for everything I paid. The inspector figured out my currency declaration, which totaled $117.00. The rest of my money would be confiscated. He shot me a steely suspicious stare and I felt my knees become rubbery. Two other male passengers were bickering over their declarations and eventually lost some of their money. I tried to pull the drama of a *sourd-muet* (deaf-mute) by gesticulating, writing, and pointing at my ear but not using my voice. Yet they wouldn't release me. My plane was

to leave in 15 minutes but two policemen made me sit down. We argued and I made the inspector double and triple check until my extra money balance dwindled to a mere $4.00, which was too measly for confiscation. After it was over, I shook like a leaf—I could have lost $223. I made a mad dash to the plane, which had been waiting for me for 45 minutes. During the flight, I sat next to a very drunk man who kept jabbing my arm and ribs with his elbow. He opened his mouth to talk to me and my finger flew to my ear as I shook my head. He left me alone after that but later knocked over his whole can of beer, dousing my knapsack.

Tanzania

Dar-es-Salaam, November 26

When I arrived, I once again ran into a tangled web of troubles since I didn't have a visa for Tanzania and was thus denied entrance. I went through the now familiar routine of arguing, showing evidence that I had a passport, running to a bank to get the money to pay for the visa. Finally I straightened everything out. The next step was to find my hotel booking. None! I threw my arms up. A youth from Canberra had the same problem. We agreed to share a taxi round trip to a beach hotel, a one-hour drive away, which had an available room for $50 a night. The airline agent said I must return to the airport at 3:30 a.m. to catch my connecting flight. That meant sleeping for only three hours! I bowed out, apologizing that I would sleep at the airport lounge. Just before midnight the whole terminal went pitch black. No one was around. My eyes bore into darkness, fearing any person could enter the unguarded terminal and find me alone. At 3 a.m., the lounge suddenly came alive with Indian tourists. They unrolled their mats, knelt down in the direction of India, and began praying.

I boarded the plane for Arusha, Tanzania. As we flew over Mount Kilimanjaro, I saw the famous snow-capped top from the window before we landed. I had a few hours until my plane took off for Kenya, so I took a taxi for a 45-minute drive to the city through a semi-desert where I saw *kraals, tukuls,* ant hills, a smatter of sparsely spaced acacia trees standing forlornly and tin-roofed farm houses. At the foothills of

Arusha, the land shifted its scenery to tropical foliage, banana trees, co-
conut trees, and gorgeous arrays of colorful flowers hanging from the
trees. I spent only a few hours meandering around this quiet city, took
a long look at majestic snow-capped mountains, and happily left
socialism-infested Tanzania.

Kenya

Nairobi, November 27

I returned to Kenya the next day. It was so good to be back with
Katherine where I felt secure and safe. She had some wonderful papers
about Total Communication to be distributed to the ministry of edu-
cation, Siriba College, and all the schools for the deaf in Kenya. She
told me that many people had seen me on television during my earlier
visit and wanted to meet me. Unfortunately, I was only going to be in
Kenya long enough to pick up my belongings so she had to make
many apologies.

Katherine, listening to the stories of all my travels, smiled when I
told her of the American embassy's help and said, "That's Uncle Sam
for you!" When I told her about sleeping in the airport lounge, she
praised, "You're a good economist!"

When I had gotten everything packed she once again drove me to the
airport and helped me get through the ticket, weight, visa, and currency
declarations. My last words to her were "Hire Michael Ndurumo!"[13]

Nigeria

Ibadan, November 28

Words could never describe how glad I was to meet Peter Mba when I
arrived in Nigeria. For eleven months I had visited hundreds of class-
rooms that lacked facilities and basic supplies—especially books, pa-
pers, and pencils—and placed more emphasis on earphones, hearing
aids, microphones, audiometers, or other audio equipment because of
their focus on speechreading and speech training. Deaf teachers were
not encouraged. Deaf children lost precious opportunities to develop
self-confidence, self-esteem, and a sense of independence in schools

without deaf teachers to serve as role models. After months of visiting orally oriented schools with only hearing teachers, and talking with hearing people who refused to learn sign language, it was a relief to see Dr. Peter Mba, a Gallaudet graduate, and his hearing friend, Mrs. Oyesola, greet me in sign language!

After Peter had acquired a doctoral degree in America, he was offered a high-paying position in the States. He was tempted to take the job but he placed duty and loyalty to his native country first and returned home to accept a similar position for a fraction of the salary. Peter was responsible for creating a teacher-training program in deaf education at the University of Ibadan, the oldest university in West Africa. Teachers trained by Peter ventured out to other Nigerian schools for the deaf and implemented the Total Communication method in those schools. He also began a long string of fights and frustrations in trying to upgrade the education of the deaf. He asked, "How come the United Kingdom could send out so many oralists and the United States couldn't do the same with advocates of Total Communication?"

At the time of my visit, I also ran into Joe Kinner, a history professor at Gallaudet who was in Nigeria at the same time I was there. When we met, I resisted the temptation to say, "Dr. Kinner, I presume!" Joe offered to interpret for me. Before I met up with him, I had taken qualified interpreters for granted. Now I realized that in Joe a qualified interpreter had been given to me in Africa on a golden platter. Joe not only interpreted mumbling speakers simultaneously but signed as he spoke to bring Peter and me into the hearing society! It was beautiful to see Joe and other hearing teachers talking to each other and signing simultaneously whether Peter and I were watching them or not! Just like the interpreters I knew in America. It took me eleven months and fourteen countries to see the light. As deaf people who used sign language, we could communicate better with hearing people through the interpreters, but orally trained deaf people could reap no such benefit.

Gabriel "Gabby" Adepoju, another top graduate of Gallaudet whom I visited during my stay in Nigeria, was the principal of Kwara State School for the Deaf in Ilorin. He told me about the long history of the fight against oralism in Nigeria. He raged about the British oralists "invading" deafness. He told me how he slowly but surely won one round after another in his battles against them, earned recognition from

Kwara Ministry of Education, and kept up a constant correspondence with Gallaudet College. He was profoundly grateful for Gallaudet's prompt replies and cooperation on spreading the word about Total Communication. He ordered films, slides, overhead projectors, filmstrips, magazines, and books to help in his fight. He and Peter had ordered 200 of the NAD's ABC books and wanted more. They believed that book helped jumpstart children's education in Total Communication. Gabby also selected a few qualified candidates out of many deaf Nigerians for scholarships to Gallaudet or any American university that included Total Communication as a teaching methodology in its curriculum. He hired trained teachers who knew manual language and developed contacts in the press to help increase the public's awareness of deaf education.

Gabby, an energetic, dynamic deaf principal, was indeed a fiery fighter for Nigerian deaf children! He wanted to return to the States to earn his doctorate but he was afraid if he left, the oralists would seize the opportunity to invade his territory, and destroy all the progress he had helped to make, which is what had happened in Ghana. Eight out of nine schools that had been founded by Dr. Tetteh-Ocloo, a deaf Ghanian who had graduated from Gallaudet, had recently bowed down to oralism. Gabby felt he had to make sure Total Communication was a strong and integral force in Nigerian deaf education before he could dare take a leave of absence. He, like Peter, had turned down well-paying professional positions in order to help Nigerian deaf children, uphold the image of the deaf intellectual, and honor his birthplace.

I observed that in the classrooms at his school, the children were encouraged to read books, write daily, and work through math problems. Most had only two years of education thus far but they accomplished far more compared to most of the schools I had seen in Asia, Africa, and even Australia! Even without acoustic aids, the teachers, who were well trained and dedicated, had successfully taught the children to pronounce spoken language well. After two short years, the older students knew addition, subtraction, multiplication, and division. When I asked them which part of arithmetic they liked best, they, with bright eyes, smiled and said, "We love all of them!"

I was invited to talk at a PTA meeting at Gabby's school, but before I began a father of a deaf pupil stood up with tears shining in his eyes. He expressed his profound gratitude for what the school had done for his son. Before the school, the father had thought his son was hopeless, and believed that God was punishing him and his wife. After two years his son's progress amazed and pleased him, especially when his son did better academically than his hearing peers. Then several other parents raised their arms, clamoring for their turns—all poured out their grateful hearts to tell us how much hope Gabby's school had brought to their children! When I then showed the film *Total Communication,* depicting the children in the Maryland classroom, everyone's eyes widened to see white deaf children. One seven-year-old boy excitedly exclaimed, "White is deaf, too! They talk with their hands like us! Rah! Rah! Rah!" and the rest rooted with him.

Later, I attended a gathering of deaf adults, which gave me an opportunity to witness the easy flow of conversation among the Nigerians, Kenyans, Ghanaians, and one person from the French colony of Togo, who spoke in French but used English signs. The Kenyans expressed their gratitude for my trip to Kenya to campaign for Total Communication. Their efforts to convince their ministry of education had failed. They were very grateful that Andrew Foster, a deaf African American man who dedicated his life to improving deaf education in Africa, brought "Gallaudet signs" so they could all communicate easily. They strenuously opposed "local natural signs" because they would hinder communication among deaf people from different locales. Why narrow down signs to a tribal language and limit the small circle of deaf society? The man from Togo grinned, "Remember Clerc came from France where l'Epée started!" He admitted many English-using deaf people did not realize he didn't know any English because he could converse freely with them. He also said those who used local signs were ignored by the English-using signers.

Throughout my stay in Nigeria, every host and hostess coddled me. Many went out of their way to make me food that tasted close to American food. I loved the long conversations I had with Joe Kinner, Gabriel and his wife Grace, and Peter Mba. When I told Peter about my narrow escape from the attacker in Mozambique, I added that I was a coward to cry. He exclaimed, "You coward? You are not!"

"But I cried for hours," I said. He explained, "What I mean, how come you stayed in Africa instead of flying straight home?" I answered, "I stayed for the sake of deaf children."

I spent a few nights at the Institute of Church and Society. One night, I decided to take a shower and wash my hair. I was careless about plugging in my hair dryer and forgot to turn the wall switch off. I received an electrical shock that knocked me unconscious. While I was out, I had a weird dream that I was hovering above myself, looking at my body lying on the floor with dripping hair. I felt like I was floating free and happy when I felt a magnetic pull upward. Suddenly I was clawing to get back to my body, thinking "Not yet! Not yet!" When I came to, I was too scared to plug the dryer back in and settled for combing my hair until it dried.

I mentioned the dream during my last conversation with Peter during that trip. He replied, "You did die" and suggested I look up the book *Life after Life*, which had just been published in America. I also remembered the end of the Ceylonese horoscope from the year earlier that included the warning "beware of reptiles and electricity, as dangers from same are shown." I suddenly realized that the reptiles represented the militant oralists I had encountered. The horoscope had proved to be eerily accurate.

Aftermath

In mid-January 1977, after one long year of introducing Total Communication and encouraging teachers and students to learn 400 signs from *A Basic Course in Manual Communication*, by Terrence J. O'Rourke, I returned to Washington, D.C. I felt my trip had been worthwhile. Faculty and staff members of Gallaudet College had extended their full support throughout my sojourn.

In the following years, the Gallaudet Department of Continuing Education, headed by Dr. Thomas Mayes, played a large role in promoting the Total Communication philosophy around the globe. The department sponsored international seminars for foreign teachers, headmasters, and principals. Dr. Mayes and Marilyn Galloway assisted

The photo on the left was taken before I began my journey in January 1976. The photo on the right was taken after I returned. I had recurring bouts of malaria and hepatitis for two to three years and intestinal parasites for fourteen after I returned.

in establishing the connection between the Peace Corps and Gallaudet College. The goal in teaching the 400 standard American signs was to enable deaf people around the world to communicate with each other. I continued to receive letters of appreciation and news of successful Total Communication projects for nearly fifteen years. Many foreign students were able to attend Gallaudet College because they already knew some American signs. They even returned home to continue the spread of the combined method.

Thailand was the first country to teach the signs from O'Rourke's book. Two teachers from the Bangkok School for the Deaf had attended the Gallaudet College Normal School (the former name of the teacher-training program), and had learned American English signs. When I visited the Bangkok school in 1974 and 1976, I was able to communicate with the school children. However, when I returned in 1993, 1998, and 2004, I noticed a drastic change in communication philosophy not only in Thailand, but in most of the countries I had visited in 1976. Instead of teaching American English signs, these countries now focus on teaching local sign languages with their native spoken

languages (in other words, bilingual education). While the teachers and students can communicate with each other, they have lost the ability to read and communicate in English. I am dismayed because these deaf children can communicate only with deaf people from their own countries. They have isolated themselves from the English-speaking and signing worlds.

Teachers, principals, and parents in Singapore, Malaysia, the Philippines, Kenya, and Ethiopia have contacted me and told me how worried and upset they are about their students' lack of English skills, and they want American English signs to be part of their curriculum. My original goal in taking my journey in 1976 was to supplement local sign languages with American English signs and improve educational opportunities for deaf people around the world. I am heartbroken at these developments.

Acknowledgments

I am extremely grateful to Brenda Brueggemann for including the story of my 1976 journey in *Deaf Women's Lives*, and to Ivey Pittle Wallace of Gallaudet University Press for recommending my manuscript to Brenda. Brenda was the angel who patiently explained to me the rules of how to write a 120-page book from my 550-page journal. I thank Ulf Hedberg, director of the Gallaudet University Archives, for retrieving my manuscript, which had been sitting in the vault for twenty-five years, and for teaching me the computer skills I needed to produce the final manuscript. Lastly, I thank Christina Robb and Deirdre Mullervy for their skillful editorial advice.

Appendix

I returned to Penang as a Peace Corps consultant in 1977 for five days of observation. I then went to Kuala Lumpur to help prepare for the impending arrival of Peace Corps volunteers from Gallaudet College. This is my report on the experience for the Peace Corps Headquarters in Washington, D.C.

REPORT TO THE PEACE CORPS

Mrs. Saleena Yahaya-Isa, principal of the Federation School for the Deaf, has proven a staunch, powerful advocate of the philosophy of

Total Communication. This is all the more impressive as she once practiced pure oralism after being brainwashed by Manchester. She is one of the rare souls who keeps in contact with her students after graduation. And she has witnessed the disastrous results when students educated with purely oral methods enter hearing society. So shortly after I instructed her teachers, she set up an "experiment" with two first-grade classes—one would be taught through the oral method and the other through Total Communication. Miss Khoo, granted the privilege of using simultaneous communication (sim-com) with her first-graders, contrasted her frustrating experience of teaching with the oral method for six years. She saw no appreciable results among her deaf pupils, with her seven months of using the sim-com method that produced tremendous results. Her tiny pupils had the ability to sign with lip movements in sentences.

Miss Khan, a Melbourne-trained teacher, described a similar experience. Miss Khan's oral class could only speak single words when shown familiar pictures illustrating those words. None of the children could speak in sentences and they all communicated through gestures. The sim-com-trained children and the oral-trained children were a study in contrasts. Miss Khan's class possessed dull, clouded, and depressed eyes and facial expressions, while Miss Khoo's class had sparkling, alert, and happy eyes and facial expressions. The vocabularies of the sim-com pupils exceeded that of the oral-trained pupils by 70 percent.

Mr. Francis, an upper-grade English instructor, had been a staunch oralist and had originally opposed using the sim-com method. Ironically, he ended up being the star student in last year's sign language class. "For six years, I couldn't get anything across to my students, and with sim-com, they get it 100 percent and learn English so rapidly," he said with an air of relief.

The deaf housemother, having learned English signs last year, approached me to express her delight and gratitude for the ability to communicate with the deaf children after trying for several years with limited gestures and no speech. She was amazed at how well they could convey abstract concepts. She now teaches the Malaysian language with American English signs to the deaf alumni of the Federation School for the Deaf. It was fascinating to see the little tots learning Malaysian with American English signs in different syntaxes (e.g., "In basket has

Left: The Penang Federation School for the Deaf Total Communication class; right: the oral class.

money" or "Boy give money that"). Any deaf American would mistake their communication method for American Sign Language!

In spite of Dr. Mahathir's verbal announcement that Total Communication would be implemented in all Malaysian deaf schools, those Manchester- and Melbourne-trained educators persisted on using the oral method. Mrs. Yahaya-Isa asked me to join her in writing letters to alert Deputy Prime Minister Mahathir that the oral method was still being used in deaf schools. He then wrote the law requiring all schools for the deaf to use Total Communication.

However, American linguists sent Deaf Studies and ASL majors to Malaysia to convince the government not to allow the schools to use American English signs in the Malaysian language. Older deaf students in Malaysia continued to use American English signs and could communicate with people in neighboring Thailand and Singapore as well as with American tourists and visitors. Younger Malaysian deaf students use Malaysian Sign Language (MSL), which doesn't follow the grammar of the Malaysian spoken language nor does it use speech. This method cuts off the easy flow of communication with people who

use American English signs. People who use MSL can only communicate with other people who use MSL.

A large number of Penang Federation School students graduated and went on to higher education at several universities, including the Rochester Institute of Technology and Gallaudet University. Many of them expressed their deep gratitude to Mrs. Yahaya-Isa, who defied the oral method and invited me to collaborate with her; otherwise they would have ended up with menial jobs in their own country.

Notes

1. When the Shah abdicated his throne, Prime Minster Hoveyda was assassinated.

2. Sadly, Julia was killed along with two of her sons, including Michael, and a friend in a small aircraft crash on a visit to northern Iran.

3. Dinaz Adenwalla was admitted to Gallaudet, made the honor roll, and became a teacher at the Rhode Island School for the Deaf. Several more deaf students from Bombay also attended Gallaudet.

4. Behroz Vasha founded the School for the Deaf and Blind, the only institute of its kind in India. She was invited to Australia, Europe, and America to expound on her teaching method. She was awarded the Nobel Prize for her work with deaf and blind children. Because of her, many schools accepted sign language in classrooms.

5. Years later, I finally had the opportunity to meet this girl, now a woman, in 1993 when she was forty years old. She looked very wizened and bony, and was bitter. When she was discarded from the street, a Christian family took her in to be their permanent housekeeper. Her employer, however, complained that she kept sneaking out to find men. I asked the ex-slave girl why she wouldn't be grateful to have a roof over her head and food in her stomach. She replied, "I ugly. I want man look me. Man take me. I feel woman. I happy."

6. The third principal, Maliwan Tammasaen, carried on the signing policy. She brought Yada, a long-time deaf teacher, with her to Gallaudet College to polish their American English signs skills as well as to learn the philosophy of Total Communication. Yada was a firm believer in simultaneous communication.

I did not know that the year following my visit, an American linguist came and researched Thai Signs. The older deaf Thais and Mr. Niram objected to his demand that English Signs no longer be used in favor of Thai Signs. The linguist and Mr. Niram fell into a heated argument that ended up with the linguist punching Mr. Niram and breaking his tooth. The assailant was handcuffed and sent to prison. He stubbornly persisted in pushing Thai Sign Language.

When Principal Tammasaeng returned to Bangkok, she broke the wonderful news that television would have an interpreter signing in American English Signs. Out of nowhere, a group of deaf people inspired by the linguist began demanding that Thai Signs replace English Signs. So now Thai Signs dominate. In 1998 I went back to Bangkok and visited Chiang Mai again. I was stunned to find I couldn't communicate with many deaf people. Still, the deaf shop owners who used American English Signs found they sold more than those who knew only Thai Signs.

7. In 1977, the following year, I returned to Penang as a Peace Corps consultant for five days of observation. I then went to Kuala Lumpur to help prepare for the impending arrival of Peace Corps volunteers from Gallaudet College. I received a gala welcome with a huge "I love you" sign. See the appendix for my report on the experience for the Peace Corps Headquarters in Washington, D.C.

8. I returned to Hong Kong in 1993 at the invitation of Father Cyril Axelrod to try to encourage the combined method system. I had warned Axelrod about the British power over deaf education in Hong Kong. He persuaded me that it would not hurt to try again.

At one meeting, a familiar woman who turned out to be the inspector from the education department breezed in. She said, "So you are back! You are wasting your time. We are getting lots of help from Australia to give our babies cochlear implants!" I smiled and answered "Cochlear implants will bring better bonding between hearing parents and deaf children, providing the parents communicate consistently in spoken language from an early age, and the surgeons do a good job."

9. SAID expanded from one small classroom (that was contributed by Eric's grandfather Sobrepena) with two pupils to a larger house with more rooms, and then to a two-story school with 100 students in 1998. Many went on to Gallaudet and other colleges in the United States. Unfortunately, some students returned home after studying ASL and convinced SAID to switch to Philippine Sign Language. For ten years Peace Corps volunteers taught deaf children not only at SAID but in to all parts of the Philippines.

10. Total Communication was fully implemented in 1977, with the inclusion of SEE 2 in 1978. The progress of the students at the Singapore School for the Deaf gave evidence to what Total Communication could help the students accomplish. From 1972, deaf students scores on the national Primary School Leaving Exam (PSLE) were 0 percent. In 1979 the academic results from the Total Communication curriculum began to become apparent—for the first time since the test was implement, deaf students received a score of 40 percent. In the following years deaf students ranged between 40 and 100 percent. Deaf students with 3 credits passed to get a place from a regular polytechnic or junior college. Heng recently updated me on the situation in Singapore: "In 1996, the number of deaf children entering the deaf secondary school began decreasing due to

the huge increase of enrollment in mainstream primary schools. At present, most new parents prefer to send their deaf children to regular schools than to special schools. The Singapore School for the Deaf has 26 deaf pupils as compared to 92 in 1990. The PSLE pass rate for the 2003 class is 43 percent (7 out of 16).

However, in 1988 a Singapore student who minored in Deaf Studies at Gallaudet graduated and returned home. He slowly planted seeds of discontent with English Signs and later created a political crisis in the Singapore Association of the Deaf. When I returned to Singapore in 1993, I saw the militancy for myself. During the Asia-Pacific World Federation of the Deaf Conference held in Kuala Lumpur in 1995, one of the detractors of English Signs from Gallaudet boasted that "local natural signing" was the ultimate answer. Mr. Peng had exclaimed, "That's old wine in new bottle!"

11. Thusara Wijatilaka was admitted to Gallaudet and proved to be a very independent student who achieved the highest grades.

12. In 1980 I returned to South Africa for a three-month stay. The head of the ministry of education granted me a pass to visit every school. He told me he'd, "like to hear your opinions about the difference between the white and the black deaf and between oral and signing." At the end of the three months, I answered him, "White deaf taught oral as young as two are way behind the black deaf student who are taught structural signing from the age of seven when first admitted to school!"

13. Katherine Abilla continued to clash with Mr. Williams. She attended International Interns at Gallaudet Continuing Education the following year. Unfortunately a few years later she died. Dr. Nduromo carried on as the head of Special Education. He was respected and listened to until the World Federation of the Deaf decided "natural signing" should be used in local schools. The Scandinavian country sponsored a school in Kenya and sent a deaf teacher as a "model."